American Foreign Policy and Its Thinkers

AMERICAN FOREIGN POLICY AND ITS THINKERS

Perry Anderson

VERSO
London • New York

This paperback edition published by Verso 2017
First published by Verso 2015
'Imperium' and 'Consilium' first published in *New Left Review* 83,
September/October 2013 and republished here by kind permission
© Perry Anderson 2015, 2017

The moral rights of the author have been asserted

1 3 5 7 9 10 8 6 4 2

Verso
UK: 6 Meard Street, London W1F 0EG
US: 20 Jay Street, Suite 1010, Brooklyn, NY 11201
versobooks.com

Verso is the imprint of New Left Books

ISBN-13: 978-1-78663-048-3
ISBN-13: 978-1-78168-668-3 (US EBK)
ISBN-13: 978-1-78168-702-4 (UK EBK)

British Library Cataloguing in Publication Data
A catalogue record for this book is available from the British Library

The Hardback Edition Has Been Cataloged by the Library of Congress as Follows

Anderson, Perry.
American foreign policy and its thinkers / Perry Anderson.
   pages cm
Originally published: London : New Left Review Ltd., 2013.
   ISBN 978-1-78168-667-6 (hardback) — ISBN 978-1-78168-668-3 (ebook)
1. United States—Foreign relations—1945–1989. 2. United States—Foreign
relations—1989- 3. Imperialism—History—20th century. 4. Imperialism—
History—21st century. I. Title.
E744.A64 2014
327.73009'04—dc23

Typeset in Minion Pro by MJ & N Gavan, Truro, Cornwall
Printed and bound by CPI Group (UK) Ltd, Croydon, CR0 4YY

CONTENTS

Preface   vii
Acknowledgements   xi

I. IMPERIUM
  1. Prodromes   3
  2. Crystallization   13
  3. Security   29
  4. Keystones   51
  5. Perimeters   69
  6. Recalibration   91
  7. Liberalism Militant   113
  8. The Incumbent   133

II. CONSILIUM
  9. Native Traditions   159
 10. Crusaders   167
 11. Realist Ideals   189
 12. Economy First   219
 13. Outside the Castle   229

Annexe   237
Postscript   255

Index   263

PREFACE

The two parts of this book, 'Imperium' and 'Consilium', offer an account of the American imperial system that reaches across the world today. It is reasonable to ask what particular contribution they could make to a subject that has attracted a large existing literature, composed essentially of diplomatic history and geopolitical strategy. The scope of 'Imperium' differs from much of the former in three ways, temporal, spatial and political. The first is a question of chronological span. An extensive body of research, much of it of the highest quality, exists on American foreign policy. But it characteristically divides into widely separate bodies of historical writing—principally, studies of US territorial and overseas expansion in the nineteenth century; analyses of US conduct in the struggle against the USSR during the Cold War; and discussions of US power projection since the last decade of the twentieth century. What is attempted here, by contrast, is a connected understanding of the dynamics of American strategy and diplomacy in a single arc from the war on Mexico to the war on Terror. The second difference is a question of geographical attention. Coverage of the exercise of US imperial power has tended to focus either on its operations in what was once the Third World of former colonial lands, or on its battle with what was once the Second World of communist states. There has on the whole been less concern with the objectives pursued by Washington within the First World of advanced capitalism itself. Here an effort is made to keep all three fronts of US expansion concurrently in focus.

Finally, there is a political difference. Much of the literature on American imperial power is critical of it, often—though, as I will note, by no means invariably—written from standpoints that can be regarded as broadly of the left, as distinct from mainstream celebrations of the role of the United States in the world, which tend to come from the centre or right of the ideological spectrum. A common characteristic of this writing on the left is not only criticism of the global hegemony of the United States, but confidence that it is in steepening decline, if not terminal crisis. Radical opposition to the American empire, however, does not require reassurance of its impending collapse or retreat. The changing balance of forces at whose centre its hegemony continues to lie must be reckoned objectively, without wishful thinking. How far much of the American elite itself is from any such sober stocktaking forms the subject of the second part of this book, 'Consilium', which looks at the current thinking of its strategists. This forms a system of discourse about which relatively little has been written. The survey of it here offers a first synoptic account. To this I have added, in an annexe, an earlier consideration of one of the best known of all its contemporary minds.

I owe composition of 'Imperium' and 'Consilium' to a year at the Institute of Advanced Studies in Nantes, finishing the last in October 2013; they first appeared in *New Left Review* in the following month. In the time that has elapsed since, the international scene has been dominated by a number of developments, in the extended Middle East, the former Soviet Union and the Far East, that have renewed debate about the condition of American power. A brief postscript considers these and their upshots, still ongoing.

Perry Anderson
October 2014

ACKNOWLEDGEMENTS

I owe special thanks to the Institut d'Etudes Avancées of Nantes, in whose ideal environment the major part of the research and writing of this book was done; to Anders Stephanson, for his critical comments; and to Susan Watkins, the editor of *New Left Review*, where the text was first published in October 2013, whose injunctions were essential to its completion.

IMPERIUM

Since the Second World War, the external order of American power has been largely insulated from the internal political system. If party competition in the domestic arena has rested on rival electoral blocs, combining significant fluidity of contours with increasing sharpness of conflicts, in the global arena such differences are far less. Commonality of outlook and continuity of objectives set the administration of empire apart from rule of the homeland.[1] In some degree, the contrast between the two is a function of the general distance between the horizons of chancelleries or corporations, and of citizens in all capitalist democracies—what happens overseas is of much greater consequence to bankers and diplomats, officers and industrialists, than to voters, issuing in correspondingly more focused and coherent outcomes.

In the American case it also follows from two further local particulars: the provincialism of an electorate with minimal

---

1   For the former: 'Homeland', *New Left Review* 81, May–June 2013. In presidential contests campaign rhetoric will routinely assail incumbents for weakness or mismanagement of foreign policy. Victors will then proceed much as before.

knowledge of the outside world, and a political system that—in strident contradiction with the design of the Founders—has increasingly given virtually untrammelled power to the executive in the conduct of foreign affairs, freeing presidencies, often baulked of domestic goals by fractious legislatures, to act without comparable cross-cutting pressures abroad. In the sphere created by these objective conditions of policy formation, there developed from mid-century around the Presidency a narrow foreign-policy elite, and a distinctive ideological vocabulary with no counterpart in internal politics: conceptions of the 'grand strategy' to be pursued by the American state in its dealings with the world.[2] The parameters of these were laid down as victory came into sight during the Second World War, and with it the prospect of planetary power.

---

2 For the general composition of foreign policy-makers, see the best succinct study of the arc of US foreign policy in the twentieth century, Thomas J. McCormick, *America's Half-Century*, Baltimore 1995, 2nd edn, pp. 13–15: one third made up of career bureaucrats, to two-thirds of—typically more influential—'in-and-outers', recruited 40 per cent from investment banks and corporations, 40 per cent from law firms, and most of the rest from political science departments.

PRODROMES

The US imperium that came into being after 1945 had a long pre-history. In North America, uniquely, the originating coordinates of empire were coeval with the nation. These lay in the combination of a settler economy free of any of the feudal residues or impediments of the Old World, and a continental territory protected by two oceans: producing the purest form of nascent capitalism, in the largest nation-state, anywhere on earth. That remained the enduring material matrix of the country's ascent in the century after independence. To the objective privileges of an economy and geography without parallel were added two potent subjective legacies, of culture and politics: the idea—derived from initial Puritan settlement—of a nation enjoying divine favour, imbued with a sacred calling; and the belief—derived from the War of Independence— that a republic endowed with a constitution of liberty for all times had arisen in the New World. Out of these four ingredients emerged, very early, the ideological repertoire of an American nationalism that afforded seamless passage to an American imperialism, characterized by a *complexio oppositorum* of exceptionalism and universalism. The United States was unique among nations, yet at the same time a lodestar for the world: an order at once historically unexampled and ultimately a compelling example to all.

These were the convictions of the Founders. The radiance of the nation would in the first instance be territorial, within the Western Hemisphere. As Jefferson put it to Monroe in 1801: 'However our present interests may restrain us within our limits, it is impossible not to look forward to distant times, when our multiplication will expand it beyond those limits, and cover the whole northern, if not the southern continent, with people speaking the same language, governed in similar forms, and by similar laws'. But in the last instance, that radiance would be more than territorial: it would be moral and political. In Adams's words to Jefferson in 1813: 'Our pure, virtuous, public spirited, federative republic will last forever, govern the globe and introduce the perfection of man'.[3] Towards mid-century, the two registers fused into the famous slogan of an associate of Jackson: 'the right of our manifest destiny to overspread and possess the whole continent that providence has given us for the great experiment of liberty and federated self-government'. For a land 'vigorous and fresh from the hand of God' had a 'blessed mission to the nations of the world'. Who could doubt 'the far-reaching, the boundless future will be the era of American greatness'?[4] The annexation of half the surface of Mexico followed in short order.

---

3   See Robert Kagan's clear-eyed *Dangerous Nation: America in the World 1600–1900*, London 2006, pp. 80, 156; for an assessment, 'Consilium', pp. 136–41, below.

4   John O'Sullivan, coiner of the slogan and author of these declarations, was an ideologue for Jackson and Van Buren: see Anders Stephanson, *Manifest Destiny: American Expansionism and the Empire of Right*, New York 1995, pp. 39–42, unsurpassed in its field.

Once the current boundaries of the United States were largely reached, the same sense of the future took more commercial than territorial form, looking west rather than south. Lincoln's secretary of state exhorted his compatriots: 'You are already the great continental power of America. But does that content you? I trust it does not. You want the commerce of the world. This must be looked for on the Pacific. The nation that draws most from the earth and fabricates most, and sells the most to foreign nations, must be and will be the great power of the earth.'[5] What Manifest Destiny and the conquest of Mexico were on land, Commodore Perry and the Open Door could be on sea—the horizon of an American marine and mercantile primacy in the Orient, bearing free trade and Christianity to its shores. With the outbreak of the Spanish–American War, classical inter-imperialist conflict brought colonies in the Pacific and the Caribbean, and full-fledged entrance into the ranks of the great powers. Under the first Roosevelt, Panama was carved out of Colombia as a US dependency to link the two seas, and race—Anglo-Saxon breeding and solidarity— added to religion, democracy and trade in the rhetoric of the nation's calling.

This was never uncontested. At each stage, eloquent American voices had denounced the megalomania of Manifest Destiny, the plunder of Mexico, the seizure of Hawaii, the slaughter in the Philippines, attacking every kind of racism and imperialism as a betrayal of the anti-colonial birthright of the republic. Rejection of foreign adventures—annexations or interventions—was not a break with national values, but always

---

5 Seward did not neglect territorial expansion, acquiring Alaska and the Midway Islands and pressing for Hawaii, but regarded this as means not end in the build-up of American power.

a possible version of them. From the beginning, exceptionalism and universalism formed a potentially unstable compound. Conviction of the first allowed for belief that the United States could preserve its unique virtues only by remaining a society apart from a fallen world. Commitment to the second authorized a messianic activism by the United States to redeem that world. Between these two poles—'separation' and 'regenerative intervention', as Anders Stephanson has described them—public opinion could more than once abruptly shift.[6]

As the US entered the new century, however, such mood swings were of less significance than the sheer economic and demographic growth of the country. By 1910, American capitalism was already in a league of its own, with an industrial magnitude larger than that of Germany and Britain combined. In an age permeated with social Darwinist beliefs in the survival of the fittest, such indices of production could only mean, for ambitious contemporaries, the coming of a power commensurate with them. As the Civil War felled half a million of his countrymen, Whitman exulted that 'we have undoubtedly in the United States the greatest military power in the world'.[7] Yet after Reconstruction, the peacetime strength of the army remained modest by international standards. The navy— marines dispatched for regular interventions in the Caribbean and Central America—had more future. Symptomatically, the entrance of the United States into the intellectual arena of

---

6 Stephanson, *Manifest Destiny*, pp. xii–xiii; it is one of the strengths of this study, which assembles a bouquet of the most extravagant pronouncements of American chauvinism, that it also supplies the (often impassioned) counterpoint of its opponents.

7 Victor Kiernan, *America: The New Imperialism: From White Settlement to World Hegemony*, London 1978, p. 57, which offers a graphic account of imperial imaginings in the 'Middle Decades' of the nineteenth century.

Weltpolitik came with the impact of Mahan's *Influence of Sea Power upon History*, closely studied in Berlin, London, Paris and Tokyo, and a touchstone for both Roosevelts, which argued that 'everything that moves on water'—as opposed to land— possessed 'the prerogative of offensive defence'.[8] A decade later, Brooks Adams laid out the global logic of US industrial preem- inence in *America's Economic Supremacy*. In 1900, he wrote, 'For the first time in human experience a single nation this year leads in the production of the precious metals, copper, iron and coal; and this year also, for the first time, the world has done its banking to the west and not to the east of the Atlantic.' In the struggle for life among nations, empire was 'the most dazzling prize for which any people can contend'. Provided the American state acquired the necessary organizational form, the US could in future surpass the imperial wealth and power of England and Rome.[9] But when war broke out in 1914, there was still a wide gap between such premonitions and any consensus that America should involve itself in the quarrels of Europe.

---

8 Captain A. T. Mahan, *The Influence of Sea Power upon History, 1660– 1783*, London 1890, p. 87. A prolific commentator on international affairs, adviser to Hay on the Open Door Notes and intimate of the first Roosevelt, Mahan was a vigorous proponent of a martial spirit and robust navalism: peace was merely the 'tutelary deity of the stock-market'.

9 'Within two generations', Adams told his readers, America's 'great inter- ests will cover the Pacific, which it will hold like an inland sea', and presiding over 'the development of Eastern Asia, reduce it to a part of our system'. To that end, 'America must expand and concentrate until the limit of the possible is attained; for Governments are simply huge corporations in competition, in which the most economical, in propor- tion to its energy, survives, and in which the wasteful and the slow are undersold and eliminated'. Given that 'these great struggles sometimes involve an appeal to force, safety lies in being armed and organized against all emergencies'. *America's Economic Supremacy*, New York 1900, pp. 194, 50–1, 85, 222. Adams and Mahan were friends, in the White House circle of TR.

II

With the arrival of Woodrow Wilson in the White House, however, a convulsive turn in the trajectory of American foreign policy was at hand. As no other president before or after him, Wilson gave voice to every chord of presumption in the imperial repertoire, at messianic pitch. Religion, capitalism, democracy, peace and the might of the United States were one. 'Lift your eyes to the horizons of business', he told American salesmen, 'and with the inspiration of the thought that you are Americans and are meant to carry liberty and justice and the principles of humanity wherever you go, go out and sell goods that will make the world more comfortable and more happy, and convert them to the principles of America.'[10] In a campaign address of 1912, he declared: 'If I did not believe in Providence I would feel like a man going blindfolded through a haphazard world. I do believe in Providence. I believe that God presided over the inception of this nation. I believe he planted in us the visions of liberty.' A 'divine destiny' was furthermore in store for America: 'We are chosen and prominently chosen to show the way to the nations of the world how they shall walk in the paths of liberty.'[11] The route might be arduous, but the bourne was clear. 'Slowly ascending the tedious climb that leads to the final uplands, we shall get our ultimate view of the duties of mankind. We have breasted a considerable part of that climb and shall presently, it may be in a generation or two, come out upon those great heights where there shines unobstructed

---

10 Address to the World's Salesmanship Congress in Detroit, 10 July 1916: *The Papers of Woodrow Wilson*, vol. 37, Princeton 1981, p. 387.

11 Campaign address in Jersey City, 26 May 1912: *Papers of Woodrow Wilson*, vol. 24, Princeton 1977, p. 443.

the light of the justice of God'.[12] After sending US troops into more Caribbean and Central American states than any of his predecessors—Mexico, Cuba, Haiti, the Dominican Republic, Nicaragua—in 1917 Wilson plunged the country into the First World War, a conflict in which America had 'the infinite privilege of fulfilling her destiny and saving the world'.[13]

If US entry into the war made victory for the Entente a foregone conclusion, imposing an American peace proved more difficult. Wilson's Fourteen Points, a hurried attempt to counter Lenin's denunciation of secret treaties and imperialist rule, were distinguished mainly by their call for a global Open Door—'the removal, so far as possible, of all economic barriers'—and 'impartial adjustment', not abolition, of 'all colonial claims'. Contrary to legend, self-determination appears nowhere in the enumeration. Wilson's bulletins of democratic deliverance were treated with disdain by his partners at Versailles. At home, the League he proposed to avert future conflicts fared no better. 'The stage is set, the destiny disclosed', he announced, presenting his arrangements for perpetual peace in 1919, 'the hand of God has led us into this way'.[14] The Senate was unmoved. America could dispense with Wilson's ambitions. The country was not ready for an indefinite extension of regenerative intervention into the affairs of the world at large. Under the next

12 Address to the Southern Commercial Congress in Mobile, 27 October 1913: *Papers of Woodrow Wilson*, vol. 28, Princeton 1978, p. 52.

13 Address in the Princess Theatre in Cheyenne, 24 September 1919: *Papers of Woodrow Wilson*, vol. 63, Princeton 1990, p. 469.

14 *Papers of Woodrow Wilson*, vol. 61, Princeton 1981, p. 436. After whipping up hysteria against anyone of German origin during the war, Wilson had no compunction in declaring that 'the only organized forces in this country' against the Versailles Treaty he presented to the Senate were 'the forces of hyphenated Americans'—'hyphen is the knife that is being stuck into the document' (*sic*): vol. 63, pp. 469, 493.

three presidents, the United States concentrated on recovering its loans to Europe, otherwise limiting its operations outside the hemisphere to ineffectual attempts to get Germany back onto its feet and restrain Japan from overdoing expansion into China. To many, capsizal to the pole of separation—in the vocabulary of its opponents, 'isolationism'—seemed all but complete.

The reality was that American entry into the First World War had answered to no determinable national interest. A gratuitous decision by its president, enforced with sweeping ethnic persecution and political repression at home, it was the product of a massive excess of US power over any material goals procurable by it. The rhetoric of American expansionism had typically projected markets overseas as if they were an external frontier, with the claim that US goods and investments now required outlets abroad that only an Open Door could assure. Yet the American economy, with its abundant natural resources and vast internal market, continued to be largely autarkic. Foreign trade accounted for no more than 10 per cent of GNP down to the First World War, when most American exports still consisted of raw materials and processed foodstuffs. Nor, of course, was there any Open Door to the US market itself, traditionally protected by high tariffs with scant regard for the principles of free trade. Still less was there the remotest threat of attack or invasion from Europe. It was this disjuncture between ideology and reality that brought Wilson's millenarian globalism to an abrupt end. The United States could afford to dictate the military outcome of war in Europe. But if the cost of its intervention was small, the gain was nil. Neither at popular nor at elite level was any pressing need felt for institutional follow-through. America could look after itself, without worrying

unduly about Europe. Under the banner of a return to normalcy, in 1920 Harding buried his Democratic opponent in the
largest electoral landslide of modern times.

But within a decade, the arrival of the Depression was
a signal that the pre-history of the American empire was
approaching its end. If the initial Wall Street crash of 1929 was
the bursting of an endogenous credit bubble, the fuse of the
bank failures that burnt the US economy into the real slump
was lit by the collapse of the Creditanstalt in Austria in 1931,
and its knock-on effects across Europe. The crisis brought home
that, however relatively insulated American factories—farms
less so—might still be from world trade, American deposits
were not from international financial markets, in a signal that
with the passing of London's role as pivot of the system, and the
default of New York as successor, the order of capital as a whole
was at risk in the absence of a stabilizing centre. The immediate
concerns of Roosevelt's first term lay in domestic measures to
overcome the crisis, prompting unceremonious abandonment
of the gold standard and brusque rejection of any coordinated
international attempt to manage exchange rates. But by previous standards the New Deal was not protectionist. The
Smoot–Hawley Act was dismantled, tariffs selectively lowered,
and an impassioned champion of free trade—to American
specifications—put in charge of foreign policy: Cordell Hull,
the 'Tennessee Cobden', becoming the longest-serving secretary of state in US history.

Towards the end of Roosevelt's second term, as war raged
in East Asia and threatened in Europe, rearmament started to
make good the weaknesses (highlighted by the recession in
1937) of domestic recovery, giving the New Deal a second wind.
The internal fortunes of the American economy and external

postures of the American state were henceforward joined as they had never been before. But though the White House was increasingly on the *qui vive* to developments abroad, and military readiness stepped up, public opinion remained averse to any prospect of a rerun of 1917–1920, and within the administration there was little or no conception of what the American role or priorities might be, should one materialize. Roosevelt had become increasingly alarmed at German and to a lesser extent Japanese belligerence. Hull was concerned above all by the retreat of national economies behind tariff walls, and the erection of trade blocs. At the War Department, Woodring resisted any thought of involvement in a new round of great power conflicts. Beyond conflicting negative apprehensions, there was not yet much positive sense of the place of American power in the world ahead.

2

CRYSTALLIZATION

The vacuum of longer-range reflections in Washington would be underlined with the appearance of a remarkable work composed before Pearl Harbour, but published shortly after it, *America's Strategy in World Politics*. Its author Nicholas Spykman—a Dutchman with a background in Egypt and Java, then holding a chair at Yale—died a year later.[1] In what remains

---

1 Spykman had a remarkable career, whose early years have aroused no curiosity in his adopted country, and later years been ignored in his native country, where he appears to be still largely unknown. Educated at Delft, Spykman went to the Middle East in 1913 at the age of twenty, and to Batavia in 1916, as a journalist and—at least in Java, and perhaps also in Egypt—undercover agent of the Dutch state in the management of opinion, as references in Kees van Dijk, *The Netherlands Indies and the Great War 1914–1918*, Leiden 2007 reveal: pp. 229, 252, 477. While in Java, he published a bilingual—Dutch and Malay—book entitled *Hindia Zelfbestuur* [Self-Rule for the Indies], Batavia 1918, advising the national movement to think more seriously about the economics of independence, and develop cooperatives and trade unions rather than simply denouncing foreign investment. In 1920 he turned up in California, completed a doctorate on Simmel at Berkeley by 1923, published as a book by Chicago in 1925, when he was hired by Yale as a professor of international relations. Not a few mysteries remain to be unravelled in this trajectory, but it is clear that Spykman was from early on a cool and original mind, who unlike Morgenthau or Kelsen, the two other European intellectuals in America with whom he might otherwise be compared, arrived in the US

perhaps the most striking single exercise in geopolitical literature of any kind, Spykman laid out a basic conceptual grid for
the understanding of contemporary relations between states,
and a comprehensive map of American positions and prospects
within it. In an international system without central authority,
the primary objective of the foreign policy of every state was
necessarily the preservation and improvement of its power, in
a struggle to curb that of other states. Political equilibrium—
a balance of power—was a noble ideal, but 'the truth of the
matter is that states are only interested in a balance which is in
their favour. Not an equilibrium, but a generous margin is their
objective'. The means of power were four: persuasion, purchase,
barter and coercion. While military strength was the primary
requirement of every sovereign state, all were instruments of
an effective foreign policy. Combining them, hegemony was a
'power position permitting the domination of all states within
its reach'.[2]

Such hegemony the United States had long enjoyed over
most of the Western hemisphere. But it was a dangerous
mistake to think that it could therefore rely on the protection
of two oceans, and the resources of the interlinked landmass
lying between them, to maintain its power position vis-à-
vis Germany and Japan. A detailed inventory of the strategic
materials needed for success in modern war showed that Latin
America, for all its valuable raw materials, could not supply
every critical item missing from North America.[3] Nor was it

not as a refugee, but as an *esprit fort* from the Indies who after naturaliza-
tion felt no inhibition in delivering sharp judgements on his host society.
2 Spykman, *America's Strategy in World Politics: The United States and the
Balance of Power*, New York 1942, pp. 7, 21, 19.
3 Six decades later, in the only serious engagement since with Spykman's
work, Robert Art has argued that his 'masterful book' erred in thinking

realistic to imagine unaffected support for the United States to the south. The record of Washington in the region, where 'our so-called painless imperialism has seemed painless only to us', precluded that. Nothing like the 'modern, capitalistic credit economy' of the United States, with its highly developed industrial system, giant corporations, militant union struggles and strikebreaker vigilantes existed in the still largely feudal societies of Latin America, while the ABC states of its far south lay 'too far from the centre of our power to be easily intimidated by measures short of war'.[4] Any purely hemispheric defence was an illusion; still more so, quarter-sphere defence confined to North America alone, if the US was to avoid becoming a mere buffer state between German and Japanese empires. American strategy would have to be offensive, striking out across the seas at the two powers now at war—by the time the book came out—against the US on the other side of the Atlantic and the Pacific.

Spykman's rebuttal of isolationism became conventional wisdom once the US entered the war. But not his wider vision, which in its cool dismissal of American verities that would be

---

North America was impregnable against military invasion, but vulnerable to economic strangulation by the Axis powers if they were victorious in Europe. The quarter-sphere, Art showed, had the raw materials to withstand any blockade: America could have stayed out of the Second World War without risk to itself. But its entry into the war was nevertheless rational, for purposes of the Cold War. 'By fighting in World War Two and helping to defeat Germany and Japan, the United States, in effect, established forward operating bases against the Soviet Union in the form of Western Europe and Japan. Having these economic-industrial areas, together with Persian Gulf oil, on America's side led to the Soviet Union's encirclement, rather than America's, which would have been the case had it not entered the war': 'The United States, the Balance of Power and World War II: Was Spykman Right?', *Security Studies*: Spring 2005, pp. 365–406, now included in Robert Art, *America's Grand Strategy and World Politics*, New York 2009, pp. 69–106.

4   Spykman, *America's Strategy in World Politics*, pp. 64, 213, 62.

recycled by the administration as wartime objectives remained incompatible with any of the doctrines that came to be formulated in Washington during the conflict. *America's Strategy in World Politics* explained that liberal democracy had become a stale myth; laissez-faire led to increasing monopoly and concentration of economic power; free trade was a fiction mocked by state subsidies; at home, class struggle, declared nonexistent, was settled by tear gas and violence; abroad, American bayonets taught lesser breeds modern accounting.[5] Declining to take the standard rhetoric of the struggle at face value, Spykman arrived at conclusions that could only be jarring to the policy-makers of the hour. The US should already be reckoning on a reversal of alliances when the war was won. In Europe, Britain would not want to see Russia any more than Germany on the shores of the North Sea, and could be counted on to build Germany back up against Russia; while in Asia, America would have to build Japan back up against China, whose potential power was infinitely greater, and once 'modernized, vitalized and militarized' would be the principal threat to the position of the Western powers in the Pacific.[6] As the Red Army fought off

5   'The whole social myth of liberal democracy has lost most of its revolutionary force since the middle of the nineteenth century, and in its present form is hardly adequate to sustain democratic practices in the countries where it originated, let alone inspire new loyalties in other peoples and other lands'. As for the country's economic creed, 'American business still believes that an invisible hand guides the economic process and that an intelligent selfishness and a free and unhampered operation of the price system will produce the greatest good for the greatest number'. Overall, 'North American ideology, as might be expected, is essentially a middle-class business ideology'—though it also included, of course, 'certain religious elements': *American Strategy in World Politics*, pp. 215–7, 258, 7. For Spykman's sardonic notations on the Monroe Doctrine, Roosevelt Corollary and the Good Neighbour policy in the 'American Mediterranean', see pp. 60–4.

6   Spykman, *American Strategy in World Politics*, pp. 460, 466–70.

the Wehrmacht at the gates of Moscow, and Japanese carriers moved towards Midway, such previsions were out of season. Their time would come.

II

The mental framework of the officials charged with American foreign policy was far from uniform. But central assumptions were widely shared. When European war broke out in 1939, virtually all its possible outcomes filled planners in Washington with alarm. Dire, certainly, would be German success: few had any illusions in Hitler. But a British victory won by statist mobilization, entrenching the sterling bloc yet further, might not be so much better. Worst of all, perhaps, would be such mutual destruction that, in the ensuing chaos, one form or another of socialism would take hold of the continent.[7] Once Washington entered the war, and alliance with London and Moscow was essential to winning it, the priorities of the battlefield took precedence over the calculations of capital. But these remained, throughout, the strategic background to the global struggle. For Roosevelt's planners the long-term priorities were two-fold.[8] The world must be made safe for capitalism at large; and within the world of capitalism, the United States should reign supreme. What would this dual objective mean for the postwar scene?

---

7 For such fears, see the abundant documentation in Patrick Hearden, *Architects of Globalism: Building a New World Order during World War II*, Lafayetteville 2002, pp. 12–17 ff, by far the best and most detailed study of the US wartime planners.

8 The critical wartime group included Hull, Welles, Acheson, Berle, Bowman, Davis and Taylor at State. Hopkins was an equerry more than a planner.

First and foremost, in point of conceptual time, the construction of an international framework for capital that would put an end to the dynamics of autarkic division and statist control that had precipitated the war itself, of which Hitler's Third Reich and Japan's Co-Prosperity Sphere had been the most destructive examples, but Britain's Imperial Preference was another retrograde case. The free enterprise system in America itself was at risk without access to foreign markets.[9] What would be needed after the war was a generalization of the Open Door that Washington had urged on its rivals in the race to seize command of markets in China: an all-round liberalization of trade, but henceforward—this was crucial—firmly embedded in new international institutions. Such an economic order would be not only a guarantee of peaceful relations between states, but allow the US to assume its natural place

9 'We need these markets for the output of the United States', Acheson told Congress in November 1944. 'My contention is that we cannot have full employment and prosperity in the United States without foreign markets'. Denied these, America might be forced into statism too, a fear repeatedly expressed at the time. In 1940, the Fortune Round Table was worrying that 'there is a real danger that as a result of a long war all the belligerent powers will permanently accept some form of state-directed economic system', raising 'the longer-range question of whether or not the American capitalist system could continue to function if most of Europe and Asia should abolish free enterprise in favour of totalitarian economics': Hearden, *Architects of Globalism*, pp. 41, 14. Concern that the US could be forced in such direction had already been voiced by Brooks Adams at the turn of the century, who feared that if a European coalition ever dominated trade with China, 'it will have good prospects of throwing back a considerable surplus on our hands, for us to digest as best as we can', reducing America to the 'semi-stationary' condition of France, and a battle with rivals that could 'only be won by surpassing the enemy with his own methods'. Result: 'The Eastern and Western continents would be competing for the most perfect system of state socialism': Adams, *America's Economic Supremacy*, pp. 52–3. In 1947 Adams's book was republished with an introduction by Marquis Childs, as a prophetic vision of the challenge of Russia to America in the Cold War.

as first among them. From the time of Jefferson and Adams onwards, conspicuous national traditions had been generically expansionist, and as now far the largest and most advanced industrial power in the world, the US could be confident that free trade would ensure its hegemony at large, as it had Britain's a century earlier. The political complement of this economic order would be founded on the principles of liberal democracy, as set forth in the Atlantic Charter.

From 1943 onwards, as victory came nearer, the requirements of this vision moved into sharper political focus. Three concerns were overriding.[10] The first was the threat to a satisfactory post-war settlement from the potential maintenance of imperial preference by Britain. Washington would brook no barrier to American exports. From the outset, the US had insisted that a condition of the lend-lease on which Britain depended for survival after 1940 must be abandonment of imperial preference, once hostilities were over. Churchill, furious at the imposition of Article VII, could only seek to weaken the American diktat with a vaguely worded temporary escape clause. The second concern, mounting as the end of the war approached, and fully shared by Britain, was the spread of resistance movements in Europe—France, Belgium, Italy, Yugoslavia, Greece—in which variegated currents of the left were leading forces, just as planners in Washington had originally feared. The third was the advance from the spring of 1944

---

10 These are the object of Gabriel Kolko's great work, *The Politics of War: The World and United States Foreign Policy, 1943–1945*, New York 1968, whose magisterial sweep remains unequalled in the literature—covering overall US economic objectives; the cutting down to size of British imperial positions; checking of the left in Italy, Greece, France and Belgium; dealing with the Soviet Union in Eastern Europe; fixing up the UN; planning the future of Germany; sustaining the GMD in China; and nuclear bombing of Japan.

of the Red Army into Eastern Europe, which soon became an acute preoccupation. If the prospect most immediately present in the minds of American planners at the start of the war was the danger of any reversion to the conditions that had produced Nazi Germany and militarist Japan, as it drew to an end a still greater threat was taking shape in the form of its most important ally in the battle against them, the Soviet Union.

For here was not just an alternative form but a negation of capitalism, intending nothing less than its overthrow across the planet. Communism was an enemy far more radical than fascism had ever been: not an aberrant member of the family of polities respecting private ownership of the means of production, but an alien force dedicated to destroying it. American rulers had, of course, always been aware of the evils of Bolshevism, which Wilson had tried to stamp out at their inception by dispatching an expedition to help the Whites in 1919. But though foreign intervention had not succeeded in strangling it at birth, the USSR of the interwar years remained an isolated, and looked a weak, power. Soviet victories over the Wehrmacht, long before there was an Anglo-American foot on European soil, abruptly altered its position in the postwar calculus. So long as fighting lasted, Moscow remained an ally to be prudently assisted, and where necessary humoured. But once it was over, a reckoning would come.

III

At the helm during the Second World War, Roosevelt had manoeuvred his country into the conflict not out of any general anti-fascist conviction—though hostile to Hitler, he had admired Mussolini, helped Franco to power, and remained on good terms with Pétain[11]—but fear of Japanese and German expansion. Nor, for his class, was he especially anti-communist: at ease with the USSR as an ally, he was scarcely more realistic about Stalin than Stalin had been about Hitler. Though fond of Churchill, he was unsentimental about the empire he upheld, and had no time for De Gaulle. Strategic thought of any depth was foreign to him. Never a particularly well-informed or consistent performer on the world stage, personal self-confidence substituting for analytic grip, his vagaries frequently dismayed subordinates.[12] But an abiding set of premises he possessed. In

11 Italy: soon after his inauguration in 1932, FDR was confiding to a friend that 'I am keeping in fairly close touch with that admirable Italian gentleman'. Asked five years later by his ambassador in Rome if 'he had anything against dictatorships', he replied, 'Of course not, unless they moved across their frontiers and sought to make trouble in other countries'. Spain: within a month of Franco's uprising, he had imposed an unprecedented embargo on arms to the Republic—'a gesture we Nationalists shall never forget', declared the Generalísimo: 'President Roosevelt behaved like a true gentleman'. France: he felt an 'old and deep affection' for Pétain, with whose regime in Vichy the US maintained diplomatic relations down to 1944, and matching detestation of De Gaulle—a 'prima donna', 'jackanapes' and 'fanatic'. See, respectively, David Schmitz, *The United States and Fascist Italy, 1922–1940*, Chapel Hill 1988, pp. 139, 184; Douglas Little, *Malevolent Neutrality: The United States, Great Britain, and the Origins of the Spanish Civil War*, Ithaca 1985, pp. 237–8, and Dominic Tierney, FDR *and the Spanish Civil War*, Durham, NC 2007, pp. 39, 45–7; Mario Rossi, *Roosevelt and the French*, Westport 1993, pp. 71–2, and John Lamberton Harper, *American Visions of Europe: Franklin D. Roosevelt, George F. Kennan and Dean G. Acheson*, Cambridge 1994, p. 113.

12 For concurrent judgements of FDR's failings as a wartime leader from antithetical observers, see Kennan: 'Roosevelt, for all his charm and skill as a political leader was, when it came to foreign policy, a very superficial man, ignorant, dilettantish, with a severely limited intellectual horizon', and Kolko: 'As a leader Roosevelt was a consistently destabilizing element in the conduct of American affairs during the war-time crises, which were intricate and often assumed a command of facts as a prerequisite for serious judgements': Harper, *American Visions of Europe*, p. 174; Kolko, *Politics of War*, pp. 348–50. Light-mindedness or ignorance led FDR to make commitments and take decisions—over Lend Lease, the

the words of the most accomplished apologist for his conduct of foreign affairs, his consistency lay simply in the fact that 'Roosevelt was a nationalist, an American whose ethnocentrism was part of his outlook': a ruler possessed of the 'calm, quiet conviction that Americanism', conceived as a 'combination of free enterprise and individual values', would be eagerly adopted by the rest of the world, once American power had done away with obstacles to its spread. Though proud of the New Deal's work in saving US capitalism, he was uncomfortable with economic questions. But 'like most Americans, Roosevelt unquestioningly agreed with the expansionist goals of Hull's economic program'. There, 'he did not lead, but followed'.[13]

The president's vision of the postwar world, formed as the USSR was still fighting for its life against the Third Reich, while the United States was basking untouched in the boom of the century, gave primacy to the construction of a liberal international order of trade and mutual security that the US could be sure of dominating. A product of the war, it marked an epochal break in American foreign policy. Hitherto, there had always been a tension within American expansionism, between the conviction of hemispheric separatism and the

---

Morgenthau Plan, Palestine, the French Empire—that often left his associates aghast, and had to be reversed.

13   Warren Kimball, *The Juggler: Franklin Roosevelt as Wartime Statesman*, Princeton 1991, pp. 185, 186, 10, 59. Culturally speaking, Roosevelt's nationalism had a persistent edge of antipathy to the Old World. The dominant pre-war outlook of his administration is described by Harper as a 'Europhobic hemispherism': *American Visions of Europe*, pp. 60 ff—'the record is full of presidential expressions of the anxiety, suspicion and disgust that animated this tendency'. At the same time, imagining that the world would fall over itself to adopt the American Way of Life, once given a chance, Roosevelt's nationalism—Kimball captures this side of him well—was easygoing in tone, just because it was so innocently hubristic.

call of a redemptive interventionism, each generating its own ideological themes and political pressures, crisscrossing or colliding according to the conjuncture, without ever coalescing into a stable standpoint on the outside world. In the wave of patriotic indignation and prosperity that followed the Japanese attack on Pearl Harbour, the conflicts of the past were washed away. Traditionally, the strongholds of isolationist nationalism lay in the small-business and farmer population of the Mid-West; the bastions of a more interventionist nationalism—in local parlance, 'internationalism'—in the banking and corporate elites of the East Coast. The war brought these together. The former had always looked more positively on the Pacific as a natural extension of the frontier, and sought no-holds-barred revenge for the attack on Hawaii. The latter, oriented to markets and investments across the Atlantic threatened by Hitler's New Order, had wider horizons. Renovated by the rise of new capital-intensive firms and investment banks committed to free trade, each a key component in the political bloc behind Roosevelt, these interests supplied the managers of the war economy. They looked forward, beyond sky-high domestic profits during the fighting, to cleaning up in Europe after it.[14]

In these conditions, the two nationalisms—isolationist and interventionist—could finally start to fuse into a durable synthesis. For Franz Schurmann, whose *Logic of World Power*

---

14 See the famous taxonomy of interests in Thomas Ferguson, 'From Normalcy to New Deal: Industrial Structure, Party Competition and American Public Policy in the Great Depression', *International Organization*, Winter 1984, pp. 41–94. In 1936, FDR could count on support from Chase Manhattan, Goldman Sachs, Manufacturers Trust and Dillon, Read; Standard Oil, General Electric, International Harvester, Zenith, IBM, ITT, Sears, United Fruit and Pan Am.

ranks with Spykman's *American Strategy* and Kolko's *Politics of War* for originality within the literature on US foreign policy, this was the true arrival of American imperialism, properly understood—not a natural outgrowth of the incremental expansionism from below of the past, but the sudden crystallization of a project from above to remake the world in the American image.[15] That imperialism, he believed, was only possible because it rested on the democratic foundations of the New Deal and the leader of genius who sought to extend it overseas in a global order of comparable popular welfare, assuring the US a consensual hegemony over postwar humanity at large. 'What Roosevelt sensed and gave visionary expression to was that the world was ripe for one of the most radical experiments in history: the unification of the entire world under a domination centred in America.'[16] In this enterprise, the contrary impulses of isolation and intervention, nationalist pride and internationalist ambition, would be joined and sublimated in the task of reorganizing the world along US lines, to US advantage—and that of mankind.

---

15 'There is an important qualitative difference between expansionism and imperialism'. Expansionism was the step-by-step adding on of territory, productive assets, strategic bases and the like, as always practised by older empires, and continued by America since the war through a spreading network of investments, client states and overseas garrisons on every continent. By contrast, 'imperialism as a vision and a doctrine has a total, worldwide quality. It envisages the organization of large parts of the world from the top down, in contrast to expansionism, which is accretion from the bottom up'. Schurmann, *The Logic of World Power*, New York 1974, p. 6.

16 'American imperialism was not the natural extension of an expansionism which began with the very origins of America itself. Nor was it the natural outgrowth of a capitalist world market system which America helped to revive after 1945. American imperialism, whereby America undertook to dominate, organize and direct the free world, was a product of Rooseveltian New Dealism': Schurmann, *The Logic of World Power*, pp. 5, 114.

Schurmann's imaginative grasp of the impending muta-
tion in the American imperium remains unsurpassed.[17] But
in its idealization of Roosevelt, however ambivalent, it outran
the time and person by a good margin. The White House still
had only sketchy notions of the order it sought when peace
was restored, and these did not include bestowing a New Deal
on humanity at large. Its concerns were focused in the first
instance on power, not welfare. The postwar system FDR had
in mind would have a place for Russia and Britain in running
the world—even *pro forma* China, since Chiang Kai-shek could
be relied on to do US bidding. But there could be no question
which among the 'four policemen', as he liked to style them,
would be chief constable. Its territory untouched by war, by
1945 the United States had an economy three times the size
of the USSR's and five times that of Britain, commanding half
of the world's industrial output and three quarters of its gold
reserves. The institutional foundations of a stable peace would
have to reflect that predominance.[18] Before he died Roosevelt
had laid down two of them. At Bretton Woods, birthplace of
the World Bank and the IMF, Britain was obliged to abandon
Imperial Preference, and the dollar installed as master of the
international monetary system, the reserve currency against
which all others had to be pegged.[19] At Dumbarton Oaks, the

---

17 Schurmann's formation set him apart from both main currents, radical
and liberal, of writing about US foreign policy. Schumpeter, Polanyi,
Schmitt, along with Marx and Mao, all left their mark on his thought:
see his self-description, *The Logic of World Power*, pp. 561–5. He was a
significant influence on Giovanni Arrighi.

18 'Roosevelt's "Four Policemen" notion had the appearance of international
equality while, in fact, it assumes a weak China and an Anglo-Soviet
standoff in Europe': Kimball, *The Juggler*, p. 191.

19 Ironically, the architect of the imposition of American will at Bretton
Woods, Harry Dexter White, a closet sympathizer with Russia, was in

structure of the Security Council in a future United Nations was hammered out, conferring permanent seats and veto rights on the four gendarmes-to-be, superimposed on a General Assembly in which two-fifths of the delegates would be supplied by client states of Washington in Latin America, hastily mustered for the purpose with last-minute declarations of war on Germany. Skirmishes with Britain and Russia were kept to a minimum.[20] Hull, awarded—the first in a long line of such recipients—the Nobel Peace Prize for his role at the birth of the new organization, had reason to deem it a triumph. By the time the UN came into being at San Francisco in 1945, it was so firmly under the US thumb that the diplomatic traffic of the delegates to its founding conference was being intercepted round the clock by military surveillance in the nearby Presidio.[21]

---

private himself a critic of the 'rampant imperialism' that was urging 'the US to make the most of our financial domination and military strength and become the most powerful nation in the world': Benn Steil, *The Battle of Bretton Woods: John Maynard Keynes, Harry Dexter White and the Making of a New World Order*, Princeton 2013, pp. 40–1. Steil's account makes clear not only how completely Keynes was outmanoeuvred by White in fumbling attempts to defend British interests in 1944, but how deluded he was in persuading himself that the proceedings of the conference reflected the utmost goodwill of the United States towards Britain.

20 To offset the entry of his *bête noire* Gaullist France into the Security Council, on which Churchill insisted, Roosevelt pressed without success for the inclusion of Brazil as another subordinate of Washington, and over British opposition sought to create 'trusteeships' to screen postwar American designs on key islands in the Pacific. The veto had to be made unconditional at Soviet insistence. For these manoeuvres, see Robert Hilderbrand's authoritative study, *Dumbarton Oaks: The Origins of the United Nations and the Search for Postwar Security*, Chapel Hill 1990, pp. 123–7, 170–4, 192–228.

21 For the lavish stage-managing and clandestine wiretapping of the Conference, see Stephen Schlesinger's enthusiastic account, *Act of*

Roosevelt was in his grave before Germany surrendered. The system whose foundations his administration had laid was incomplete at his death, with much still unsettled. Neither Britain nor France had consented to part with Asian or African colonies he viewed as an anachronism. Russia, its armies nearing Berlin, had designs on Eastern Europe. It might not fit so readily into the new architecture. But with its population decimated and much of its industry in ruins as the Wehrmacht retreated, the USSR would not represent a significant threat to the order to come, and might over time perhaps be coaxed towards it. Moscow's exact role after victory was a secondary preoccupation.

Creation: The Founding of the United Nations, Boulder 2003, *passim*, and Peter Gowan's scathing reconstruction, 'US: UN', *New Left Review* 24, Nov–Dec 2003.

3

SECURITY

Roosevelt's insouciance did not survive him. Once the Red Army was entrenched in Eastern Europe, and Communist regimes set up behind it, with mass Communist parties active to the west and north, in France, Italy and Finland, priorities in Washington were reversed. Meeting the Soviet threat was more urgent than fine-tuning a Pax Americana, some of whose principles might have to be deferred in resisting it. Winning what became the Cold War would have to come first. Truman, who had once rejoiced at the Nazi invasion of the Soviet Union, hoping that each state would destroy the other, was well equipped for the change of direction.[1] Within four days of the German surrender, he had cut off Lend-Lease to Russia

---

1 Famously: 'If we see that Germany is winning we ought to help Russia and if Russia is winning we ought to help Germany, and that way let them kill as many as possible': speech in the Senate, 5 June 1941. In the White House, he would more than once cite the forged Testament of Peter the Great—a nineteenth-century Polish counterpart of the *Protocols of the Elders of Zion*—as the blueprint for Soviet plans of world conquest. In the severe judgement of his most lucid biographer, whose conclusions from it are damning, 'Throughout his presidency, Truman remained a parochial nationalist': Arnold Offner, *Another Such Victory: President Truman and the Cold War, 1945–1953*, Stanford 2002, p. 177.

without warning. At first insecure, tacking between bluster and joviality, his own temperament and that of his predecessor, once US nuclear weapons had shown what they could do in Japan, he scarcely looked back. By the spring of 1946, conciliatory relations with Moscow of the kind Roosevelt had vaguely envisaged, and Stalin doubtfully hoped, were finished. Within another year, the Truman Doctrine blew the bugle for a battle to defend free nations everywhere from aggression and subversion by totalitarianism, the president relishing his role in waking the country from its slumber.[2]

In the Cold War now set in motion, the two sides were asymmetrical. Under Stalin, Soviet foreign policy was essentially defensive: intransigent in its requirement of a security *glacis* in Eastern Europe to prevent any repetition of the invasion it had just suffered, no matter what degree of political or military repression was required to enforce this, but more than willing to ditch or hobble any revolution—in Greece or China—outside this zone that threatened to provoke trouble with a West plainly so much more powerful than itself.[3] The USSR was still only

2   The crudity and violence of Truman's outlook distinguished him from Roosevelt, entitling him to high marks from Wilson Miscamble's vehement *From Roosevelt to Truman: Potsdam, Hiroshima and the Cold War*, Cambridge 2007, whose only complaint is that he did not break fast enough with Roosevelt's collaboration with Stalin: pp. 323–8. FDR would have been unlikely, in dismissing a member of his Cabinet, to rage at 'All the "Artists" with a capital A, the parlour pinkos and the soprano-voiced men' as a 'national danger' and 'sabotage front' for Stalin. See Offner, *Another Such Victory*, p. 177.

3   In the last months of the war, Stalin had been so concerned with maintaining good relations with the allies that he bungled the capture of Berlin when Zhukov's Army Group was a mere forty miles from the city across open country, with orders from its commander on February 5 to storm it on February 15–16. Stalin cancelled these instructions the following day, for fear of ruffling Allied feathers at Yalta, where the Big Three had just started to convene, and he received no favours in return. Had he let his

building—re-building after Nazi wreckage—socialism in one country. Stalin never abandoned the Bolshevik conviction that communism and capitalism were mortal antagonists.[4] But the ultimate horizon of a worldwide free association of producers —the classless society Marx had envisaged—lay far off. For the time being, the balance of forces remained lopsided in favour of capital. In the longer run inter-imperialist contradictions would flare up again and weaken the enemy, as they had twice done in the past, shifting the advantage to labour.[5] In the interim, it was vital that revolutionary forces outside the perimeter of the Soviet bloc should neither threaten its security by provoking imperialism prematurely, nor question the authority of the CPSU over them.

In doctrine as in power, the position of the United States was altogether distinct. Ideologically, two universalisms were locked in struggle during the Cold War. But there was an ontological

---

generals advance as he had earlier agreed, the whole Soviet bargaining position in postwar Germany would been transformed. 'Towards the end of March, Zhukov found him very tired, tense and visibly depressed. His anguish was hardly alleviated by the thought that all the uncertainties might have been avoided if he had allowed the Red Army to attack Berlin and possibly end the war in February, as originally planned': Vojtech Mastny, *Russia's Road to the Cold War. Diplomacy, Warfare and the Politics of Communism, 1941–1945*, New York 1979, pp. 238–9, 243–4, 261. This would not be his only disastrous blunder, not of aggressive over-reaching, but anxious under-reaching, as World War Two came to a close.

4 For a penetrating depiction of Stalin's outlook at the close of the War, see Vladislav Zubok and Constantine Pleshakov, *Inside the Kremlin's Cold War*, Cambridge, MA 1996, pp. 11–46.

5 This was the theme of his speech to the Supreme Soviet of 9 February 1946. Since the first inter-imperialist war had generated the October Revolution, and the second taken the Red Army to Berlin, a third could finish off capitalism—a prospect offering ultimate victory without altering strategic passivity. To the end of his life, Stalin held to the position that inter-imperialist contradictions remained for the time being primary, contradictions between the capitalist and socialist camp secondary.

difference between them. In Stephanson's trenchant formulation: 'Whereas the Soviet Union, representing (it claimed) the
penultimate stage of history, was locked in a dialectical struggle for the final liberation of humankind, the United States *is*
that very liberation. It is the end, it is already a world empire,
it can have no equal, no dialectical Other. What is not like the
United States can, in principle, have no proper efficacy. It is
either a perversion or, at best, a not-yet'.[6] Materially, furthermore, there was no common measure between the rival states
as they emerged from the war. The USSR of 1946–1947 had not
the remotest hope of the ambition on which American grand
strategy was fixed: a 'preponderance of power' across the world,
its annunciation staged over Hiroshima and Nagasaki. The initiative in the conflict between the two lay with the stronger
party. Its ideological label was 'containment', as if the aim of US
planners was to stem a tide of Soviet aggression. But the substance of the doctrine was far from defensive. Nominally, it was
a counsel of firmness and tactical patience to wear the enemy
down, by 'the adroit and vigilant application of counterforce at
a series of constantly shifting geographical and political points',
as its originator put it. But from the beginning, the objective
was not to check, but delete the adversary. Victory, not safety,
was the aim.[7]

---

6 'If the end of history as emancipated humankind is embodied in the
"United States", then the outside can never be identical or ultimately
equal. Difference there is, but it is a difference that is intrinsically unjust
and illegitimate, there only to be overcome and eradicated'. These pas-
sages come from Stephanson, 'Kennan: Realism as Desire', in Nicolas
Guilhot, ed., *The Invention of International Relations Theory*, New York
2011, pp. 177–8.

7 'A battle to the death the Cold War certainly was, but to a kind of abstract
death. Elimination of the enemy's will to fight—victory—meant more
than military victory on the battlefield. It meant, in principle, the very

In later years Kennan would represent his conception of containment as a political strategy of limited geographical application—not a call for worldwide armed activity, as charged by Lippmann, a rare early critic—and contrast it as a stance of prudent defence with the adventurist notions of 'roll-back' advocated by Dulles, and 'flexible response' by Kennedy. Legend has since canonized the image of a sober adviser whose counsels of moderation and wisdom were distorted into a reckless anti-communist activism that would bring disasters against which he spoke out, remaining true to himself as a critic of American hubris and intransigence. The reality was otherwise. Unstable and excitable, Kennan lacked the steadiness of his friend and successor Nitze, but in his days of power in Washington was a Cold Warrior *à l'outrance*, setting the course for decades of global intervention and counter-revolution.[8] At

---

liquidation of the enemy whose right to exist, let alone equality, one did not recognize. Liquidation alone could bring real peace. Liquidation is thus the "truth" of the Cold War': Stephanson, 'Fourteen Notes on the Very Concept of the Cold War', in Gearóid Ó Tuathail and Simon Dalby, *Rethinking Geopolitics*, London 1998, p. 82.

8   In the extravagance of his fluctuations between elated self-regard and tortured self-flagellation—as in the volatility of his opinions: he would frequently say one thing and its opposite virtually overnight—Kennan was closer to a character out of Dostoevsky than any figure in Chekhov, with whom he claimed an affinity. His inconsistencies, which made it easier to portray him in retrospect as an oracle of temperate realism, were such that he could never be taken as a simple concentrate or archetype of the foreign-policy establishment that conducted America into the Cold War, his role as policy-maker in any case coming to an end in 1950. But just insofar as he has come to be represented as the sane keeper of the conscience of US foreign policy, his actual record—violent and erratic into his mid-seventies—serves as a marker of what could pass for a sense of proportion in the pursuit of the national interest. In the voluminous literature on Kennan, Stephanson's study *Kennan and the Art of Foreign Policy*, Cambridge, MA 1989 stands out as the only serious examination of the intellectual substance of his writings, a courteous but devastating

the outset of his career as a diplomat, he had decided that the Bolsheviks were 'a little group of spiteful Jewish parasites', in their 'innate cowardice' and 'intellectual insolence' abandoning 'the ship of Western European civilization like a swarm of rats'. There could be no compromise with them. Stationed in Prague during the Nazi takeover of Czechoslovakia, his first reaction was that Czechs counted German rule a blessing; later, touring occupied Poland—he was now *en poste* in Berlin—he felt Poles too might come to regard rule by Hans Frank as an improvement in their lot. When Hitler attacked the Soviet Union, he told his superiors that, from Scandinavia to the Black Sea, Russia was everywhere feared more than Germany, and must bear the 'moral consequences' of Operation Barbarossa alone, with 'no claim on Western sympathies'.[9]

---

deconstruction of them. An acute, not unsympathetic, cultural-political portrait of him as a conservative out of his time is to be found in Harper's *American Visions of Europe*, pp. 135–232. In later life, Kennan sought to cover his tracks in the period when he held a modicum of power, to protect his reputation and that of his slogan. We owe some striking pages to that impulse, so have no reason to complain, though also none to take his self-presentation at face value. His best writing was autobiographical and historical: vivid, if far from candid *Memoirs*—skirting *suggestio falsi*, rife with *suppressio veri;* desolate vignettes of the American scene in *Sketches from a Life*; and the late *Decline of Bismarck's European Order: Franco-Russian Relations 1875–1890*, Princeton: Princeton University Press, 1979.

9 Under Nazi rule, 'the Czechs enjoyed privileges and satisfaction in excess of anything they "dreamed of in Austrian days"', and could 'cheerfully align themselves with the single most dynamic movement in Europe', as the best account of this phase in his career summarizes his opinion. In Poland, Kennan reported, 'the hope of improved material conditions and of an efficient, orderly administration may be sufficient to exhaust the aspirations of a people whose political education has always been primitive': see David Mayers, *George Kennan and the Dilemmas of US Foreign Policy*, New York: Oxford University Press, 1988, pp. 71–3. For Kennan's letter on 24 June 1941, two days after the launching of Hitler's attack on the USSR, described simply as 'the German war effort', see his *Memoirs, 1925–1950*, New York: Little, Brown & Co., 1968, pp. 133–4, which give

After the war, promoted to Deputy Commandant of the National War College, he declared that if Russian military industry should make faster progress than American, 'we would be justified in considering a preventive war', unleashing nuclear weapons: 'with probably ten good hits with atomic bombs you could, without any great loss of life or loss of the prestige or reputation of the United States, practically cripple Russia's war-making potential'.[10] At the head of the Policy Planning Staff in the State Department, and as *consigliere* to Acheson, he initiated covert paramilitary operations in Eastern Europe; advocated, if need be, US military intervention in Southern Europe and Southeast Asia; urged support for French colonialism in North Africa; supervised cancellation of reforms in Japan; endorsed repression in Latin America; proposed American seizure of Taiwan; exulted when US troops were dispatched to Korea.[11] Containment was limited neither

no hint of his initial response to the Nazi seizure of what remained of Czechoslovakia, and make no mention of his trip to occupied Poland.

10 C. Ben Wright, 'Mr "X" and Containment', *Slavic Review*, March 1976, p. 19. Furious at the disclosure of his record, Kennan published a petulant attempt at denial in the same issue, demolished by Wright in 'A Reply to George F. Kennan', *Slavic Review*, June 1976, pp. 318–20, dotting the i's and crossing the t's of his documentation of it. In the course of his critique of Kennan, Wright accurately observed of him: 'His mastery of the English language is undeniable, but one should not confuse gift of expression with clarity of thought'.

11 Taiwan: 'Carried through with sufficient resolution, speed, ruthlessness and self-assurance, the way Theodore Roosevelt might have done it', conquest of the island 'would have an electrifying effect on this country and throughout the Far East': Anna Nelson, ed., *The State Department Policy Planning Staff Papers*, New York 1983, vol. III, PPS 53, p. 65. Korea: 'George was dancing on air because MacArthur's men were mobilized for combat under auspices of the United Nations. He was carrying his balalaika, a Russian instrument he used to play with some skill at social gatherings, and with a great, vigorous swing, he clapped me on the back with it, nearly striking me to the sidewalk. "Well, Joe," he cried, "What do

in its range nor in its means. It was an *Ermattungskrieg*, not a *Niederwerfungskrieg*, but the objective was the same. America could hope that 'within five or ten years' the USSR would be 'overwhelmed by clouds of civil disintegration', and the Soviet regime soon 'go down in violence'. Meanwhile 'every possible means' should be set in motion to destabilize Moscow and its relays in Eastern Europe.[12] In their intention, containment and rollback were one from the start.

II

A bureaucratic euphemism, containment was too arid a term to galvanize popular opinion for the launch to Cold War. But it could readily be translated into what was henceforward the centrepiece of the American imperial ideology: security. In the critical years 1945–1947, this became the key slogan linking internal atmospherics and external operations into a single front, and assuring passage from the New Deal to the Truman Doctrine.[13] The Social Security Act had been the most popular

---

you think of the democracies now?'": Joseph Alsop, *'I've Seen The Best of It'. Memoirs*, New York 1992, pp. 308–9. Alsop, with prewar memories of the young Kennan telling him that 'the United States was doomed to destruction because it was no longer run by its "aristocracy"', reminded him tartly of his excoriations of democracy only a few days earlier: pp. 274, 307. Two million Koreans perished during an American intervention whose carpet-bombing obliterated the north of the country over three successive years: see Bruce Cumings, *The Korean War*, New York 2010, pp. 147–61.

12 David Foglesong, 'Roots of "Liberation": American Images of the Future of Russia in the Early Cold War, 1948–1953', *International History Review*, March 1999, pp. 73–4; Gregory Mitrovich, *Undermining the Kremlin: America's Strategy to Subvert the Soviet Bloc, 1947–1956*, Ithaca 2009, pp. 6, 29, 180, who observes: 'There would be no delay: containment and a "compellent" strategy would be pursued in parallel, not in sequence'.

13 It was Schurmann who first saw this, and put it at the heart of his account

reform of the Roosevelt era, enshrining a new value in the vocabulary of domestic politics. What more natural complement than a National Security Act, to meet the danger, no longer of depression, but subversion? In March 1947 came Truman's speech warning of the apocalyptic dangers of communism in the Mediterranean, designed by Acheson 'to scare the hell out of the country' with a message that was perforce 'clearer than truth'. Calling his countrymen to battle in the Cold War, Kennan expressed 'a certain gratitude to Providence which, by providing the American people with this implacable challenge, has made their entire security as a nation dependent on their pulling themselves together and accepting the responsibilities of moral and political leadership that history plainly intended them to bear'.[14] In the same month, the National Security Act created the Defence (no longer War) Department, the Joint Chiefs of Staff, the National Security Council and—the *pièce de résistance*—the Central Intelligence Agency. Around this institutional complex developed the permanent ideology of national security presiding over the American empire to this day.[15] If the depth of its grip on the national imaginary was a product of the Cold War, the fears on which it played had a long pre-history,

---

of American imperialism: 'A new ideology, different from both nationalism and internationalism, forged the basis on which bipartisanship could be created. The key word and concept in that new ideology was *security*': *The Logic of World Power*, pp. 64–8.

14 "X", 'The Sources of Soviet Conduct', *Foreign Affairs*, July 1947, p. 582.

15 For the bureaucratic background to the Act, and the ideology that both generated and crystallized around it, the essential study is Michael Hogan, *A Cross of Iron: Harry S. Truman and the Origins of the National Security State, 1945–1954*, Cambridge 1998: its title a poignant allusion to Bryan's famous cry, 'You shall not crucify mankind upon a cross of gold'. Forrestal was the principal architect of the Act, becoming the country's first Secretary of Defence, before personal and political paranoia exploded in a leap to his death from a hospital window.

in alarmist scenarios of US vulnerability to external attack and magnification of foreign dangers, from Lodge through Wilson to Roosevelt.[16] Masking strategies of offence as exigencies of defence, no theme was better calculated to close the potential gap between popular sentiments and elite designs. The most authoritative study of the Truman administration's entry into the Cold War offers a critique of the 'expanded' conception of national security that came to take hold in Washington. But the ideology of national security, US-style, was inherently expansionist.[17] 'There is literally no question, military or political, in which the United States is not interested', Roosevelt cabled Stalin in 1944, during a global conflict it had not initiated. *A fortiori,* in a Cold War it had.

The organization of the postwar discourse of empire around security did not, of course, mean that the foundational themes of American patriotism were eclipsed by it. The legitimations of US expansionism had always formed a mobile complex of ideologemes, their order and emphasis shifting kaleidoscopically according to the historical conjuncture. The primacy of

16 The extensive record of such scares is surveyed in John A. Thompson, 'The Exaggeration of American Vulnerability: The Anatomy of a Tradition', *Diplomatic History*, Winter 1992, pp. 23–43, who concludes: 'The dramatic extension of America's overseas involvement and commitments in the past hundred years has reflected a growth of power rather the decline of security. Yet the full and effective deployment of that power has required from the American people disciplines and sacrifices that they are prepared to sustain only if they are persuaded the nation's safety is directly at stake'. Among the results have been 'the expansion of national security to include the upholding of American values and the maintenance of world order', and 'the recurrent tendency to exaggerate the country's vulnerability to attack'.

17 For the leading Cold War historian John Lewis Gaddis this was, admirably, a long-standing tradition of the country: 'Expansion, we have assumed, is the path to security': *Surprise, Security and the American Experience*, Cambridge, MA 2004, p. 13.

security after 1945 altered the hierarchy of appeals, without purging them. Immediately below it, now came democracy—the American gift to the world that security served to protect. What had to be secured—that is, expanded—against the total-itarian threat of communism was a Free World in the image of American liberty. In the struggle of the US with the USSR, the force of the claim to be what the enemy was not, a liberal democracy, was plain: where there was any experience or pros-pect of representative government, typically a trump card. In private, of course, the managers of national security were often contemptuous of the democracy they were supposedly defending. Kennan, an admirer of Schuschnigg and Salazar, rulers who showed that 'benevolent despotism had greater pos-sibilities for good' than democracy, argued on the eve of the Second World War that immigrants, women and blacks should be stripped of the vote in the United States. Democracy was a 'fetish': needed was 'constitutional change to the authoritar-ian state'—an American *Estado Novo*.[18] After the war Kennan compared democracy to 'one of those prehistoric monsters with a body as long as this room and a brain the size of a pin', and never lost his belief that the country was best governed by an enlightened elite immune to popular passions. Acheson dismissed 'the premise that democracy is some good', remark-ing 'I don't think it's worth a damn'—'I say the Congress is too damn representative. It's just as stupid as the people are; just

---

18 'Fair Day Adieu!' and 'The Prerequisites: Notes on Problems of the United States in 1938', documents still kept under wraps—the fullest summary is in Mayers, *George Kennan and the Dilemmas of US Foreign Policy*, pp. 49–55. For a cogent discussion of Kennan's outlook in these texts, see Joshua Botts, '"Nothing to Seek and ... Nothing to Defend": George F. Kennan's Core Values and American Foreign Policy, 1938–1993', *Diplomatic History*, November 2006, pp. 839–66.

as uneducated, just as dumb, just as selfish'.[19] Such confidences were not for public consumption. Officially, democracy was as prominent a value in the American mission to the world as in the time of Manifest Destiny.

That destiny, however, had undergone a change. After the Spanish–American War, it had ceased to be territorial, becoming with Wilson all but metaphysical. During the Cold War, it was articulated with less rapture, in a moral-political register occupying a lower position in the ideological hierarchy. But the connexion with religion remained. In his final inaugural address of 1944, Roosevelt had declared: 'The Almighty God has blessed our land in many ways. He has given our people stout hearts and strong arms with which to strike mighty blows for our freedom and truth. He has given to our country a faith which has become the hope of all peoples in an anguished world.' Truman, speaking on the day he dropped the second atomic bomb on Nagasaki, was equally forthright about the country's strong arms: 'We thank God that it [the atomic bomb] has come to us, and not our enemies; and we pray that He may guide us to use it in His Ways and for His purposes.' Amid the postwar ruins, the president was more expansive. 'We are going forward to meet our destiny, which I think Almighty God intended us to have', he announced: 'We are going to be the leaders.'[20] Viewing the destruction in Germany, Kennan

19 Acheson: interview with Theodore Wilson and Richard McKinzie, 30 June 1971. Johnson was cruder still: 'We pay a lot of good American dollars to the Greeks, Mr Ambassador', he told an envoy, after drawling an expletive, 'If your Prime Minister gives me talk about democracy, parliament and constitution, he, his parliament and his constitution may not last long': Philip Deane [Gerassimos Gigantes], *I Should Have Died*, London 1976, pp. 113–4. Nixon and Kissinger could be no less colourful.
20 John Fousek, *To Lead the Free World: American Nationalism and the Cultural Roots of the Cold War*, Chapel Hill 2000, pp. 44, 23; Lloyd

found himself 'hushed by the realization that it was we who had been chosen by the Almighty to be the agents of it',[21] but in due course uplifted by the awesome challenge that the same Providence had granted Americans in the form of the Cold War. Since then, the deity has continued to guide the United States, from the time of Eisenhower, when 'In God We Trust' was made the official motto of the nation, to Kennedy exclaiming: 'With a good conscience our only sure reward, with history the final judge of our deeds, let us go forth to lead the land we love, asking His blessing and His help, but knowing that here on earth God's work must truly be our own'—down to the declaration of the younger Bush, that 'Our nation is chosen by God and commissioned by history to be a model for the world', and Obama's confidence that God continues to call Americans to their destiny: to bring, with His grace, 'the great gift of freedom' to posterity.[22] America would not be America without faith in the supernatural. But for obvious reasons this component of the national ideology is inner-directed, without much appeal abroad, and so now relegated to the lowest rung in the structure of imperial justification.

Gardner, in Gardner, Schlesinger, Morgenthau, *The Origins of The Cold War*, Ann Arbor 1970, p. 8. In 1933, Roosevelt could in all seriousness warn Litvinov that on his deathbed he would want 'to make his peace with God', adding 'God will punish you Russians if you go on persecuting the church': David Foglesong, *The American Mission and the 'Evil Empire'*, Cambridge 2007, p. 77.

21 Kennan, *Memoirs, 1925–1950*, New York 1968, p. 429.

22 Kennedy inaugural, 20 January 1961: 'The rights of man come not from the generosity of the state, but from the hand of God'; George W. Bush, speech to the International Jewish B'nai B'rith Convention, 28 August 2000; Obama inaugural, 20 January 2009: 'This is the source of our confidence: the knowledge that God calls on us to shape an uncertain destiny'—an address reminding his audience, *inter alia*, of the heroism of those who fought for freedom at Gettysburg and Khe Sanh.

To be effective, an ideology must reflect as well as distort, or conceal, reality. At the outset, as at the conclusion, of the Cold War, the United States possessed few colonies, was indeed an electoral democracy, did confront a sociopolitical system that was not, and as in the past enjoyed extraordinary natural advantages of size, location and endowments. All these could be, and were, synthesized into an imperial ideology commanding popular consensus, if never unanimity, at home, and power of attraction, if never ubiquitous, abroad. But the ultimately determinant instance in the formation of American foreign policy lay elsewhere, and could receive only circumspect articulation until the Cold War was won. So long as communism was a threat, capitalism was all but a taboo term in the vocabulary of the West. In the US itself, the virtues of free enterprise were certainly always prominent in the national liturgy, but even in this idiom were rarely projected as *leitmotifs* of the global defence of liberty against the totalitarian danger. The managers of the empire were aware that it would be counterproductive to foreground them. Early drafts of the presidential speech that would become the Truman Doctrine, prepared by his aides Clifford and Elsey, presented Greece as a strategic line of defence for access to oil in the Middle East and, noting that 'there has been a world-wide trend away from the system of free enterprise', warned that 'if, by default, we permit free enterprise to disappear in the other nations of the world, the very existence of our own economy and our own democracy will be gravely threatened'. This was speaking too plainly. Truman objected that it 'made the whole thing sound like an investment prospectus', and Acheson made sure such cats were not let out of the bag.[23] Even free trade, however essential to a

---

23 McCormick, *America's Half-Century*, p. 77. *Business Week* could afford to

Pax Americana, was not accorded top billing as an ideological imperative. But what, for the time being, was least conspicuous in the hierarchy of its legitimations would, as events were going to show, be most decisive in the map of its operations. For the moment, the Cold War had to be won, and the catechism of security was paramount.

III

The Great Contest, as Deutscher called it, is still generally taken as the defining framework of American grand strategy in the postwar epoch. But the exigencies of the struggle against communism, all-consuming as these became, were only one, if protracted, phase within a longer and wider arc of American power-projection, which has outlived them by half as many years again. Since it came to an end, the Cold War has produced an often remarkable body of international scholarship. But this has nearly always remained unseeing of the dynamic predating, encompassing and exceeding it. For all its scope and intensity, the Cold War was—in the words of an outstanding exception to this literature—'merely a sub-plot' within the larger history of American global domination.[24]

That exception came from the tradition which pioneered modern study of American imperialism, founded in Wisconsin by William Appleman Williams in the fifties. Williams's *American–Russian Relations* (1952), *Tragedy of American Diplomacy* (1959) and *The Contours of American History*

---

be blunter, observing that the task of the US government was 'keeping capitalism afloat in the Mediterranean—and in Europe', while in the Middle East 'it is already certain that business has an enormous stake in whatever role the United States is to play'.

24 McCormick, *America's Half-Century*, p. xiii.

(1961) argued that the march to the internal frontier within North America, allowing a settler society to escape the contradictions of race and class of an emergent capitalist economy, had been extended across the Pacific in the drive for an Open Door empire of commerce, and then in the *fuite en avant* of a bid for global dominion that could not brook even a defensive Soviet Union. For Williams, this was a morally disastrous trajectory, generated by a turning away from the vision of a community of equals that had inspired the first arrivals from the Old World. Produced before the US assault in Vietnam, Williams's account of a long-standing American imperialism struck with prophetic force in the sixties. The historians who learnt from him—Lloyd Gardner, Walter LaFeber, Thomas McCormick, Patrick Hearden—shed the idealism of his explanatory framework, exploring with greater documentation and precision the economic dynamics of American diplomacy, investment and warfare from the nineteenth to the end of the twentieth century. The Wisconsin School was not alone in its critical historiography of empire. Kolko's monumental *Politics of War* shared the same political background, of revulsion at the war in Vietnam, if not intellectual affiliation.

To the regnant liberalism of the time, and since, this was an aberrant optic for viewing America's postwar role in the world. It was not requirements of profitability, but of security that formed the guideline of US foreign policy, set by the conflict of the Cold War rather than the objectives of the Open Door. Leading the reaction was John Lewis Gaddis, who over four decades has tirelessly upheld patriotic truths about his country and the dangers it faced. The Cold War, he explained at the peak of the US bombing of Vietnam in 1972, had been forced on a reluctant American government that did not want it, but wanted insecurity even less. Responsibility for the conflict fell on a Soviet dictator who was not answerable to any public opinion, and so could have avoided a confrontation that democratic rulers in Washington, who had to heed popular feelings outraged by Russian behaviour, could not. The domestic political system, rather than anything to do with the economy, determined the nation's conduct of foreign affairs.[25] If there was such a thing as an American empire—perhaps 'revisionism', after all, had a case there—it was one by invitation, freely sought in Western Europe from fear of Soviet aggression, unlike the Russian empire imposed by force on Eastern Europe.[26] American policy towards the world, he insisted a decade later, had always been primarily defensive. Its leitmotif was containment, traceable across successive declensions from the time of Truman to that of Kissinger, in an arc of impressive restraint and clairvoyance.[27]

Another ten years on, the Cold War now won, Gaddis could reveal what '*We Now Know*' of its real nature: a battle of good against evil as contemporaries saw it, in which American conceptions of collective security, embodied in a NATO alliance inspired by federal principles akin to those of the US

25 Gaddis, *The United States and the Origins of the Cold War 1941–1947*, New York 1972, pp. 353, 356–8, 360–1. In a preface to the re-edition of the book in 2000, Gaddis congratulated himself on his good fortune, as a student in Texas, in feeling no obligation 'to condemn the American establishment and all its works': p. x.

26 Gaddis, 'The Emerging Post-Revisionist Synthesis and the Origins of the Cold War', *Diplomatic History*, July 1983, pp. 181–3.

27 Gaddis, *Strategies of Containment*, New York 1982, p. viii, *passim*. Gaddis had by then become Kennan's leading exegete, earning his passage to official biographer, and the sobriquet 'godfather of containment'. For the latter, see Sarah-Jane Corke, *US Covert Operations and Cold War Strategy: Truman, Secret Warfare and the CIA, 1945–1953*, pp. 39–42 ff.

Constitution, had triumphed over narrow Soviet conceptions of unilateral security, and in doing so diffused democracy across the world. The nuclear arms race alone had deferred a collapse of the USSR that would otherwise have occurred much earlier.[28] But not all dangers to freedom had been laid to rest. In 2001 the terrorists who attacked the Twin Towers and the Pentagon, like the Japanese who bombed Pearl Harbour, had 'given the US yet another chance to lead the world into a new era', and George W. Bush—the underestimated Prince Hal of the hour—was rising to the challenge of creating an 'empire of liberty', in keeping with the nation's calling as, in Lincoln's words, 'the last, best hope of mankind'.[29]

By the time of these pronouncements, the intellectual climate had changed. From the mid-eighties onwards, the record of the American state during the Cold War came to be viewed in a more sceptical light. Its performance in two theatres of its operation attracted particular criticism in much subsequent scholarship, as overly and unnecessarily aggressive. The first was the role of the US at the inception of the Cold War in Europe, the second its subsequent interventions in the Third World. Studies of these have flowed in turn into a general broadening and deepening of the historiography of the Cold War, enabled by the opening of Soviet and Chinese archives as well as a more critical sense of Western

---

28 Gaddis, *We Now Know: Rethinking Cold War History*, Oxford 1997, pp. 51, 199–201, 280, 286–7, 292.

29 Gaddis, 'And Now This: Lessons from the Old Era for the New One', in Strobe Talbott and Nayan Chanda, eds, *The Age of Terror*, New York 2001, p. 21; Gaddis, *Surprise, Security, and the American Experience*, pp. 115, 117. For 'one of the most surprising transformations of an underrated national leader since Prince Hal became Henry V', prompting comparison of Afghanistan with Agincourt, see pp. 82, 92; and further pp. 115, 117. In due course Gaddis would write speeches for the Texan president.

sources.[30] The imposing three-volume *Cambridge History of the Cold War* (2010), a monument to current research, is testimony to the change; and its co-editors, Melvyn Leffler and Odd Arne Westad, can stand as illustrations of the advance the new literature represents, and its limits. Each is author of the finest single work in their respective fields, in both cases deeply felt, humane works of historical reflection: Leffler's *A Preponderance of Power: National Security, the Truman Administration and the Cold War* (1992) and Westad's *The Global Cold War: Third World Interventions and the Making of Our Times* (2005). Leffler's massive, meticulous analysis of American doctrines and actions in the first five years of the Cold War left no doubt of Washington's drive for global hegemony—'preponderance' at large—and dismissal of the predictable apprehensions it aroused in Moscow, in the wake of one invasion from Germany and fear of another, as the US divided the country to keep the Ruhr securely within its grasp.[31] Westad's study broke decisively from a conventional focus on Europe, for a powerful narrative of the battlefields of the Third World, treated as the most important single front of the Cold War, and most disastrous for the peoples caught in the crossfire of American and Soviet attempts to control their fate.

---

30 For the successive phases of this historiography, see Stephanson, 'The United States', in David Reynolds, ed., *The Origins of the Cold War in Europe: International Perspectives*, New Haven 1994, pp. 25–48. A shorter update is contained in John Lamberton Harper, *The Cold War*, Oxford 2011, pp. 83–9, a graceful work that is now the best synthesis in the field.

31 For the degree of Leffler's rejection of Gaddis's version of the Cold War, see his biting demolition of *We Now Know*: 'The Cold War: What Do "We Now Know"?', *American Historical Review*, April 1999, pp. 501–24. He had started to question it as early as 1984: 'The American Conception of National Security and the Beginnings of the Cold War, 1945–48', *American Historical Review*, April 1984, pp. 346–81.

Commanding though each of these works is on its terrain, that remains delimited. In historical scope, neither matches Kolko's integration within a single compass of the full range of American strategic aims and actions while the Red Army fought the Wehrmacht, with a full sense of popular experiences of suffering and revolt from the Yangzi to the Seine, in the world beyond Washington.[32] The forty pages of bibliography in the first volume of the *Cambridge History* contain no reference to *The Politics of War*, a telltale omission. At its best, this literature has produced major works of clear-minded political history. But while no longer apologetic, often dwelling on unwarranted blunders and excesses of American foreign policy that compromised the chance of better diplomatic outcomes after the war, or crimes committed in fear of worse in the underdeveloped world, it has proved consistently unable to come to terms with the matrix that rendered these rational enough for their purposes. The symptom of this inability is the general silence with which it has treated the cumulative work of those US historians who have made that the principal object of their research. Distortions of ideology and exaggerations of insecurity are the acceptable causes of American misjudgement or misconduct abroad. The political logic of a dynamic continental economy that was the headquarters of world capital is matter—at best—for evasion or embarrassment.[33]

---

32 In 1990, Kolko added a preface to the re-publication of *The Politics of War* that extends its argument to comparative reflections on the German and Japanese regimes and their rulers, and the differing political outcomes of French and German popular experiences of the war: a text of exceptional brilliance.

33 Tackled by Bruce Cumings for his failure either to address or even mention the work of Kolko, or more generally the Wisconsin School of historians descending from Williams, Leffler could only reply defensively that for him, 'the writings of William Appleman Williams still provide

That was not the case in the early seventies, when the influ-ence of Williams was at its height. At that time, two penetrating critiques of the Wisconsin School appeared, whose clarity and rigour are in notable contrast with the foot-shuffling that fol-lowed. Robert Tucker and John Thompson each took aim at the elisions of the term 'expansion' in Wisconsin usage, pointing out that territorial expansion across North America, or even the

the best foundation for the architectural reconfigurations that I envision', since 'Williams captured the essential truth that American foreign policy has revolved around the expansion of American territory, commerce and culture'—a trinity, however, of which only the last figures significantly in his work on the Cold War. See, for this exchange, Michael Hogan, ed., *America in the World: The Historiography of American Foreign Relations since 1941*, Cambridge 1995, pp. 52–9, 86–9. For his part, Westad could write wide-eyed as late as 2000 that 'American policy-makers seem to have understood much more readily than most of us have believed that there was an intrinsic connection between the spread of capitalism as a system and the victory of American political values': Westad, ed., *Reviewing the Cold War: Approaches, Interpretations, Theory*, London 2000, p. 10. Five years later, *The Global Cold War* contains a few nervous, indecisive pages on economic considerations in US foreign policy, without significant bearing on the subsequent narrative, before con-cluding with perceptible relief at the end of it, that—as exemplified by the invasion of Iraq—'freedom and security have been, and remain the driving forces of US foreign policy': pp. 27–32, 405. A discreet footnote in Kimball informs us that 'historians have only begun to grapple with the intriguing questions posed by William Appleman Williams', and taken up Gardner and Kolko, as against 'the more commonly accepted viewpoint which emphasizes power politics and Wilsonian idealism' and does not 'really deal with the question of America's overall economic goals and their effect on foreign policy'—a topic handled somewhat gingerly, if not without a modicum of realism, in the ensuing chapter on Lend-Lease: *The Juggler*, pp. 218–9, 43–61. Of the typical modulations to traditional Cold War orthodoxy, McCormick once justly observed: 'While post-revisionists may duly note materialist factors, they then hide them away in an undifferentiated and unconnected shopping-list of variables. The operative premise is that multiplicity, rather than articulation, is equiva-lent to sophistication': 'Drift or Mastery? A Corporatist Synthesis for American Diplomatic History', *Reviews in American History*, December 1982, pp. 318–9.

Pacific, did not mean the US economy required foreign markets to thrive in either the nineteenth or first half of the twentieth century, nor that mistaken beliefs by politicians or businessmen to the contrary could be adduced as evidence of any purposeful continuity in American foreign policy, conspicuously absent. Expansion, Tucker readily conceded, there had been. But it was better understood, not as a projection of the socioeconomic structure of American capitalism, but of the sheer growth of American power and the dynamics of inter-state competition, accompanied by ideas of a mission to spread American values abroad. For Thompson, any number of beliefs were expressed by Americans as justifications of their country's foreign policy, and there was no reason to attach *a priori* more importance to commercial than to strategic or moral or political arguments for them. Considerations of security, often invoked, were among the repertoire. Legitimate up to the mid-fifties, in Tucker's view, these had become excessive thereafter, abandoning the rational pursuit of a balance of power for the will to hegemony of an expansionist globalism. In that respect, the Wisconsin critique of American foreign policy in the Cold War was sound. 'To contain the expansion of others, or what was perceived as such, it became necessary to expand ourselves. In this manner, the course of containment became the course of empire.'[34]

---

34 Robert W. Tucker, *The Radical Left and American Foreign Policy*, Baltimore 1971, pp. 11, 23, 58–64, 107–11, 149: a conservative study of great intellectual elegance. Likewise, from an English liberal, John A. Thompson, 'William Appleman Williams and the "American Empire"', *Journal of American Studies*, April 1973, pp. 91–104, a closer textual scrutiny.

4

KEYSTONES

Left unresolved in the exchanges of that period were both the general structure of the relations between state and capital in the modern era, and the particular historical form these had taken in the United States. That the pattern of incentives and constraints to which the two were subject could never be identical was written into the independent origins of each. Capitalism, as a system of production without borders, emerged into a European world already territorially divided into a plurality of late feudal states pitted in rivalry against each other, each with its own means of aggression and systems of coercion. In due course, when absolutist monarchies became capitalist nation-states, economic and political power, fused in the feudal order, became structurally separated. Once direct producers were deprived of the means of subsistence, becoming dependent for their livelihoods on a labour market, extra-economic coercion was no longer required to exploit them. But their exploiters were still divided into the multiplicity of states they had inherited, along with the tensions between them. The result, as classically formulated by Robert Brenner, was twofold.[1] On the one hand,

1   Robert Brenner, 'What Is, and What Is Not, Imperialism?', *Historical Materialism*, vol. 14, no. 4, 2006, pp. 79–95, esp. pp. 83–5.

such states could not contradict the interests of capital without undermining themselves, since their power depended on the prosperity of an economy governed by the requirements of profitability. On the other hand, the activities of states could not be subject to the same set of incentives and constraints as those of firms. For while the field of inter-state—like that of inter-firm—relations was also one of competition, it lacked either the institutional rules of a market or the transparency of a price mechanism for adjudicating claims of rationality or efficiency. There was no external counterpart to the internal settlement of the coordination problem. The consequence was a continual risk of miscalculations and sub-optimal—at the limit, disastrous—outcomes for all contending parties.

The aim of capital is profit. What is the comparable objective of the state? In polite parlance, 'security', whose arrival as the conventional definition of the ultimate purpose of the state coincided, after 1945, with the universal sublimation of Ministries of War into Ministries of Defence. Nebulous as few others, the term was—as it remains—ideally suited for all-purpose ideological use.[2] Spykman had coolly noted the reality behind it: 'The struggle for power is identical with the struggle for survival, and the improvement of the relative power position becomes the primary objective of the internal and external

---

2   For a contemporary adept of the locution, Joseph Nye—chairman of the National Intelligence Council under Clinton—'security is like oxygen: you tend not to notice until you lose it': 'East Asian Security—The Case for Deep Engagement', *Foreign Affairs*, July–August 1995, p. 91. As Lloyd Gardner remarked of Gaddis's ubiquitous use of the term, 'it hangs before us like an abstraction or, with apologies to T. S. Eliot, "shape without form, shade without colour"': 'Responses to John Lewis Gaddis', *Diplomatic History*, July 1983, p. 191. For Gaddis's elaboration, two decades later, that American security has always meant expansion, see note 52 above.

policy of states', for 'there is no real security in being just as strong as a potential enemy; there is security only in being a little stronger'.[3] After 1945, even that 'little' would become an archaism. Leffler's study of the Truman years can be read as a vast scholarly exfoliation of Tucker's incisive conclusion twenty years earlier: the meaning of national security had been extended to the limits of the earth.[4] Conceptually, however, Leffler's work retained a prudent ambiguity. 'Fear and power', he wrote—'not unrelenting Soviet pressure, not humanitarian impulses, not domestic political considerations, not British influence'—were 'the key factors shaping American policies'.[5] Fear and power—the need for security, the drive for primacy: were they of equal significance, or was one of greater import than the other? The title and evidence of Leffler's book point unambiguously one way; the judicious casuistics of its ending, the other.

In postwar Washington, a 'preponderance of power' was not simply, however, the standard goal of any major state— the pursuit, as Spykman put it, 'not of an equilibrium, but a generous margin' of strength. Objectively, it had another meaning, rooted in the unique character of the US as a

3 Spykman, *America's Strategy in World Politics*, pp. 18, 20.

4 Tucker's critique of this inflation was the more radical: 'By interpreting security as a function not only of a balance between states but of the internal order maintained by states, the Truman Doctrine equated America's security with interests that evidently went well beyond conventional security requirements. This conception cannot be dismissed as mere rhetoric, designed at the time only to mobilize public opinion in support of limited policy actions, though rhetoric taken seriously by succeeding administrations. Instead, it accurately expressed the magnitude of America's conception of its role and interests in the world from the very inception of the Cold War': *The Radical Left and American Foreign Policy*, p. 107.

5 Leffler, *A Preponderance of Power*, p. 51.

capitalist state not only encompassing far the largest and most self-sufficient industrial economy in the world, but sheltering behind its oceans from any credible attack by rival or enemy. On the plane of *Weltpolitik* there thus emerged a wide gap between the potential power of the American state and the actual extent of American interests. Entry into the Second World War narrowed the distance and transformed the structure of the relationship between them. The Depression had made it clear to policy-makers that the US economy was not insulated from shockwaves in the worldwide system of capital, and the outbreak of war that autarkic trading blocs not only threatened exclusion of US capital from large geographical zones, but risked military conflagrations that could endanger the stability of bourgeois civilization at large. Thereafter, participation in the war yielded a double bonus: the American economy grew at a phenomenal rate under the stimulus of military procurements, GNP doubling between 1938 and 1945; and all three of its main industrial rivals—Germany, Britain, Japan—emerged from the conflict shattered or weakened, leaving Washington in a position to reshape the universe of capital to its requirements.

The elites of the Great Power that acquired this capacity were closer to business and banking than those of any other state of the time. The highest levels of policy-making in the Truman administration were packed with investment bankers and corporate lawyers, leading industrialists and traders: Forrestal, Lovett, Harriman, Stettinius, Acheson, Nitze, McCloy, Clayton, Snyder, Hoffman—a stratum unlikely to overlook the interests of American capital in redesigning the postwar landscape. Free enterprise was the foundation of every other freedom. The US alone could assure its preservation and extension worldwide, and was entitled to the benefits of doing so. In the immediate aftermath of the war, when fears of a possible return to depression in the wake of demobilization were common, the opening of overseas markets to US exports—an *idée fixe* within the wartime State Department—was widely regarded as vital for future prosperity.

The Cold War altered this calculus. Economic recovery of Western Europe and Japan had always been seen as a condition of the free-trade system in which American goods could flow to consumer markets restored to solvency abroad. But the Red Army's arrival on the Elbe and the PLA's crossing of the Yangzi imposed a different kind of urgency—and direction—on the building of a liberal international order. For the time being, the Open Door would have to be left somewhat ajar, European and Japanese markets more protected than American, or foreseen, if a totalitarian adversary of markets of any kind was to be defeated. There the preponderance of American power over American interests became for the first time fully functional, in the shape of an imperial hegemony. The US state would henceforward act, not primarily as a projection of the concerns of US capital, but as a guardian of the general interest of all capitals, sacrificing—where necessary, and for as long as needed—national gain for international advantage, in the confidence of ultimate pay-off.

It could afford to do so, because after the war, as before it, the measure of American power—now not simply economic, but military and political—was still far in excess of the reach of American banks and corporations. There was a lot of slack available for the concessions to subaltern states, and their ruling groups, essential for the construction of a hegemonic system. Their consent to the new order was not bought only with these: they had as much reason to fear the common enemy as the superordinate state that now became their shield. They too needed the armed force that is inseparable from any hegemony. A new kind of war was under way, requiring the strong nerves of a superpower. The strategic means and ends of the American empire to come were resumed by Forrestal: 'As long as we can outproduce the world, can control the sea and can strike inland with the atomic bomb, we can assume certain risks otherwise unacceptable in an effort to restore world trade, to restore the balance of power—military power—and to eliminate some of the conditions which breed war'.[6] In that agenda, restoring the balance of power belonged to the same lexicon of euphemisms as containment: as Spykman had noted, 'states are only interested in a balance in their favour'. That was understood in Moscow as well as Washington, and in neither capital was there by then any illusion as to what it implied. Capitalism and communism were incompatible orders of society, as their rulers knew, each bent on bringing—sooner or later: sooner for the first, much later for the second—the other to an end. So long as the conflict between them lasted, the hegemony of America in the camp of capital was assured.

II

At the outset, the overriding task for Washington was to make sure that the two advanced industrial regions that lay between the US and the USSR, and had detonated the war, did not fall into the hands of Communism. Their historically high levels of economic and scientific development made Western Europe

---

6   Letter to Chandler Gurney, chairman of the Senate Armed Services Committee, 8 December 1947: Walter Millis, ed., *The Forrestal Diaries*, New York 1951, p. 336. For Forrestal, the struggle with the Soviet Union was best described, more bluntly, as 'semi-war', rather than Cold War.

and Japan the great prizes in any calculus of postwar power. Reconstruction of them under American guidance and protection was thus the top priority of containment. Stripped of their conquests, the former Axis powers needed to be rebuilt with US aid as prosperous bulwarks of the Free World and forward emplacements of American military might; and the former Allied powers, less damaged by the war, supported in their return to normal economic life. Western Europe, the larger of the two trophies, and vulnerable to land attack by the Red Army as insular Japan was not, required most attention and assistance. This was, Acheson explained to Congress, 'the keystone of the world'.[7]

In 1946–47 Britain became the proving ground for the abrupt alterations of American policy demanded by the Cold War. Financially bankrupted by its second struggle against Germany, the UK was forced in mid-1946 to submit to draconian conditions for an American loan to keep itself afloat: not only interest payments against which it protested, but the scrapping of import controls and full convertibility within a year. With American prices rising, the British import bill soared, plunging the country into a massive balance of payments crisis. The Attlee government was forced to suspend convertibility within a few weeks of introducing it.[8] Hull's free-trade maximalism had overshot its imperial objectives, and become counterproductive. There was no point in ruining a former ally if it was to become a viable protectorate. *A fortiori* the more precarious countries of Western Europe, above all France and Italy, yet

---

7 Leffler, *A Preponderance of Power*, p. 277.

8 'Truman's signing of the British loan legislation on July 15, 1946 launched the pound sterling on an agonizing yearlong death march', remarks Steil, *The Battle of Bretton Woods*, p. 309—apt phrasing for the ruthlessness of the American diktat.

weaker economically than Britain, and less secure politically. By 1947, the dollar gap between Europe's imports from the US and its ability to pay for them was yawning, and a change of course indicated. The Marshall Plan funnelled some $13 billion into counterpart funds for European recovery—controlled by US corporate executives and tied to purchase of American goods—dropping insistence on immediate abolition of tariffs and exchange controls, and instead bringing pressure to bear for fiscal retrenchment and European integration.[9] The corollary did not wait long. Marshall funds brought economic succour, NATO a military buckler. The Atlantic Pact was signed in the spring of 1949.

Germany, divided between four occupying powers, with a third of the country under Soviet control, could not be handled in quite the same way. The Western zone, covering the Ruhr, was too valuable a holding to be foregone in any unification in which Moscow would have a say. In mid-1947 Washington made it clear that Russia could expect no reparations for the vast destruction visited on it by the Third Reich, while the US had been luxuriating in its wartime boom, and that the Western zone was scheduled for separation from the Eastern zone as a new German polity within Anglo-American jurisdiction.[10] But even

---

9   Also, of course, congenial electoral outcomes: 'The Marshall Plan sent a strong message to European voters that American largesse depended on their electing governments willing to accept the accompanying rules of multilateral trade and fiscal conservatism', while at the same time sparing them drastic wage repression that might otherwise have caused social unrest: McCormick, *America's Half-Century*, pp. 78–9; Offner, *Another Such Victory*, p. 242. That the actual economic effect of Marshall aid on European recovery, well underway by the time it arrived, was less than advertised, has been shown by Alan Milward: 'Was the Marshall Plan Necessary?', *Diplomatic History*, April 1989, pp. 231–52. What was critical was its ideological, more than its material, impact.

10 See the definitive account in Carolyn Eisenberg, *Drawing the Line: The*

in reduced form as the Federal Republic, Germany remained an object of fear to its neighbours as Japan did not. Rebuilding it as a bastion of freedom thus required not just American aid and armour, but its integration into a European system of mutual security, within which German industrial might could help revive neighbouring economies, and German rearmament strengthen barriers to the Red Army. Washington was thus from the start a patron of every step towards European unity. Once its most favoured version—the military project of a European Defence Community—was blocked in France in 1954, it brought West Germany into NATO. But economic integration remained a key objective, giving State and Defense no reason to quibble over the tariffs set up around the Common Market by the Treaty of Rome, despite protests from the Commerce Department. The imperatives of free trade had not been neglected as the Cold War set in—GATT was signed soon after the Marshall Plan, the Kennedy Round followed in due course—but were no longer the main front. Derogations from them had to be accepted in the interests of assuring the stability of capitalism in the major industrial centres at each end of Eurasia.

American Decision to Divide Germany, 1944–1949, Cambridge 1996, *passim*. The case that US reneging on the reparations promised the USSR at Yalta—not only eminently justifiable, but perfectly feasible—was the decisive act in launching the Cold War, is made by Stephanson, *Kennan and the Art of Foreign Policy* pp. 127–32. In his view, the US refusal after mid-1947 to engage in normal diplomacy was the defining element of the Cold War, and must be seen as a 'development of the concept of "unconditional surrender", taken directly from the Civil War', and proclaimed by Roosevelt at Casablanca: see 'Liberty or Death: The Cold War as American Ideology', in Westad, ed., *Reviewing the Cold War*, p. 83. More powerfully and clearly than any other writer, Stephanson has argued that 'the Cold War was from the outset not only a US term but a US project'. For this, see his 'Cold War Degree Zero', in Joel Isaac and Duncan Bell, eds, *Uncertain Empire*, Oxford 2012, pp. 19–49.

Yet more so in the other major prize of the peace. Japan, sur-
rounded by sea, was secure against the risk of Soviet invasion.
There, where the US was the sole occupying power, American
political control was tighter and economic assistance less than
in Europe. Postwar reforms were abruptly cancelled after a
descent by Kennan had installed the Reverse Course, preserving the *zaibatsu* and reinstating the prewar political class with
its Class A war criminals, as was not possible in Germany.
The Occupation, he remarked, could 'dispense with bromides
about democratization'.[11] The Dodge Plan was more a conventional stabilization programme than a replication of Marshall
Aid, and the Security Treaty came a decade later than NATO.
But amid a much more devastated postwar landscape, where
a major labour insurgency had to be crushed, Washington
made no difficulty over a model of development based on a
high degree of *de facto* protection and state intervention, at
notable variance with the liberal economic order enforced
elsewhere. Dirigisme was a small price to pay for immunity
to revolution.

Overall, in this advanced industrial zone, American objectives met with complete success. From the outset, these were
societies with business elites that were natural allies of the US,

11 Confident that he had 'turned our whole occupation policy', Kennan
regarded his role in Japan as 'the most significant constructive contribution I was ever able to make in government': Gaddis, *George F. Kennan*,
pp. 299–303. Miscamble—an admirer—comments: 'Kennan evinced no
real concern for developments in Japan on their own terms. He appeared
not only quite uninterested in and unperturbed by the fact that the
Zaibatsu had proved willing partners of the Japanese militarists but also
unconcerned that their preservation would limit the genuine openness
of the Japanese economy. He possessed no reforming zeal or inclination':
George F. Kennan and the Making of American Foreign Policy, Princeton
1992, p. 255. The PPS paper Kennan delivered on his return from Tokyo
called for the purge of wartime officials to be curtailed.

extensive middle classes and generally (if not invariably) moderate labour movements, with a prewar past of parliamentary
institutions and competitive elections. When postwar reconstruction released twenty years of fast economic growth and
rising living standards, their transformation into thriving protectorates within the American ecumene was achieved with
scarcely a hitch. In Japan, where the party that continues to rule
the country was put together by the Occupier, significant quo-
tients of coercion and corruption were initially needed to set
up a satisfactory regime. In Western Europe, on the other hand,
the amount of pressure required to lock local societies into the
US security system was never great. Force determined the
outcome only in the impoverished periphery of Greece, where
the British had led the way for military counterrevolution.[12]
Elsewhere—principally Italy and France—covert American
funding of parties, unions and periodicals helped the anti-
communist cause. Military intervention, though on standby,
was not required.[13] The balance of domestic opinion in each

12 From the outset, Roosevelt had backed Churchill's dispatch of British
    troops in 1944 to crush the main body of the Greek resistance. Under
    Truman the country became the Very light for American advance to
    the Cold War, Acheson telling Congressmen that failure to maintain
    a friendly government in place might 'open three continents to Soviet
    penetration. Like apples in a barrel infected by one rotten one, the cor-
    ruption of Greece would affect Iran and all to the East'. Nothing less than
    the fate of 'two thirds of the area of the world' was at stake. Marshall
    was soon instructing the American embassy 'not to interfere with the
    administration of Greek justice', as mass execution of political prisoners
    proceeded. Twenty years later, with a junta in power in Athens, Acheson
    instructed locals that there was 'no realistic alternative to your colonels',
    since Greece was 'not ready for democracy': Lawrence Wittner, *American
    Intervention in Greece, 1943–1949*, New York 1982, pp. 12–3, 71, 145;
    Gigantes, *I Should Have Died*, pp. 122–4.

13 See, for such contingencies, Kennan's cable to Acheson, 15 March 1948:
    'Italy is obviously key point. If Communists were to win election there

country was favourable enough on its own. Fundamentally, the process was consensual: capitalist democracies freely accepting their place in an imperial order in which they prospered. It was not 'empire by invitation', in the fulsome phrase of a Norwegian admirer.[14] The invitation came from, not to, the empire, and was the kind that could not be refused. Germany and Japan, defeated powers now stripped of their conquests, had little reason to do so: helped back on their feet by the US, and sheltering under its nuclear umbrella, they were freed to devote themselves single-mindedly to their economic miracles. The rulers of Britain and France, victor powers still in control of overseas possessions, would for a time have more autonomy, with its potential for friction. All four, along with lesser European states, were entitled to a measure of diplomatic tact, as auxiliaries in the battlefield of the Cold War. Command remained American.

---

our whole position in Mediterranean, and possibly Western Europe as well, would be undermined. I am persuaded that the Communists could not win without strong factor of intimidation on their side, and it would clearly be better that elections not take place at all than that the Communists win in these circumstances. For these reasons I question whether it would not be preferable for Italian Government to outlaw Communist Party and take strong action against it before elections. Communists would presumably reply with civil war, which would give us grounds for reoccupation of Foggia fields and any other facilities we might wish. This would admittedly result in much violence and probably a military division of Italy; but we are getting close to a deadline and I think it might well be preferable to a bloodless election victory, unopposed by ourselves, which would give the Communists the entire peninsula at one coup and send waves of panic to all surrounding areas': Stephanson, *Kennan and the Art of Foreign Policy*, p. 99.

14 Geir Lundestad, *The United States and Western Europe Since 1945*, Oxford 2003, pp. 2–3, *passim*.

III

The war was cold, but still a war. The USSR was not just a state whose rulers were committed to the political overthrow of capitalism. That the Soviet Union had been since the October Revolution. It was a formidable military power which had broken Hitler's armies at a time when America was little more than a spectator in Europe, and now enjoyed an overwhelming advantage in conventional force ratios on the continent. The threat posed by the Red Army had to be deterred with a superior arsenal of destruction. With the obliteration of Hiroshima and Nagasaki, Washington appeared to possess that: a warning to Moscow even before the Pacific War had ended, which Truman hoped would cut off Russian entry into it.[15] For four years, the

---

15 There was never any question that America would use its atomic weapons on Japan, regardless of either military requirements or moral considerations: 'The war had so brutalized the American leaders that burning vast numbers of civilians no longer posed a real predicament by the spring of 1945'. Two months before they were used, Stimson recorded a typical exchange with Truman: 'I was a little fearful that before we could get ready the Air Force might have Japan so thoroughly bombed out that the new weapon would not have a fair background to show its strength'. To this, the president 'laughed [*sic*] and said he understood'. Kolko, *The Politics of War*, pp. 539–40. Jubilant at what Stimson called the 'royal straight flush' behind his hand at Potsdam, Truman sailed home on the battleship *Augusta*. 'As the *Augusta* approached the New Jersey coast on August 6, Map Room watch officer Captain Frank Graham brought first word that the atomic bomb had been dropped on Hiroshima. Ten minutes later a cable from Stimson reported that the bombing had been even more "conspicuous" than in New Mexico. "This is the greatest thing in history", Truman exclaimed to Graham, and then raced about the ship to spread the news, insisting that he had never made a happier announcement. "We have won the gamble", he told the assembled and cheering crew. The President's behaviour lacked remorse, compassion or humility in the wake of nearly incomprehensible destruction—about 80,000 dead at once, and tens of thousands dying of radiation': Offner, *Another Such Victory*, p. 92, who adds that the number of American deaths supposedly

US had a monopoly of the atom bomb. Then in 1949, much earlier than American intelligence expected, came the first Soviet test of one. But the Pentagon had not been idle, and by 1952 had tested a hydrogen bomb. This time, the Soviet riposte was even quicker, with a rudimentary explosion in 1953. But the US was still far ahead—the device it exploded over Bikini the following year would be thirty times more destructive than the Soviet counterpart of 1955.

Nuclear weapons had to be not just developed, but delivered. There too, America maintained for twenty years a continuous lead, punctuated by repeated claims that it was falling behind. In the mid-fifties, the legend of a 'bomber gap' led to the construction of over two thousand strategic bombers at a time when Russia had no more than twenty. The launching of a *Sputnik* satellite by the USSR, quickly overtaken by more powerful US rockets in the space race, spurred a large expansion of military spending on the back of claims that Moscow had opened up a 'missile gap' in American defences, when there were just four Soviet prototype ICBMs, and the stockpile of American warheads was nearly ten times that of the USSR. Soon thereafter, Pentagon development of MIRV technology put the US ahead again. By the early seventies, when Russia had finally caught up with America in nuclear megatonnage and number, if not quality, of launchers, and was claiming strategic parity, US warheads were still treble its own.

Nor, of course, was the overall strategic balance ever simply a question of rockets. America was a maritime power in command of the world's oceans: its fleets patrolling waterways

averted by the nuclear attacks on Japan, the standard rationale for them, would have been nowhere near Truman's subsequent claim of 500,000 GI lives saved, or Stimson's 1,000,000—perhaps 20,000: p. 97.

from the East China Sea to the Mediterranean, the Atlantic to the Persian Gulf, aircraft carriers cresting the waves, nuclear submarines—five times more than Russia—gliding below them. On land and in the sky, before the war had even ended in 1945 the Joint Chiefs of Staff were planning for a global network of bases and military transit rights covering Latin America, North Africa, the Mediterranean, the Middle East, South Asia and the Far East, and by 1946 already had 170 active airfields in operation at overseas locations.[16] By the mid-sixties, the United States controlled some 375 major bases and 3,000 lesser military facilities around the globe, encircling the Soviet bloc on all sides including even the impassable Arctic.[17] A much poorer and more backward society, the USSR was by comparison a regional power, connected to a set of oppositional movements beyond its borders by a common ideology, where the US was a global power with client regimes in every continent. In the unequal rivalry between them, the vastly greater extent of its strategic empire could be borne at far lower cost by America, as a proportion of its wealth, than its much smaller version could be by Russia. The economic effort required to compete against such odds was enormous.

'Without superior aggregate military strength, in being and readily mobilizable, a policy of "containment"—which is in effect a policy of calculated and gradual coercion—is no more than a policy of bluff', declared the authoritative

---

16 Leffler, *A Preponderance of Power*, pp. 56–9, 135, 171. The planners of 1945 had, of course, not only the USSR in mind. 'In designating bases in the Pacific, for example, Army and Navy officers underscored their utility for quelling prospective unrest in Northeast and Southeast Asia and for maintaining access to critical raw materials': p. 56.

17 C. T. Sandars, *America's Overseas Garrisons: The Leasehold Empire*, Oxford 2000, p. 9.

statement of US strategy in the high Cold War, drafted largely by Nitze in the spring of 1950, and calling for a tripling of the defence budget. But more was required than simply amassing military strength. The battle against the USSR was indivisibly political and ideological as well, in an existential struggle between 'the marvelous diversity, the deep tolerance and the lawfulness of the free society' and 'the idea of slavery under the grim oligarchy of the Kremlin'. At stake was nothing less than 'the fulfillment or destruction not only of this Republic, but of civilization itself'.[18] Politically, the priority was to 'place the maximum strain on the Soviet structure of power and particularly on the relationships between Moscow and the satellite countries', by waging 'overt psychological warfare to encourage mass defections from Soviet allegiance', and deploying 'covert means of economic warfare and political and psychological warfare with a view to fomenting and supporting unrest and revolt in selected strategic satellite countries'. Covert operations against Russia had a pre-history under Wilson, who preferred clandestine to overt means of overthrowing Bolshevik power, and made ample use of them, bequeathing both methods and personnel to their renewal thirty years later.[19] Set in place two

---

18 'Our free society finds itself mortally challenged by the Soviet system. No other value system is so wholly irreconcilable with ours, so implacable in its purpose to destroy ours, so capable of turning to its own uses the most dangerous and divisive trends in our own society, no other so skillfully and powerfully evokes the elements of irrationality in human nature everywhere'. NSC–68 was initially rejected by Nitze's superiors as overwrought, then ratified by Truman in the autumn, after the Cold War had finally exploded into fighting in the Far East. The document was top secret, an *arcanum imperii* only declassified a quarter of a century later.

19 Allen Dulles, one of the products of this experience, would later say: 'I sometimes wonder why Wilson was not the originator of the Central Intelligence Agency'. His brother was equally keen on the dispatch of operatives to subvert Bolshevism. See Foglesong, *America's Secret War*

years before NSC–68 by Kennan,[20] such operations escalated through the fifties, in due course becoming the public objective of a strategy of rollback, depicted by Dulles as a tougher response to Moscow than containment. By then, the slogan was bluster. When revolts did break out in Eastern Europe—in East Germany and Hungary; later Czechoslovakia—they were left to their fate by Washington. Military encirclement of the Soviet bloc was practicable, political intervention was not. That left ideological warfare. The United States was defending not capitalism—the term was carefully avoided, as vocabulary of the enemy—but a Free World against the totalitarian slavery of communism. Radio stations, cultural organizations, print media of every kind, were mobilized to broadcast the

---

against Bolshevism, pp. 126–9, who provides full coverage of Wilson's projects, 'shrouded by a misty combination of self-deception and expedient fictions': p. 295. Leffler's exonerations of Wilson's role in the Russian Civil War—'he viewed the Bolsheviks with contempt. But he did not fear their power'—appeared before the publication of Fogelsong's book, which makes short work of the conventional apologies for Wilson in the literature. Leffler's version of these can be found in *The Spectre of Communism: The United States and the Origins of the Cold War 1917–1953*, New York 1994, pp. 8–9 ff.

20 For Kennan's role in introducing the term and practice of clandestine 'political warfare', and launching the paramilitary expeditions of Operation Valuable into Albania, see Corke, US *Covert Operations and Cold War Strategy*, pp. 45–6, 54–5, 61–2, 84; and Miscamble, *George F. Kennan and the Making of American Foreign Policy*, pp. 110–1: 'Kennan approached covert operations with enthusiasm in 1948 and does not appear to have made apparent any sentiment on his part that covert operations would be limited in extent. Nor did he display any reservations concerning the extralegal character of much of what the OPC would undertake'. For the recruitment of ex-Nazis to its work, see Christopher Simpson, *Blowback*, New York 1988, pp. 112–4. Kennan's connexions to the underworld of American intelligence, foreign and domestic, went back to his time in Portugal during the war, and would extend over the next three decades, to the time of the Vietnam War.

contrast.[21] In the advanced industrial societies of Western Europe and Japan, where the Cold War could be readily projected as a straightforward conflict between democracy and dictatorship, the battle of ideas was won without difficulty. But what of the world beyond them that was also declared free? What did freedom signify there?

---

21 The front organizations set up by the CIA for cultural penetration at home and abroad—the Congress for Cultural Freedom and the like— were another initiative of Kennan, an enthusiast for this kind of work: see Hugh Wilford, *The Mighty Wurlitzer*, Cambridge, MA 2008, pp. 25–8.

5

PERIMETERS

Securing the industrialized flanks of Eurasia against communism, and building a superior strike-capacity and set of strategic revetments against the Soviet Union, were the most urgent tasks for postwar planners in Washington, dominating their immediate attention. Each was achieved in short order. Though successive false alarms would punctuate the arms race, and shadowboxing continue over Berlin, the lines of conflict drawn in 1947–1948 were soon essentially static, an indefinite war of position setting in. From the start, however, American strategists were conscious that the overall battlefield was wider. Another landscape confronted them across vast territories in Asia, Africa and Latin America. These possessed no centres of major industry, had low levels of literacy, and were far more backward in social structure. At the same time, they were a treasury of the natural resources needed to run advanced economies and develop powerful military technologies—petroleum in the Middle East, tin and rubber in Southeast Asia, uranium and cobalt in Central Africa, copper and bauxite in South America, and much more. They also contained the great majority of the world's population. It was obviously critical to hold them.

That posed a more complicated set of problems than reviving Western Europe and Japan, or upgrading a nuclear arsenal. Looking out from the parapets of Washington as the Cold War set in, the panorama of what would later become the Third World was composed of four principal zones. In Asia, European colonial empires that had been shaken or overrun by Japan during the Second World War confronted nationalist movements—some predating the war, others galvanized by it—demanding independence. In the Middle East, weak semi-colonial states—sovereign but tied to former mandatory or supervisory powers—predominated. In Africa, European imperial authority had been little affected by the war, and nationalist movements were still modest. In Latin America, independent republics older than most European states were long-term US clients. Nowhere was there anything approaching the stable representative systems of what would become the First World.

Across this variegated scenery, it was the colonial empires of Britain and France—much the largest—that raised the trickiest issues for Washington. Both countries had been greatly weakened by the war, and were reminded without ceremony of their reduced economic circumstances by the US, which made it plain it would brook no return to their traditional pretensions. Within the Atlantic community over which America would henceforward preside, mustering the capitalist states of the West against the Soviet Union, they could find a place as favoured subordinates. But what was to happen to their imperial booty in the tropics? The US, though late in the day it had acquired colonies of its own in the Pacific and Caribbean, defined itself ideologically as an anti-colonial power, the 'first new nation' to gain independence from the Old World, and had no intention of allowing prewar spheres of influence or control of raw materials to be restored. Its mastery of the Western hemisphere, where Latin America had long been a satellite zone of the United States, showed the way forward, in principle: formal independence of onetime colonies, informal reduction of them to US clients.

A political century later, however, that might not prove so easy. For now anti-colonialism, no doubt acceptable enough in itself, was all too often contaminated by confused ideas of anti-capitalism, leaving struggles for national liberation prey to communist infiltration. The task for American grand strategy was thus a delicate one. The European colonial powers were loyal auxiliaries of the US in the Cold War, which could not be brushed aside or humiliated too brutally. Moreover, where the nationalist movements they confronted were indeed led by communists, colonial counterinsurgency deserved the full backing of the US. On the other hand, where this threat had not yet crystallized, European imperialism risked, in clinging onto its possessions, provoking just what had to be averted, the radicalization of an eclectic nationalism into an insurrectionary socialism. To stem this danger, the colonial empires would have to pass away, and their legacies be developed under new management. That, inevitably, would require a great deal of intervention—economic, political and military—by the United States, to assure safe passage from European domination to American protection, and with it the common interests of the West.

In the process, the US would have to find effective agents of its design where it could. There was no point in being finicky about these. Oligarchs and dictators of one kind or another, many exceptionally ruthless, had long been staples of its Good

Neighbour system in Latin America. Now colonial governors and viceroys, where still in place, might for a time have to be helped. Monarchs, police chiefs, generals, sheikhs, gangsters, latifundists: all were better than communists.[1] Democracy was certainly the ideal political system. Where it was firmly established, in the advanced industrial countries, markets were deepest and business was safest. But where it was not, in less developed societies, matters were otherwise. There, if elections were not proof against attempts on private property, they were dispensable. The Free World was compatible with dictatorship: the freedom that defined it was not the liberty of citizens, but of capital—the one common denominator of its rich and poor, independent and colonial, temperate and tropical regions alike. What was incompatible with it was not absence of parliaments or rights of assembly, but abrogation of private ownership of the means of production. But of the dangers of that there were plenty. In backward societies, not only was the spectre of communism abroad. In the bid to overcome underdevelopment, nationalism itself was subject to statist temptations —arbitrary confiscations and the like, destroying the confidence of foreign investors—against which guard had also to be maintained.

---

1   In his critique of Kennan's 'X' article, Walter Lippmann had foreseen this landscape from the outset. 'The Eurasian continent is a big place and the military power of the United States, though it is very great, has certain limitations which must be borne in mind if it is to be used effectively', he observed dryly. 'The counterforces which Mr X requires have to be composed of Chinese, Afghans, Iranians, Turks, Kurds, Arabs, Greeks, Italians, Austrians, of anti-Soviet Poles, Czechoslovaks, Bulgars, Yugoslavs, Albanians, Hungarians, Finns and Germans. The policy can be implemented only by recruiting, subsidizing and supporting a heterogeneous array of satellites, clients, dependents and puppets': *The Cold War: A Study in US Foreign Policy*, New York 1947, pp. 11, 14.

For operations on this uncertain terrain, the US developed a toolbox of policies and instruments specific to the colonial world and its sequels. Conventional land wars, precluded in the First World, lay at one end of the spectrum; purchase of leaders and suborning of opinion—helpful at the outset in the First World, too—at the other.[2] In between full mechanized violence and selective corruption, a wide range of other methods for enforcing its will would come to be employed: aerial bombardment, military coup, economic sanction, missile attack, naval blockade, honeycomb espionage, torture delegated or direct, assassination. Common to all these forms, across the spectrum, was resort in one way or another to coercion, in a war of movement shifting rapidly from one geographical theatre to the next. The widespread consent on which American imperial power could rely in the First World was missing in the Third. There, it would mostly have to be extorted or counterfeited. The US would not be without genuine friends and loyal relays among regional elites. There would be many of those. But where popular forces came into play, force and fraud were never far away.

---

2   For Gramsci, corruption as a mode of power lay between consent and coercion. Logically enough, therefore, its use has spanned the entire arc of imperial action, across all zones of the Cold War. The worldwide role of the clandestine distribution of money in securing the American empire—Spykman's 'purchase'—has tended to be cast into the shadow by the role of covert violence. More discreet, its scale remains more secret than that of resort to force, but has been more universal, extending from the financing of parties of the postwar political establishment in Italy, France, Japan and cultural institutions throughout the West, to renting of crowds in Iran and rewards for officers in Latin America, subsidies for Afghan warlords or Polish dissidents, and beyond. A full reckoning of it remains, of course, to date impossible, given that even the overall budget of the CIA, let alone its record of disbursements, is a state secret in the US.

II

The first challenge came in the Far East. There, the impact of the Japanese empire that had conquered Asia from Seoul to Mandalay—supplanting Western colonialism across Southeast Asia, and battering the GMD regime in China close to destruction—had by the end of the Pacific War created a unique situation. Over the larger part of the Co-Prosperity Sphere, the most effective form of nationalism had become communism, mustered in resistance movements on the Allied side against Tokyo. Of these forces the most formidable, with the longest history and widest mass organization, was the CCP. Aware of the danger it posed to the GMD regime that Roosevelt had seen as a reliable support of the US, when the Pacific War came to an end the Truman administration kept Japanese forces in China at the ready under its command; dispatched 50,000 marines to hold the Tianjin–Beijing area for Chiang Kai-shek, and another 100,000 troops to occupy Shandong; airlifted half a million GMD soldiers to Manchuria to prevent it falling to the Communists; and over the next three years funnelled some \$4 billion to prop up Chiang. American arms and assistance gave the GMD an initial edge, but wartime destruction and postwar corruption had rotted Chiang's regime so far that the tide soon turned. As Communist advances from base areas close to the Soviet Union accelerated, direct American intervention in such a vast country looked too uncertain of outcome to be risked. The loss of China could not be stopped. To planners in Washington at the time, the victory of the Chinese Revolution, heavy a blow as it might be, was still strategically a sideshow.[3]

---

3   Kennan, whose opinions about China skittered wildly from one direction to another in 1948–1949, could write in September 1951: 'The less

What mattered was keeping control of the industrial heartlands of the West and the Far East. But Asian communism, unlike European, was on the march.

Korea, the oldest Japanese conquest, would left to itself have been the scene of a revolution before China. After the Japanese surrender, only allocation of the South to occupation by the US and the North by the USSR prevented a victory of Korean communism, the strongest native force to emerge after the war, throughout the peninsula.[4] Five years later, the regime set up under Russian protection in the North, emboldened by the triumph of the PLA and the semi-encouragement of Stalin, invaded the South in the hope of rapidly knocking over the unpopular counterpart set up by the US across the border. This was a direct assault on an American creation, in

we Americans have to do with China the better. We need neither covet the favour, nor fear the enmity, of any Chinese regime. China is not the great power of the Orient': Gaddis, *Strategies of Containment*, p. 45. There was no doubt an element of sour grapes, along with blindness, in this pronouncement, at which Spykman might have smiled.

4   Not least because of the 75,000–100,000 Korean veterans who fought alongside the PLA in China during the Anti-Japanese and Civil Wars; the indigenous culture of the regime set up in the North; and the strength of postwar guerrillas in the South: see Bruce Cumings, *Korea's Place in the Sun: A Modern History*, New York 1997, pp. 199, 239–42 ff; Charles Armstrong, *The North Korean Revolution 1945–1950*, Ithaca 2003, pp. 241–4, *passim*. In November 1947, Kennan lugubriously concluded that whereas communists were 'in their element' in Korea, 'we cannot count on native Korean forces to hold the line against Soviet expansion': *State Department Policy Planning Staff Papers*, vol. I, p. 135. Division of the country was one of Stalin's two great timorous blunders in the last months of the war, its consequences more disastrous than his failure at Berlin. Without any necessity, as Khrushchev later complained, he acceded to an American request that US troops occupy the southern half of the country, when none were anywhere near it, and the Red Army could without breaking any agreement have strolled to Pusan. Naturally, Truman did not reciprocate the favour and allowed not so much as a Soviet military band into Japan.

a more manageable space, with easy access from Japan. At Truman's orders a counterattack rolled the enemy up the length of the peninsula, before being checked just short of the Yalu by Chinese entry into the war, and driven back close to the original lines dividing the country, where stalemate set in. Frustrating though the final upshot proved, saturation bombing by the USAF long after a truce became possible destroyed most of the North, saving the South for what would eventually become a showcase of capitalist development, and kick-starting high-speed growth in Japan with a boom in military procurements. Diplomatically, as a US war waged under the nominal banner of the UN, it laid down a marker for the future.

In the tropics, the threat came not in the form of regular armies in a civil war, but communist guerrilla forces newly sprung from the anti-Japanese resistance, fighting for independence against Western colonial powers restored to their prewar possessions. Even where colonial evacuation was swift, they could persist. In the Philippines, rigged elections after independence installed a compliant regime, but the Huks were not put down till 1955. In Burma, White Flag Communists were still in the field twenty years after the British had left. The major dangers, however, lay where the European powers clung on. In Malaya, where tin and rubber wealth ruled out any quick colonial exit, Britain had no little difficulty crushing a Communist movement rooted only in the Chinese minority of the population. Most precarious of all was Indochina. There France was bogged down in a war to reconquer a colony where the Communist party led a national liberation struggle in Vietnam that was not only based squarely on the majority of the population, but could rely on substantial military assistance from the CCP across the border. Funded by Washington,

French repression was a losing battle. After contemplating a nuclear strike to save the day, the US drew back, joining France and Britain at Geneva in 1954 to impose division of the country along Korean lines—the best of a bad job, for the time being.

Financing the French war had been cheaper for Washington, and domestically less conspicuous, than fighting it. But the upshot was plainly shakier. If the South had been kept out of the hands of the Vietminh, there was no DMZ to seal it off from the North in future. The Republic proclaimed by Ho in 1945, before the French arrived back to reclaim it, had extended throughout the country, and enjoyed a nationwide legitimacy that the DPRK, founded after division in 1948, had never possessed. Elections in the South, supposedly scheduled at Geneva, had to be cancelled in view of the certain result, and a weak Catholic regime in Saigon propped up with funds and advisers against mounting guerrilla attacks by the Vietminh. There could be no question of letting it go under. As early as 1949, Kennan had urged American support 'to ensure, *however long it takes*, the triumph of Indochinese nationalism over Red imperialism.'[5] Within a dozen years, Kennedy had dispatched

---

5   Kennan, 'United States Policy Towards South-East Asia', PPS 51, in Nelson, ed., *The State Department Policy Planning Staff Papers,* vol. III, p. 49. See, on this document, Walter Hixson, 'Containment on the Perimeter: George F. Kennan and Vietnam': *Diplomatic History*, April 1988, pp. 151–2, who italicizes the phrase above. In the same paper, Kennan explained that Southeast Asia was a 'vital segment in the line of containment', whose loss would constitute a 'major political rout, the repercussions of which will be felt throughout the rest of the world, especially in the Middle East and in a then critically exposed Australia' [*sic*]. Kennan would later support Johnson's expansion of the war after the Tonkin Gulf Resolution, endorsing the massive bombing of the DRV— Operation Rolling Thunder—in February 1965 as a weapon to force, Kissinger-style, the enemy to the negotiating table. Though increasingly critical of the war as damaging to the national interest, it was not until

American forces to help hold the fort. Under Johnson they rose to over half a million, the number sent to Korea. But despite more tonnage of high explosives dropped on Indochina than the US had unloaded during the whole of the Second World War, with a destructive force equivalent to 200 Hiroshima-type atomic bombs; routine massacres by US troops; systematic use of torture by CIA interrogators and proxies; and some two to three million killed, the Vietnamese Revolution could not be broken.[6] By the turn of the seventies, domestic opposition had made continuation of the war impossible, and once America withdrew, the regime in Saigon collapsed. It was the heaviest defeat of the United States in its history.

But no domino effect followed. British and French colonialism had perforce both enjoyed unstinting support in Southeast Asia, once they were battling communism, the former with ultimate success, the latter—faced with a much more powerful movement—with failure requiring an American relay. For two reasons, Dutch colonialism was another matter. Relatively speaking, beside Britain or France, the Netherlands was a *quantité négligeable* on the European chequerboard,

---

November 1969 that Kennan called for US withdrawal from Vietnam. At home, meanwhile, he wanted student protesters against the war to be locked up, and collaborated with William Sullivan, head of COINTEL-PRO, a longtime associate, in the FBI's covert operations against student and black opponents of the government. See Nicholas Thompson, *The Hawk and the Dove: Paul Nitze, George Kennan and the History of the Cold War*, New York 2009, pp. 221–2—a characteristic exercise in *New Yorker* schlock, by a staffer who is Nitze's grandson, that sporadically contains material at variance with its tenor.

6 For documentation, see Nick Turse, *Kill Anything That Moves: The Real American War in Vietnam*, New York 2013, pp. 11–15, 79–80, 174–91, based on, among other sources, discovery of 'the yellowing records of the Vietnam War Crimes Working Group', a secret Pentagon task force, whose findings lay hidden for half a century, as well as extensive interview material.

which could be given instructions without ceremony; while in the Dutch East Indies, unlike in Malaya or Vietnam, nationalist forces put down a communist uprising during the anti-colonial struggle.[7] As Marshall's undersecretary Lovett gratefully acknowledged, the nascent Indonesian Republic— still at war with the Dutch—was 'the only government in the Far East to have crushed an all-out Communist offensive'. Six months later, NSC–51 determined it imperative to pressure the Dutch to hand over power to those who had shown 'unexcelled skill' in liquidating a revolt instigated by the Kremlin. Within two days Acheson told the Dutch that no Marshall Aid would be forthcoming unless they quit.[8] Independence did not, however, quell communism in Indonesia, which within another decade had become the strongest mass force in the country. The tolerance of the PKI by Sukarno's regime prompted an unsuccessful CIA bid to overthrow it in the late fifties. But the growth of the party alarmed the hardened Indonesian military no less. Within a few months of US troops disembarking at Da Nang in 1965, the largest Communist party in the Free World was wiped out, half a million of its members and their families massacred by an army which needed little prompting from the CIA to do its work, if some assistance in targeting PKI leaders.

7   The presence of communists in the anti-colonial struggle had been cause for acute alarm in Washington—Kennan deciding, in typical vein, that Indonesia was 'the most crucial issue of the moment in our struggle with the Kremlin'. Its fall would lead to nothing less than 'a bisecting of the world from Siberia to Sumatra', cutting 'our global east–west communications', making it 'only a matter of time before the infection would sweep westwards through the continent to Burma, India and Pakistan': Miscamble, *Kennan and the Making of American Foreign Policy*, p. 274.

8   Robert McMahon, *Colonialism and Cold War: The United States and the Struggle for Indonesian Independence, 1945–49*, Ithaca 1971, pp. 242–4, 290–4.

The slaughter accomplished, the Suharto dictatorship received every benefaction from Washington.

The pogrom in Indonesia, a country with nearly three times the population of Vietnam, more than counterbalanced the setbacks in Indochina. With the destruction of the PKI, the danger of revolutionary contagion in the zone where communism and nationalism had fused most directly was over. By the end of the war in Indochina, any threat to capital in Southeast Asia had been defused. Where the Japanese armies had stopped, there was no comparable tinderbox. In the Subcontinent, the British could transfer power to national movements above suspicion of any radical temptations. In Pakistan, Washington had a staunch ally from the start. In India, Congress might make the occasional anti-American noise, but it could be counted on to give short shrift to communism.

III

The Middle East presented an altogether different scene. There the imprint of European imperialism was shallower. Egypt had been put under British tutelage in the late nineteenth century, though never annexed, and British protectorates managed from India stretched along the Gulf coast. But for the rest of the region the arrival of European colonialism came late, with the breakup of the Ottoman Empire at the end of the First World War, and camouflaged under mandates, was brief. Largely untouched by the Second World War, by its aftermath the whole region was composed of formally independent states, except the British colony in Aden, all ruled by conservative monarchies or emirates of one kind or another, except for Syria, where French colonial rule had been republican, and Lebanon, which the French had succeeded in detaching from it as a separate unit on exiting. Popular risings in Iraq and Palestine had been crushed by the British before the war, nationalist currents had not been steeled in resistance movements during the war, and the influence of communism was generally modest. So far, so good. But the region was close to the Soviet Union, as Southeast Asia had not been. It contained the largest oil reserves on earth, whose Saudi fields were early designated by Hull 'one of the world's greatest prizes',[9] their ruler courted by Roosevelt on his way home from Yalta. It now further contained a state that owed its existence to Truman, who had steamrollered a partition of Palestine through the UN for the creation of Israel. But in Washington there was no overall scheme for the region. Roosevelt had made the Saudi connexion. Truman bequeathed the Israeli. In the cartography of American power, these were still scattered bivouacs between the great emplacements of Eurasia.

But if in the first phase of the Cold War, while not a blank zone, the Middle East had relatively low salience for the US,

---

9   Hearden, *Architects of Globalization*, p. 124. Hull's overriding concern was to keep Saudi petroleum out of British hands: 'the expansion of British facilities serves to build up their post-war position in the Middle East at the expense of American interests'. As early as February 1943 Roosevelt issued a finding that 'the defence of Saudi Arabia' was 'vital to the defence of the United States': see David Painter, *Oil and the American Century: The Political Economy of US Foreign Oil Policy, 1941–1954*, Baltimore 1986: 'the idea that the United States had a preemptive right to the world's oil resources was well entrenched by World War II': pp. 37, 208. Such was the spirit in which FDR told Halifax: 'Persian oil is yours. We share the oil of Iraq and Kuwait. As for Saudi Arabian oil, it's ours'. In August 1945, Ibn Saud granted Washington its first military base in the region, in Dhahran. But it was still British bases in the Cairo–Suez area that counted as the Cold War got under way. 'From British-controlled airstrips in Egypt, US bombers could strike more key cities and petroleum refineries in the Soviet Union and Romania than from any other prospective base in the globe': Leffler, *A Preponderance of Power*, p. 113.

one country was a concern from the beginning. Iran was not only the world's second largest petroleum producer. It abutted directly onto the USSR, and harboured the only communist movement in the region with a significant following in the aftermath of the war. There in 1951 the Mossadegh government nationalized the British-owned and controlled oilfields in Abadan. In London, Bevin wanted to dispatch the Royal Navy to repossess them. For Washington, this could only worsen matters, inflaming a Persian nationalism already subject to contagion from communism in the shape of the local Tudeh Party.[10] The solution was not gunboats, but covert action. In 1953, the CIA and MI6 orchestrated a military coup to oust Mossadegh, installing in power the young Pahlavi Shah, whose regime made short work of the Tudeh.[11] For its services, the

10 Kennan was indignant, arguing in 1952 that the US should give full support to a British expedition to recapture Abadan. Only 'the cold gleam of adequate and determined force' could save Western positions in the Middle East. 'Abadan and Suez are important to the local peoples only in terms of their *amour propre* … To us, some of these things are important in a much more serious sense, and for reasons that today are sounder and better and more defensible than they ever were in history', he wrote to Acheson. 'To retain these facilities and positions we can use today only one thing: military strength, backed by the resolution and courage to use it': Mayers, *Kennan and the Dilemmas of US Foreign Policy*, pp. 253–5. Kennan went on to deplore the Republican Administration's opposition to the Anglo-French-Israeli attack on Egypt, and applaud its landing of troops in the Lebanon.

11 Of the coup, the CIA could record in its secret history of the operation: 'It was a day that should never have ended. For it carried with it such a sense of excitement, of satisfaction and of jubilation that it is doubtful if any other can come up to it': see Lloyd Gardner, *Three Kings: The Rise of an American Empire in the Middle East after World War II*, New York 2009, p. 123. For a recent neo-royalist attempt, by a former functionary of the Shah, to downplay the role of the CIA in the coup, on the grounds that Mossadegh had aroused opposition in the Shi'a hierarchy, see Darioush Bayandor, *Iran and the CIA: The Fall of Mossadeq Revisited*, New York 2010, and successive rebuttals in *Iranian Studies*, September 2012.

Eisenhower administration forced a reluctant Whitehall to give the American oil majors a cut of the British stake in Abadan.

Where there was no direct communist threat on the ground, there was less need for collaboration with older empires, whose interests might conflict with US objectives. Three years later, the potential for tension between these exploded when Egypt nationalized the Suez Canal. The US had no time for Nasser, who had rejected its insistence that he enter secret talks with Israel and give Moscow a cold shoulder. But it feared that any overt military assault to regain the Canal might align the entire Third World against the West in its battle with the Soviet Union.[12] Furious that Eden ignored his warnings, Eisenhower brought the Anglo-French-Israeli attack on Egypt to an abrupt halt by cutting off support for sterling, leaving London high and dry. The real position of its European allies within the postwar American order, normally enveloped in the decorous fictions of Atlantic solidarity, was made brutally plain.

But there was a cost to the operation. Having defied the West, Nasser's prestige in the Arab World soared, fanning a more radical nationalism in the region, with fewer inhibitions about close ties with the USSR. After getting rid of Mossadegh, the US had sought to create a *cordon sanitaire*

12 Should Britain and France send in troops, Eisenhower cautioned Eden on September 2, 'the peoples of the Near East and of North Africa and, to some extent, of all of Asia and all of Africa, would be consolidated against the West to a degree which, I fear, could not be overcome in a generation and, perhaps, not even in a century, particularly having in mind the capacity of the Russians to make mischief.' Counselling patience, US policy-makers believed the crisis could be resolved by diplomacy and covert action. 'The Americans' main contention', Eden remarked on September 23, 'is that we can bring Nasser down by degrees rather on the Mossadegh lines': Douglas Little, 'The Cold War in the Middle East: Suez Crisis to Camp David Accords', in Leffler and Westad, eds, *The Cambridge History of the Cold War*, vol. II, Cambridge 2010, p. 308.

against communism with the Baghdad Pact, putting together Turkey, Iraq, Iran and Pakistan. In 1958 the scheme collapsed with an Iraqi Revolution that overthrew the monarchy, and brought to power a military regime well to the left of Nasser's, supported by what was now the strongest communist movement in the Middle East. In response, the US landed 14,000 marines in the Lebanon to defend its Maronite president from the spectre of subversion. Five years later came the putsch that first brought the Baath to power in Baghdad, of which the CIA was given advance knowledge, supplying in return lists of Iraqi communists to be killed in the slaughter that followed it. None of the military regimes of the time—Syria was now under Baath control too—could be trusted by Washington, however, since no matter how they treated their own communists, they were no friends of free enterprise or foreign investment, and all alike not only welcomed arms and assistance from Moscow, but menaced reliable neighbouring dynasties.

In this unsatisfactory scene, the Israeli blitz of June 1967, wiping out the Egyptian air force in a few hours and seizing Sinai, the Golan Heights and the West Bank in less than a week, struck like a political thunderbolt. Nasser, whose bungled support for a Yemeni republic that was feared by the Saudi monarchy had long been an irritant, was now a busted flush in the Arab world, while Israel emerged as overwhelmingly the strongest military power in the region. After the Tripartite attack on Egypt of 1956, France—along with Britain—had helped Israel to become a clandestine nuclear power, as part of the secret pact between the three that launched the Suez expedition, and for a time Paris had been Israel's closest ally in the West. But the spectacular success of the Six-Day War altered all calculations in the US, where the Jewish community was buoyed with new enthusiasm for the homeland of Zionism, and the Pentagon saw a prospective regional partner of formidable punitive strength. Henceforward, American policy in the Middle East pivoted around an alliance with Israel, confident that the Arab oil kingdoms would have to put up with it.

There remained the problem of the flow of Soviet arms and personnel to Egypt and Syria, stepped up after the Arab disaster of 1967, and viewed in Washington as the spearhead of Russian penetration of the Middle East. To win American favour, Sadat expelled all Soviet advisors from Egypt in 1972, and a year later launched a joint attack on the Israeli gains of 1967 with Syria and Jordan. This time a massive airlift of US tanks and aircraft saved the day for Israel, whose counterattack was only stopped from crossing the Canal and annihilating the Egyptian army by last-minute American dissuasion. The 1973 war yielded a near-perfect result for Washington, demonstrating that no amount of Soviet armour could compete with combined American and Israeli capabilities in the region, and putting the Egyptian military regime into its pocket as henceforward a US dependent.

IV

Remote from the Soviet Union, clear of European empires, unscathed by the war, Latin America was home territory for Washington, the province of the Monroe doctrine and Olney's famous corollary: 'The United States is practically sovereign on this continent and its fiat is law upon the subjects to which it confines its interposition', since 'its infinite resources combined with its isolated position render it master of the situation'. From the last years of the nineteenth century to

the Great Depression, the US had dispatched troops and war-
ships to crush strikes, put down risings, oust rulers or occupy
territories in the Caribbean and Central America, with unin-
hibited regularity. Since then there had been no obvious call
to do so. The US had made sure of the allegiance of a Latin
American *cortège*—numerically the largest single bloc—in the
UN before it was even founded, with the Act of Chapultepec
in early 1945. The Rio Treaty of Inter-American Defence followed in 1947, capped by the formation of the Organization
of American States, headquarters in Washington and expressly
devoted to the fight against subversion, in 1948. Two years later
Kennan, warning against 'any indulgent and complacent view
of Communist activities in the New World', made it clear that
ruthless means might be required to crush them: 'We should
not hesitate before police repression by the local government.
This is not shameful since the Communists are essentially trai-
tors', he told US ambassadors to South America summoned to
hear him in Rio. 'It is better to have a strong regime in power
than a liberal government if it is indulgent and relaxed and
penetrated by Communists'.[13]

13 See Walter LaFeber, *Inevitable Revolutions*, New York 1993, p. 109. On
getting back to Washington, Kennan hammered his message home:
'Where the concepts and traditions of popular government are too
weak to absorb successfully the intensity of the communist attack, then
we must concede that harsh measures of repression may be the only
answer; that these measures may have to proceed from regimes whose
origins and methods would not stand the test of American concepts of
democratic procedures; and that such regimes and such methods may be
preferable alternatives, and indeed the only alternatives, to communist
success': see Roger Trask, 'George F. Kennan's Report on Latin America
(1950)', *Diplomatic History*, July 1978, p. 311. The Southern hemisphere,
in Kennan's view, was an all-round cultural disaster zone: he doubted
whether there existed 'any other region of the earth in which nature and
human behaviour could have combined to produce a more unhappy and
hopeless background for the conduct of life'.

At the time, with the notable exception of Perón's regime in Argentina, virtually all Latin American governments, a medley of conservative autocracies of one kind or another—traditional dictators, neo-feudal oligarchies, military juntas, single-party rule—with a sprinkling of narrowly based democracies, were more or less congenial helpmeets of US business and diplomacy. Living standards, however low for the majority of the population, were nevertheless on the whole somewhat higher than in Southeast Asia or the Middle East. In the first years of the Cold War, the region offered fewer reasons for alarm than any other in the postcolonial world.

The election of a left-wing government in Guatemala, nationalizing landholdings of the United Fruit Company and legalizing the local Communist Party, changed this. Mounting a land invasion by mercenaries, backed by a naval blockade and bombing from the air, the CIA ousted the Arbenz regime in 1954, the *New York Times* exulting that this was 'the first successful anti-Communist revolt since the war'.[14] Six years later, when the victory of the Cuban Revolution brought expropriation of American capital to the doorstep of the US,[15] the

---

14 In 1952, Truman had already approved a plan developed by Somoza after a visit to the president for a CIA operation to overthrow Arbenz, countermanded at the last minute by Acheson, probably out of fear it would fail: Piero Gleijeses, *Shattered Hope: The Guatemalan Revolution and the United States 1944–1955*, Princeton 1992, pp. 228–31. Richard Helms, promoted to chief of operations at the CIA the following year, explained to Gleijeses: 'Truman okayed a good many decisions for covert operations that in later years he said he knew nothing about. It's all presidential deniability': p. 366.

15 At which the overthrow of the regime in Havana rapidly became 'the top priority of the US government', in the younger Kennedy's words: 'All else is secondary. No time, money, effort, or manpower is to be spared.' Kennan, consulted by the elder Kennedy before his inauguration, approved an invasion of Cuba, provided it was successful: Thompson, *The Hawk and the Dove*, p. 172.

Kennedy administration attempted without success a larger CIA invasion to crush it, and then imposed a naval blockade to stop Soviet missiles arriving in the island, whose withdrawal had to be exchanged for abandonment of further military action against Cuba. With this, Latin America moved to the top of the Cold War agenda in Washington. Inspired by the Cuban Revolution, guerrilla movements sprang up across the continent, while the US touted an Alliance for Progress as the liberal alternative to their radical goals, and armed counterinsurgency campaigns in one country after another—Venezuela, Peru, Bolivia, Guatemala—to root them out.

But the traditional forces of the Latin American right—the army, the church, latifundists, big business—were quite capable of taking the initiative to destroy any threat from the left, with or without it taking up arms, in the knowledge that they could count on the blessing, and where need be, material backing of the US. In 1964, the Brazilian military staged the first of the counterrevolutionary coups against an elected government that swept the major societies of the continent, while the aircraft carrier *Forrestal* and supporting destroyers hovered offshore in case help was required.[16] A year later, US marines waded into the Dominican Republic to repel an imaginary communist danger, Brazilian troops returning the favour in

16 McGeorge Bundy to the NSC, 28 March 1964: 'The shape of the problem in Brazil is such that we should not be worrying that the military will react; we should be worrying that the military will not react': Westad, *Global Cold War*, p. 150. On April 1, Ambassador Lincoln Gordon could teletype Washington that it was 'all over', with the democratic rebellion already 95 per cent successful', and the next day celebrate 'a great victory for the free world', without which there could have been 'a total loss to the West of all South American Republics'. For these and other particulars of 'Operation Brother Sam', see Phyllis Parker, *Brazil and the Quiet Intervention, 1964*, Austin 1979, pp. 72–87.

their train. In Uruguay, Argentina and Chile, whether popular hopes for an alternative order took shape in urban guerrillas, populist labour movements, socialist or communist parties, all were crushed by ferocious military dictatorships, acting with the support of the US. By the mid-seventies, the Cuban Revolution had been isolated and the continent was armour-plated against any further challenge to capital.

As a theatre of the Cold War, Latin America saw the widest breadth of political forms and energies pitted against the American imperial order, and least connected—ideologically or materially—with the distant Soviet state. To Cuba, Moscow supplied an economic lifeline without which it could scarcely have survived, but strategically it was at variance with Havana, deploring its revolutionary activism throughout. The letter of the Olney Corollary no longer held—the juntas in Brasília or Santiago were not mere subjects of the US, and Cuba could not be retaken. But its logic was still in place. To all appearances, in the first quarter of a century of the Cold War, nowhere was American victory so complete.

6

RECALIBRATION

In the history of the postwar American empire, the early seventies was a watershed. For twenty years after the onset of the Cold War, the alternation of incumbents in the White House scarcely affected the continuity of the strategy laid out in NSC–68. At the turn of the seventies, however, deep changes in the environment of US global power coincided with a presidency less committed to the pious fictions and policy fixations of its predecessors, capable of pursuing the same ultimate ends with notably more flexible—if also, where required, yet more ruthless—means. As no American ruler before or after him has been, Nixon was an innovator. But his departures from the handbook for running the Free World came from the opportunities and constraints of the conjuncture. On all three fronts of US grand strategy, the years 1971–1973 saw dramatic changes.

The first came where everything had hitherto gone most smoothly. The reconstruction of Western Europe and Japan, the highest American priority after the war, had been a resounding success. But after two decades, the former Axis powers were now—thanks to US aid, access to US markets and borrowing of US technology, combined with reserve armies of low-wage labour and more advanced forms of industrial organization than the US possessed—outcompeting American firms in one branch of manufacturing after another: steel, auto, machine tools, electronics. Under this German and Japanese pressure, the rate of profit of US producers fell sharply, and a US trade deficit opened up.[1] Compounding this relentless effect of the uneven development of capitalism during the long postwar boom were the costs of the domestic reforms with which Nixon, like Johnson, sought to consolidate his electorate and tamp down opposition to the war in Vietnam, itself a further drain on the US Treasury. The upshot was escalating inflation and a deteriorating balance of payments. To cap matters, France—under De Gaulle and Pompidou, the one Western state to regain, for a season, real political independence from Washington—had started to attack the dollar with increasing purchases of gold. The latitude of American power over American interests, the remit of the imperial state beyond the requirements of national capital, was for the first time under pressure.

Nixon's response was draconian. The principles of free trade, the free market and the solidarity of the free world could not stand in the way of the national interest. Wasting no time on diplomatic consultation, in a four-minute television address to a domestic audience he jettisoned the Bretton Woods system, cutting the link of the dollar to gold, imposed a tariff surcharge on all imports, and decreed a wage and price freeze. In the short run, devaluation restored the competitive punch of US exporters, and in the long run, delinkage of the dollar from gold gave the US state greater freedom of economic manoeuvre

---

1 For this development, the indispensable account is Robert Brenner, *The Economics of Global Turbulence*, London and New York 2006, pp. 99–142.

than ever before. The real structure of the liberal international order projected in 1943–1945 stood momentarily revealed. But this impressive success in the exercise of national egoism could only mask for a limited spell the irreversible alteration in the position of the United States in the world economy, of which Nixon was aware.

A month before delivering the American quietus to Bretton Woods, Nixon had startled the world with another, no less drastic reorientation of US policy, the announcement that he would shortly be travelling to Beijing. The victory of the Chinese revolution had been the worst blow Washington had ever suffered in the Cold War. Regarding the CCP as a more bitter enemy even than the CPSU, it had refused to recognize Mao's regime, maintaining that the real China was its ward in Taiwan, and ignoring the split between Beijing and Moscow that became public in the early sixties and worsened steadily thereafter. Nixon now became determined to capitalize on this. Still mired in Vietnam, where the DRV was receiving assistance from both Russia and China, his aim was to increase his leverage on both powers, playing them off against each other to secure a settlement that would preserve the South Vietnamese state and American military credibility in Southeast Asia. In February 1972 his cordial reception by Mao in Beijing marked a diplomatic revolution. The two leaders agreed on the threat posed by the Soviet Union, laying the basis for a tacit alliance against it. Having obtained this understanding, Nixon proceeded to Moscow three months later, where—reminding Brezhnev of the potential dangers from China—he signed the first SALT agreement, amid much celebration of *détente*. The treaty did not halt the arms race, and the atmospherics of *détente* were of less effect than intended in neutralizing domestic opposition to the war in Indochina. But the basic strategic gain of Nixon's turn was enormous, and would last. The Communist world was no longer just divided. Henceforward China and Russia would compete for privileged relations with the United States.

What this transformation of the dynamics of the Cold War could not deliver was Nixon's immediate objective, a stalemate in Vietnam. Though Moscow and Beijing both urged another Geneva-style arrangement on Hanoi, they were not in a position to impose one. A further massive American bombing campaign failed to buckle the DRV. In January 1973, accords had to be signed in Paris for a withdrawal of US troops from Vietnam in sixty days, sealing the fate of the southern regime. But the inglorious end of the long American intervention in Vietnam was rapidly recouped elsewhere. In September the Allende regime, the most advanced, freely elected socialist experience in South America, from whose example capital had most to fear, and whose fall Nixon had demanded from the start, was destroyed by the Chilean military.[2] A month later, the Egyptian army was routed by the Israeli offensive across the Canal, and the Arab nationalism embodied by Nasser's regime

2   The director of the CIA cabled its station chief in Santiago on 16 October 1970: 'It is firm and continuous policy that Allende be overthrown by a coup. It would be much preferable to have this transpire prior to 24 October, but efforts in this regard will continue vigorously beyond this date. We are to continue to generate maximum pressure towards this end utilizing every appropriate resource. It is imperative that these actions be implemented clandestinely and securely so that USG and American hand be well hidden.' See Peter Kornbluh, *The Pinochet File: A Declassified Dossier on Atrocity and Accountability*, New York 2003, p. 64. In dealing with Chile, Kissinger was true to Kennan's recommendations two decades earlier. In 1971, Kennan remarked: 'Henry understands my views better than anyone at State ever has', and eight days after the coup in Chile wrote to Kissinger, who had just become secretary of state, 'I could not be more pleased than I am by this appointment': Gaddis, *George F. Kennan*, p. 621.

was finished, leaving the United States diplomatic master of the Middle East.

II

Nixon's departure was followed, after a brief interim, by a tonal and tactical reversion to more standard styles of American *Weltpolitik*. In a typical bout of domestic positioning, *détente* soon came under Democratic attack as an unprincipled sell-out to Moscow. In late 1974 the Jackson–Vanik amendment blocked the granting of MFN status to the USSR for obstructing Jewish emigration from Russia to Israel. A year later, SALT II was dead in the water. Nixon had not held high enough the banners of the Free World—in particular the cause of human rights, picked out by Jackson and blazoned by Carter in his campaign for the White House, which henceforward became an ideological staple of all regimes in Washington. The Cold War was not to be waged as a mere power-political contest. It was a moral-ideological battle for civilization, as Nitze had seen.

Strategically, little altered. Nixon's legacy was not discarded, but substantively consolidated. There would be no return to benevolent American indifference—let alone assistance—to the economic rise of Japan or Germany. The First World had become a clear-cut arena of inter-capitalist competition in which US predominance was at stake, to be assured where necessary without compunction. Nixon had cut the dollar free from gold, and shown scant respect for laissez-faire totems at home or abroad, but the oil shock of 1973 had compounded the underlying economic downturn in the US with a steep burst of inflation, which the floating exchange rates instituted at the Smithsonian in 1971 did little to improve. By the end of the decade the temporary boost to American exports from the 1971 devaluation was exhausted, and the dollar dangerously low. With Volcker's arrival at the Fed under Carter, there was an abrupt change of course. Interest rates were driven sky-high to stamp out inflation, attracting a flood of foreign capital, and putting massive pressure on dollar-denominated Third World debts. But once the dollar strengthened again—US manufacturers paying the price, the trade deficit widening—the Reagan administration did not stand on ceremony. After ruthless arm-twisting, Japan and Germany were forced to accept enormous revaluations of the yen and the Mark to make American exports competitive once more.[3] The Plaza Accords of 1985, clinching the relative economic recovery of the US in the eighties, left no doubt who was master in the liberal international order, and intended to remain so.

Beyond the First World, Nixon's two other great legacies each required completion. In the Far East, China had been wooed into an unspoken entente with America, but there were still no diplomatic relations between the two states, Washington maintaining formal recognition of the GMD regime in Taiwan as the government of China. In the Middle East, Israel had been handed victory, and Egypt saved from disaster, but a settlement between the two was needed for the US to capitalize fully on its command of the situation. Within a few months of each other, unfinished business in both theatres was wrapped up. In the autumn of 1978 Sadat and Begin signed a US-monitored agreement at Camp David returning Israeli-occupied Sinai to Egypt in exchange for the abandonment by Egypt of the allies who had fought with it, whose territories Israel continued to

---

3 Brenner, *Economics of Global Turbulence*, pp. 190, 206–7; *The Boom and the Bubble*, London and New York 2002, pp. 60–1, 106–7, 122–3, 127.

occupy, and of empty promises to the Palestinians, promptly discarded. A deluge of US military aid to both countries followed, as henceforward interconnected, if incommensurate ramparts of the American system in the Middle East: Israel an ally more than capable of independent action, Egypt a pensionary incapable of it.

In the Far East, China was easier game. Some tractations were needed to finesse the problem of Taiwan, but once Beijing made no case of continued American commercial and material support for the island, provided Washington withdrew recognition of the ROC, the way was clear for the establishment of formal diplomatic relations between the two powers on the first day of 1979. Two weeks later, Deng Xiaoping arrived in the US for a tour of the country and talks at the White House, aiming not only for a compact with America as a strategic counterbalance to Russia, as Mao had done, but integration into the global economic system headed by the US—an Open Door in reverse—which Mao had not. The entrance ticket he offered was a Chinese attack on Vietnam to punish it for having overthrown the Pol Pot regime, a protégé of Beijing, in Cambodia. The US, still smarting from its humiliation in Indochina, was happy to accept it. The Chinese invasion of Vietnam did not go well, and had to be called off with heavy casualties and little to show for it. But it served its political purpose, blooding China as a reliable US partner in Southeast Asia, where the two powers joined forces to sustain the Khmer Rouge along the Thai border for another dozen years, and entitling the PRC to the full benefit of American investors and American markets. Carter—human rights a better magic cloak for Pol Pot than Chicago economics for Pinochet—had proved an effective executor of Nixon.

III

Further strengthening of positions in the Middle and Far East was no guarantee of security elsewhere in the Third World. The late seventies and eighties saw not a contraction, but an expansion of danger-zones for the US into areas hitherto little touched by the Cold War.[4] Africa had long been the continent least affected by it. The Algerian Revolution, the one mass armed struggle of the late fifties and early sixties, had caused some anxiety, but the rapid capture of power by an intro-verted military regime with few ideological ambitions allayed these. Elsewhere, there was no comparable scale of European settlement, with the exception of the white racist stronghold of South Africa, which could look after itself. In between, French and British colonies run by a handful of administrators,

4   Though, of course, never entirely out of sight in Washington. There is no better illustration of how imaginary is the belief that Kennan's doctrine of containment was geographically limited, rather than uncompromis-ingly global, than PPS 25 of March 1948 on North Africa, which—after remarking that 'the people of Morocco can best advance under French tutelage'—concluded: 'The development of the US into a major world power together with the wars that have been fought by this country to prevent the Atlantic littoral of Europe and Africa from falling into hostile hands, the increasing dependency of England upon the US and the situ-ation brought about by the rise of air power and other technological advances, have made it necessary that a new concept should be applied to the entire group of territories bordering on the Eastern Atlantic at least down to the "Bulge" of Africa. The close interflexion of the French African territories bordering on the Mediterranean must also be considered an integral part of this concept. This would mean, in modern terms, that we could not tolerate from the standpoint of our national security the exten-sion into this area of any system of power which is not a member of the Atlantic community, or a transfer of sovereignty to any power which does not have full consciousness of its obligations with respect to the peace of the Atlantic order': Anna Kasten Nelson, ed., *State Department Policy Planning Staff Papers*, vol. II, pp. 146–7.

undisturbed by any wartime radicalization, covered most of the vast sub-Saharan spaces. There, decolonization could be handled without much difficulty, with a controlled transfer of power to generally moderate elites still highly dependent, materially and culturally, on the former metropoles.

There were two other colonial powers, however, of lesser size and self-confidence, who in opposite ways flubbed this process, putting Washington on the alert. Belgium, having for years made no effort to prepare a suitable postcolonial landing in the Congo, granted it independence overnight in 1960. When amid chaotic conditions following a mutiny of the ex-colonial gendarmerie against its white officers, Lumumba—elected leader of the country—appealed for Soviet aid, the CIA was instructed to poison him. After this came to nothing, the US—in effective control of the UN operation ostensibly sent to stabilize the situation—orchestrated a seizure of power by troops under Mobutu, a CIA asset, ensuring Lumumba's death *par pouvoir interposé*, and the dictatorship in the Congo of their parachutist commander for thirty years.[5]

---

5   The UN bureaucracy and the US secret state were in full agreement, Hammarskjöld opining that 'Lumumba must be broken', his American deputy Cordier that Lumumba was Africa's 'Little Hitler', and Allen Dulles cabling the CIA station chief in Leopoldville: 'In high quarters here it is held that if [Lumumba] continues to hold office, the inevitable result will at best be chaos and at worst pave the way to Communist takeover of the Congo with disastrous consequences for the prestige of the UN and for the interests of the free world generally. Consequently we conclude that his removal must be an urgent and prime objective.' In Washington, Eisenhower gave a green light to the disposal of Lumumba, and an emissary was dispatched to poison him. The best documentation of his fate is Ludo De Witte, *The Assassination of Lumumba*, London and New York 2001, pp. 17–20 ff and *passim*. The Congo operation was much more important in setting a benchmark for subsequent use of the UN as an instrument of American will than its function as an international fig leaf for the war in Korea.

Portugal, itself a dictatorship dating back to fascist times, whose identity as a European power was inseparable from its African empire, had no intention of relinquishing its colonies, and by outlasting France and Britain on the continent for over a decade, created the conditions for a radicalized anti-imperialism looking for aid and inspiration to the USSR, otherwise present elsewhere only in South Africa. When, after a dozen years of armed struggle, a metropolitan revolution finally brought decolonization, the richest Portuguese possession of Angola was divided between three movements for independence, two of the right, backed by the Congo and the PRC, and one of the left, backed by Russia. Alarmed at the prospect of this last winning the contest between them, in 1975 Washington supplied its opponents with funds, weapons and officers in a covert CIA operation from the north, while inciting South Africa to invade the colony from the south. Before Luanda could fall, Cuban troops ferried from the Caribbean in Soviet transports arrived in strength, clearing the north and obliging the South African column to withdraw. For the US, defeat in Angola was consignment of the country to communism, and in the eighties it stepped up support for the rival force remaining in the field, led by Pretoria's ally Savimbi. A second South African invasion, assisted by Savimbi, was halted thirteen years later by another Cuban expedition, larger than the first. In Angola, by the time Reagan left office, America had been worsted.[6]

The only African arena to have escaped European colonization prior to the First World War, and then been only briefly conquered after it, predictably became the other proving

---

6   See the fine account in Westad, *The Global Cold War*, pp. 218–46, 390–2.

ground of the last phases of the Cold War, as a feudal kingdom overdue for explosion. The Ethiopian revolution that toppled the archaic local dynasty in 1974 became steadily more radical as the group of junior officers who took power underwent a series of convulsive purges, ending in a regime that not only called for Soviet military assistance, but—rather than talking vaguely of African socialism, as many others had done— proclaimed the goal of creating a society based on scientific socialism, Soviet-style. Imperial Ethiopia had, traditionally, been a *plaque tournante* of American strategic dispositions in the Horn. When it appeared to have capsized into communism, the US instigated an invasion by Somalia in 1977 to reclaim the Ogaden region. As in Angola, the incursion was beaten back by a combination of Cuban troops and much more Soviet armour and oversight, a bitter pill for Washington to swallow. At the helm of the NSC, Brzezinski declared the death of *détente* in the sands of the Ogaden. Success in the Congo had confirmed the value of the UN as a cover for US operations in the Third World. Setbacks in Angola and Ethiopia offered lessons in how better to run proxy wars.

Across the Atlantic, South America had been so scoured of threats to capital by the late seventies that the military regimes which had stamped them out could withdraw, their historical task accomplished, leaving democratic governments in place, safe from any temptation of radical change. Central America, however, lay in a different political time zone. Long a political backwater, home to some of the most benighted tyrants on the continent, its brief episodes of insurgency quickly snuffed out, most of the region had remained quiet during the period of high revolutionary activism to the south. The overthrow by Sandinista rebels in 1979 of the Somoza dynasty in Nicaragua, whose rule under American patronage dated from the time of Roosevelt, brought the country into the full glare of US counterinsurgency.[7] The Nicaraguan revolutionaries were closely linked to Cuba, and in 1981 their victory set off an insurrection in El Salvador that developed into a civil war lasting a decade, and a briefer uprising in Guatemala—where guerrillas were an older phenomenon—broken by all-out repression. Local oligarchs and officers reacted to the wave of regional radicalization with death-squads, disappearances, torture, massacres. In these two countries, the Carter administration supplied American training and assistance. Reagan, no less determined to hold the line in El Salvador and Guatemala, decided to tackle the root of the problem in Nicaragua itself.

From 1982 onwards, the US assembled an army of counter-revolutionaries, well funded and equipped, in Honduras and Costa Rica to destroy the Sandinista regime. Cross-border raids and attacks multiplied, with widespread sabotage of communications, destruction of crops and economic installations, and assassination of civilians, in a campaign under direct American

7   Somoza, to whom Stimson had taken a liking on a visit during the second US occupation of Nicaragua in 1927, became the first head of the National Guard created by the Marines as Roosevelt took office. After murdering Sandino in 1934, he was in due course welcomed to Washington in unprecedented style by the president: 'Plans called for Roosevelt, for the first time since entering office in 1933, to leave the White House to greet a chief of state. The vice-president, the full cabinet, and the principal leaders of Congress and the judiciary were all scheduled to be present for the arrival of Somoza's train. A large military honour guard, a twenty-one gun salute, a presidential motorcade down Pennsylvania Avenue, a state dinner, and an overnight stay at the White House were all part of the official itinerary', with 'over five thousand soldiers, sailors and Marines lining the streets and fifty aircraft flying overhead. Government employees released from work for the occasion swelled the crowds along the procession': Paul Coe Clark, *The United States and Somoza: A Revisionist Look*, Westport 1992, pp. 63–4.

control and design. Without being able to hold large swathes of territory, the Contras put the country under siege. Privation and fatigue gradually weakened popular support for the Sandinista government, until at the end of the decade it agreed to elections if the Contras were stood down, and was defeated by the candidate of the State Department, who alone could deliver an end to the American embargo impoverishing the country. Central America was not Africa. The US could fight a proxy war against a small opponent to complete success—rounding off its grip on the region with an invasion of Panama straight out of the twenties, before Nicaraguans even went to the polls, to get rid of an unsatisfactory strongman.[8]

---

8 'Between the onset of the global Cold War in 1948 and its conclusion in 1990, the US government secured the overthrow of at least twenty-four governments in Latin America, four by direct use of US military forces, three by means of CIA-managed revolts or assassination, and seventeen by encouraging local military and political forces to intervene without direct US participation, usually through military coups d'état … The human cost of this effort was immense. Between 1960, by which time the Soviets had dismantled Stalin's gulags, and the Soviet collapse in 1990, the numbers of political prisoners, torture victims, and executions of nonviolent political dissenters in Latin America vastly exceeded those in the Soviet Union and its East European satellites. In other words, from 1960 to 1990, the Soviet bloc as a whole was less repressive, measured in terms of human victims, than many individual Latin American countries. The hot Cold War in Central America produced an unprecedented humanitarian catastrophe. Between 1975 and 1991, the death toll alone stood at nearly 300,000 in a population of less than 30 million. More than 1 million refugees fled from the region—most to the United States. The economic costs have never been calculated, but were huge. In the 1980s, these costs did not affect US policy because the burden on the United States was negligible': John Coatsworth, 'The Cold War in Central America, 1975–1991', in Leffler and Westad, eds, *Cambridge History of the Cold War*, vol. 3, pp. 220–1.

IV

Much more was at stake in the other zone to open up as a
front in the last decade of the Cold War. Between the Arab
world and the Subcontinent lay two states that had never been
subject to European mandate or conquest, though each had
been the object of repeated intrusion and manipulation by
imperial powers. Since its installation by US and British intelligence in the fifties, the royal dictatorship in Iran had become
the linchpin of American strategy in the region surrounding
the Gulf, recipient of every kind of favour and assistance from
Washington. In Afghanistan, the monarchy had been terminated by a dynastic cousin seeking to update the country with
Soviet aid. In January 1978, massive demonstrations broke out
against the Pahlavi regime, long a byword for tyranny and corruption, and within a year it was finished, the shah fleeing into
exile and the Shi'a cleric Khomeini returning from it to head
a revolutionary regime of unexpected Islamist stamp, equally
hostile to the Iranian left and to the American superpower.[9]
In April 1978, Afghan communists targeted for a purge hit
back with a coup that put them in power overnight. Though
not equivalent, both upheavals were blows. Afghanistan might
have semi-lain within Moscow's diplomatic sphere of influence, but the establishment of a Communist regime there
was another matter, a threat to Pakistan and unacceptable in

---

9   On the last day of 1977, Carter had toasted the shah in Teheran—'there
     is no leader with whom I have a deeper sense of personal gratitude and
     personal friendship'—as a fellow-spirit in the cause of 'human rights',
     and a pillar of stability in the region, upheld by 'the admiration and love
     your people give to you': see Lloyd Gardner, *The Long Road to Baghdad*,
     New York 2008, p. 51. When the US embassy in Teheran was seized by
     students two years later, Kennan urged an American declaration of war
     on Iran: Thompson, *The Hawk and the Dove*, p. 278.

principle. But the country was poor and isolated. Iran, double in size and population, and one of the world's largest oil producers, was neither. In itself, no doubt, an Islamic regime was less dangerous than a Communist one, but its anti-imperialist fervour could prove the more destabilizing, if unchecked, in the Middle East. The US embassy was seized and its staff held hostage in Teheran, not Kabul.

Fortuitously, the problem of how to deal with the Iranian Revolution found a happy solution within less than a year of the overthrow of the shah, with the all-out attack on Iran launched by Iraq in September 1980, in the belief Teheran was much weakened by a Khomeinist regime still preoccupied by repression of a range of internal oppositions. Saddam Hussein's bid to seize the oil-rich, predominantly Arab, province of Khuzestan unleashed the second-longest conventional war of the twentieth century, with undercover US encouragement and assistance.[10] Calling on every reserve of Iranian patriotism, the Khomeinist system survived the assault. But for American purposes, the war was cost-effective. Without the commitment of any US troops, or even CIA operatives, disabled within the country, the Iranian Revolution was pinned down within its own borders for nearly a decade, and its external impetus largely exhausted by the struggle for defensive survival. When the war finally came to an end in 1988, the clerical regime was still in place, but it had been contained, and with the proclamation of the Carter Doctrine and its implementation by Reagan, the Gulf converted into a military walkway for US power in the region.

Afghanistan could be tackled more ambitiously than Iran, along Central American rather than Southern African lines.

10 See Bruce Jentleson, *With Friends Like These: Reagan, Bush and Saddam, 1982–1990*, New York 1994, pp. 42–8.

If Baghdad was an arm's length Pretoria, Islamabad would be a close-range Tegucigalpa, from which the US could mount a proxy war against Communism with an army of Contras who, however, would become more than mercenaries. As early as July 1979, before the monarchy had collapsed in Iran or Soviet tanks were anywhere near Kabul, the US was bankrolling religious and tribal resistance to the Saur Revolution. When Moscow reacted to fratricide in Afghan communism with a full-scale military intervention in December, Washington saw the chance to pay the USSR back in its own coin: this would be the Soviet Union's Vietnam. Under the benevolent awning of the Zia dictatorship in Pakistan, massive transfers of money and advanced weaponry were funnelled to *mujahedin* fighters against atheism. Divided from the start, Afghan communism had tried to compensate for the weakness of its basis in a still overwhelmingly rural and tribal society with the ferocity of its repression of opposition to it, now superimposed with the ponderous weight of an alien army. In these conditions, the US had little difficulty sustaining hi-tech guerrilla attacks on it for over a decade, irrigated with CIA and Saudi funding, but grounded in passionate religious-popular sentiment. Dependent for military survival on Soviet air and land power, the regime in Kabul was politically doomed by it.

V

In their long contest with the United States, the rulers of the Soviet Union believed by the mid-seventies that they had achieved strategic nuclear parity, and therewith recognition by Washington of political parity as a superpower of equal standing at large. *Détente*, in their eyes, signalled its acceptance of these realities. So they saw no reason why the USSR should act with less freedom than the US where the frontiers between the two blocs were not, as in Europe, fixed fast by mutual agreement. Central America was within the hemispheric domain of the US and they would not interfere. But Africa was a *terrain vague*, and Afghanistan a borderland of the USSR in which the US had never been greatly involved. Military power-projection in such regions was not a provocation, but within the rules of the game as understood by Moscow.

These were illusions. What Brezhnev and his colleagues believed was a strategic turning point was for Nixon and Kissinger a tactical construction. No American administration had any intention of permitting Moscow to act in the Third World as Washington might do, and all had the means to see that it would come to grief if it tried to do so. The apparent Soviet gains of the seventies were built on sands, brittle regimes that lacked either disciplined communist cadres or nation-wide mass movements behind them, and would fall or invert in short order once support from Moscow was gone. The ultimate disparity between the two antagonists remained as great as it had ever been at the dawn of the Cold War, before Mao's victory in China altered the extent of the imbalance for a time. Even with lines of communication as short as those to Afghanistan, Moscow was trapped as Brzezinski had intended. The Red Army had no remedy against Stinger missiles. To demoralization beyond the perimeters of Stalin's rule was added fraying within them. Eastern Europe had long been off-limits to the US, which had stood by when East German workers rose in 1953, Hungary revolted in 1956 and Czechoslovakia was invaded in 1968. But *détente*, which had deluded Soviet leaders into thinking they could act with less inhibition in the Horn or the Hindu Kush, where it had no bearing for Washington, allowed the US to act with less inhibition in Europe. There the Helsinki Accords, where Moscow paid for formal recognition of territorial borders that were never in real dispute with formal recognition of human rights that eminently were, had changed the coordinates of the Cold War. This time, when Solidarity erupted in Poland, there could be no Iron Curtain. American subventions, sluiced through the Vatican, could not be stopped, nor a rolling Polish insurgency broken.

Along with military wounds and political troubles came economic pressures. In the seventies, rising oil prices had compounded recession in the West. In the eighties, falling oil prices hit Soviet trade balances that depended on hard currency earnings from the country's energy sector to pay for medium-tech imports. If the origins of the long downturn in the OECD lay in the dynamics of uneven development and over-competition, its consequences could be checked and deferred by a systemic expansion of credit, to ward off any traumatic devalorization of capital. In the USSR, a long economic downturn began earlier—growth rates were already falling in the sixties, if much more sharply from the second half of the seventies; and its dynamics lay in plan-driven lack of competition and over-extension of the life span of capital.[11] In the thirties, Trotsky had already observed that the fate of Soviet socialism would be determined by whether or not its productivity of labour surpassed that of advanced capitalism. By the eighties, the answer

---

11 Vladimir Popov, 'Life Cycle of the Centrally Planned Economy: Why Soviet Growth Rates Peaked in the 1950s', CEFIR/NES Working Paper no. 152, November 2010, pp. 5–11—a fundamental diagnosis, showing that in effect the Soviet economy suffered from its own, much more drastic, version of the same problem that would slow American growth rates from the seventies onwards, in Robert Brenner's analysis.

was clear. The GNP and per capita income of the USSR were half those of the US, and labour productivity perhaps 40 per cent. Central to that difference was a still larger one, in reverse. In the much richer American economy, military expenditures accounted for an average of some 6–7 per cent of GDP from the sixties onwards; in the Soviet economy, the figure was over double that—15–16 per cent.

Since the fifties, American grand strategy had classically aimed to 'put the maximum strain', as NSC–68 had enjoined, on the Soviet system. The Reagan administration, mauling its flanks in Central Asia and infiltrating its defences in Eastern Europe, also piled on economic pressure, with a technological embargo striking at Russian oil production, and a quadrupling of Saudi output that lowered oil prices by 60 per cent. But its decisive move was the announcement of a Strategic Defense Initiative to render the US invulnerable to ICBM attack. Originating in an evaluation of the Soviet threat by Team B within the CIA that rang the alarm at a 'window of vulnerability' —yet another avatar of the bomber and missile gaps of the fifties and sixties—which Moscow could use to obliterate or blackmail the West, SDI was a technological scarecrow whose putative costs were enormous. That it could not actually be built was of little importance. What mattered was that it intimidate a cornered Soviet leadership, now flailing about in bungled attempts to revive the economy at home, and increasingly desperate for Western approval abroad.

Aware that the USSR could no longer hope to match so costly a programme, Gorbachev travelled to Reykjavik to try to deliver his country from the crippling weight of the arms race altogether.[12] There US officials were stunned as he made

12 Gorbachev to the Politburo in October 1986: 'We will be pulled into an

one unilateral concession after another. 'We came with nothing to offer, and offered nothing', one negotiator remembered. 'We sat there while they unwrapped their gifts'.[13] But it was no dice. SDI would not be abandoned: Gorbachev came away empty-handed. Two years later, a ban on intermediate-range missiles was small consolation. It had taken thirty years for the Soviet Union to achieve formal nuclear parity with the United States. But the goal was overvalued and the price ruinous. American encirclement of the USSR had never been primarily conceived as a conventional *Niederwerfungskrieg*. From the start, it was a long-term *Ermattungskrieg*, and victory was now at hand.

Amid a continually worsening crisis of material provision at home, as the old economic system was disrupted by addled reforms incapable of giving birth to a new one, withdrawal from Afghanistan was followed by retreat from Eastern Europe. There the regimes of the Warsaw Pact had never enjoyed much native support, their peoples rebelling whenever they had a chance of doing so. In 1989, emboldened by the new conjuncture, one political breakout followed another: within six months, Poland, Hungary, East Germany, Czechoslovakia,

---

arms race that is beyond our capabilities, and we will lose it, because we are at the limit of our capabilities. Moreover, we can expect that Japan and the FRG could very soon add their economic potential to the American one. If the new round begins, the pressure on our economy will be unbelievable': Vladislav Zubok, *A Failed Empire: The Soviet Union in the Cold War from Stalin to Gorbachev*, Chapel Hill 2007, p. 292. As Reagan candidly recalled: 'The great dynamic success of capitalism had given us a powerful weapon in our battle against Communism—*money*. The Russians could never win the arms race; we could outspend them forever': *An American Life*, New York 1990, p. 267.

13 'Secretary Schultz, not then deep in nuclear matters, nevertheless caught the drift. We had triumphed': Kenneth Adelman, *The Great Universal Embrace*, New York 1989, p. 55. Adelman was arms control director under Reagan.

Bulgaria, Romania. The signal for the upheaval came in the spring, when the Hungarian government was secretly paid a billion Deutschmarks by Kohl to open its border with Austria, and young East Germans started to pour across it.[14] In Moscow, Gorbachev let matters take their course. Making no attempt to negotiate Soviet exit from the region, he placed his trust in Western gratitude for a unilateral withdrawal of the 500,000 Red Army troops stationed in it. In exchange, Bush Sr offered a verbal promise that NATO would not be extended to the borders of Russia, and declined to supply any economic aid until the country was a free market economy.[15] His call for Europe to be whole and free was met. For the USSR itself to become free, it would have to be divided. Gorbachev survived his unrequited pursuit of an entente with America by little more than a year. What remained of the Soviet establishment could see where his conception of peace with honour was leading, and in trying to depose him, precipitated it. In December 1991, the USSR disappeared from the map.

---

14 Harper, *The Cold War*, p. 238.

15 'Disappointed by the failure of his personal relations with Western leaders to yield returns, Gorbachev tried to make a more pragmatic case for major aid. As he told Bush in July 1991, if the United States was prepared to spend $100 billion on regional problems (the Gulf), why was it not ready to expend similar sums to help sustain perestroika, which had yielded enormous foreign-policy dividends, including unprecedented Soviet support in the Middle East? But such appeals fell on deaf ears. Not even the relatively modest $30 billion package suggested by American and Soviet specialists—comparable to the scale of Western aid commitments to Eastern Europe—found political favour': Alex Pravda, 'The Collapse of the Soviet Union, 1990–1991', in Leffler and Westad, eds, *Cambridge History of the Cold War*, vol. 3, p. 376.

7

LIBERALISM MILITANT

The end of the Cold War closed an epoch. The United States now stood alone as a superpower, the first in world history. That did not mean it could rest on its laurels. The agenda of 1950 might be complete. But the grand strategy of the American state had always been broader. The original vision of 1943 had been put on hold for an emergency half-century, but never relinquished: the construction of a liberal international order with America at its head. Communism was dead, but capitalism had not yet found its accomplished form, as a planetary universal under a singular hegemon. The free market was not yet worldwide. Democracy was not invariably safe. In the hierarchy of states, nations did not always know their place. There was also the detritus of the Cold War to be cleared away, where it had left relics of a discredited past.

In the immediate aftermath of the Soviet collapse, the last were details that took care of themselves. By 1992, the regimes in South Yemen, Ethiopia and Afghanistan had all fallen, Angola had come to its senses, and Nicaragua was back in good hands. In the Third World, scarcely a government was left that any longer cared to call itself socialist. There had always, however,

been states which without making that misstep were unacceptable in other ways, some failing to respect liberal economic
principles, others the will of what could now be called, without
fear of contradiction, the 'international community'. Few had
consistently defied Washington, but nationalist posturing of
one kind or another might still lead them in directions that
would need to be stopped. The Panamanian dictator Noriega
had long been on the CIA payroll, and supplied valuable help
in the undeclared war against the Sandinistas. But when he
resisted pressure to drop his take of the drug trade, and started
to edge away from Washington, he was summarily removed
with a US invasion in late 1989.

A much larger offence was committed by the Iraqi dictatorship in seizing Kuwait the following year. The Baath regime
headed by Saddam Hussein had also enjoyed CIA assistance
in coming to power, and played a useful role in pinning down
the Iranian revolution in protracted trench warfare. But though
merciless to communists, as to all other opponents, the regime
was truculently nationalist, permitting no foreign oil companies to operate on its soil and, unlike the Egyptian dictatorship,
no American control of its decisions. Whatever the historic
rights and wrongs of Baghdad's claims to the sheikhdom to the
south, a British creation, there could be no question of allowing it to acquire the Kuwaiti oilfields in addition to its own,
which could put Iraq in a position to threaten Saudi Arabia
itself. Mobilizing half a million troops, topped up with contin-
gents from thirty-odd other countries, after five weeks of aerial
bombardment Operation Desert Storm routed the Iraqi army
in five days, restoring the Sabah dynasty to its throne. The cost
to the US was nugatory: 90 per cent of the bill was picked up by
Germany, Japan and the Gulf states.

The Gulf War, the first Bush proclaimed, marked the arrival of a New World Order. Where only a year earlier the invasion of Panama had been condemned by majorities in both the General Assembly and the Security Council of the UN (Russia and China joining every Third World country to vote for the resolution, the UK and France joining the US to veto it), the expedition to Iraq sailed through the Security Council, Russia approving, China abstaining, America tipping Third World states for their service. The end of the Cold War had changed everything. It was as if Roosevelt's vision of the world's posse had arrived.[1] To cap the US triumph, within a few months of these victories, the Nuclear Non-Proliferation Treaty, hitherto an ineffectual residue of the late sixties, was transformed into a powerful instrument of American hegemony with the submission of France and China to it, sealing a nuclear oligarchy in the Security Council, under which signature of the treaty would henceforward become a condition of international respectability for lesser states, save where Washington wished to waive it—Israel was naturally exempted.[2] In four short years, the colourless elder Bush could be accounted the most successful foreign policy president since the war.

1   Bush: 'A world once divided into two armed camps now recognizes one sole and preeminent superpower: the United States of America. And they regard this with no dread. For the world trusts us with power—and the world is right. They trust us to be fair and restrained; they trust us to be on the side of decency. They trust us to do what's right': State of the Union Address, January 1992.

2   Susan Watkins, 'The Nuclear Non-Protestation Treaty', *New Left Review* 54, Nov–Dec 2008—the only serious historical, let alone critical, reconstruction of the background and history of the treaty.

II

Clinton, profiting from a third-party candidate, was elected on a dip in the domestic economy, the recession of 1991. But like every contender for the White House since the fifties, he assailed the incumbent for weakness in fighting America's enemies abroad, calling for tougher policies on Cuba and China, in a stance backed by Nitze, Brzezinski and fellow-spirits, for whom Bush had been too soft on dictators and insufficiently resolute in pursuing violators of human rights.[3] In office, however, Clinton's first priority was to build out the liberal order of free trade into an encompassing global system under US command. Bush had not neglected this front, but lost power before he could finalize either the creation of a regional economic bloc welding Mexico and Canada to the United States, or the protracted negotiations to wrap up the Uruguay Round at GATT. Clinton, overriding opposition in his own party, pushed through NAFTA and the transformation of GATT into the WTO as the formal framework of a universal market for capital to come. Within that framework, the US could now play a more decisive role than ever in shaping an emergent pan-capitalist world to its own requirements.

In the first decades of the Cold War, American policies had been permissive: other industrial states could be allowed, even assisted in the face of Communist danger, to develop as they judged best, without undue regard for liberal orthodoxy. From the seventies onwards, American policies became defensive: US interests had to be asserted against competitors within the

---

3   Derek Chollet and James Goldgeier, *America Between the Wars: From 11/9 to 9/11*, New York 2008, pp. 35–7. Robert Kagan was another supporter of Clinton in 1992.

OECD, if necessary with brutal *coups d'arrêt*, but without undue intervention in the rival economies themselves. By the nineties, Washington could move to the offensive. The neoliberal turn had deregulated international financial markets, prising open hitherto semi-enclosed national economies, and the United States was strategically master of a unipolar world. In these conditions, the US could for the first time apply systematic pressure on surrounding states to bring their practices into line with American standards. The free market was no longer to be trifled with. Its principles had to be observed. Where protection, either social or national, infringed on them, it should now be phased out. The Washington Consensus—imperatives shared by the IMF, the World Bank and the US Treasury—laid down the appropriate rules for the Third World. But it was the Mexican and Asian financial crises, each a direct result of the new regime of footloose global finance, that gave the Clinton administration the real opportunity to drive American norms of market-friendly conduct.[4] With far the deepest capital markets of any major economy, and the global reserve currency, the United States stood for the moment controller of the very turbulence its model of accumulation was unleashing. The triumvirate of Greenspan, Rubin and Summers could be billed by the local press as the 'Committee to Save the World'.

Mexico, Korea, Indonesia: these were important targets for IMF mediation. But the leading object of US concern was naturally Russia, where the collapse of communism did not *ipso facto* ensure a smooth passage to capitalism, essential for the consolidation of victory in the Cold War. For the Clinton administration, the maintenance of a political regime in

---

4   For the latter, see Peter Gowan, *The Global Gamble*, London and New York 1999, pp. 76–9, 84–92, 103–15.

Moscow willing to make a complete break with the past was a priority. Yeltsin might be drunk, corrupt and incompetent, but he was a convert to the cause of anti-communism, who had no qualms about shock therapy—overnight freeing of prices and cutting of subsidies—or the handing-over of the country's principal assets for nominal sums to a small number of crooked projectors, advisers seconded from Harvard taking a cut. When he bombarded the Russian parliament with tanks and faked victory in a constitutional referendum to stay in power, Clinton's team warmly congratulated him. His reelection in danger, a timely American loan arrived, with political consultants from California to help his campaign. His obliteration of Grozny accomplished, Clinton celebrated its liberation. Russian finances melting down in 1998, the IMF stepped into the breach without conditionality. In exchange, Yeltsin's diplomatic alignment with Washington was so complete that Gorbachev, no enemy of the US, could describe his foreign minister as the American consul in Moscow.

The worldwide extension of neoliberal rules of trade and investment, and the integration of the former Soviet Union into its system, could be seen as fulfilments of the long-range vision of the last years of Roosevelt's presidency. But much had changed since then, in the reflexes and ambitions of US elites. The Cold War had ended in the economic and political settlement of an American peace. But that did not mean a return to arcadia. American power rested not simply on force of example—the wealth and freedom that made the US a model for emulation and natural leader in the civilization of capital—but also, inseparably, force of arms. To the expansion of its economic and political influence could not correspond a contraction of its military reach. The one, its strategists had long insisted, was a condition of the other. For the Clinton regime, the disappearance of the Soviet threat was thus no reason for withdrawal of forward US positions in Europe. On the contrary: the weakness of Russia made it possible to extend them. NATO, far from being dismantled now that the Cold War was over, could be enlarged to the doorstep of Russia.

To do so would put a safety-catch on any attempt to revive Muscovite aspirations of old, and reassure newly liberated East European states that they were now behind a Western shield. Not only this. The expansion of NATO to the East represented an assertion of American hegemony over Europe, at a time when the end of the Soviet Union risked tempting traditional US partners in the region to act more independently than in the past.[5] To make the continental point clear, NATO was extended to Eastern Europe before the EU got there. At home, NATO enlargement enjoyed bipartisan support at congressional level—Republicans were as ardent for it as Democrats. But at elite level, where grand strategy was debated, it caused the sharpest *ex ante* split since the Second World War, many hardened Cold Warriors—Nitze, even Clinton's own defence secretary—judging it a dangerous provocation of Russia, liable to weaken its newfound friendship with the West and foster a resentful revanchism. To help Yeltsin's reelection in 1996, Clinton postponed it for a year.[6] But he knew his partner: only token protests were forthcoming. In due course, NATO

5   'A final reason for enlargement was the Clinton Administration's belief that NATO needed a new lease of life to remain viable. NATO's viability, in turn, was important because the alliance not only helped maintain America's position as a European power, it also preserved America's hegemony in Europe': Robert Art, *America's Grand Strategy and World Politics*, p. 222. Art is the most straightforward and lucidly authoritative theorist of US power-projection today. See 'Consilium', pp. 150–5 below.

6   Chollet and Goldgeier, *America Between the Wars*, pp. 124, 134.

enlargement was then doubled, as 'out of area' military operations without even a façade of defence—Balkans, Central Asia, North Africa—expanded the geopolitical projection of the 'Atlantic' alliance yet further.

Meanwhile, the new unipolar order had brought a third innovation. Federal Yugoslavia, communist but not part of the Soviet bloc, disintegrated in the last period of the Bush administration, its constituent republics breaking away along ethnic lines. In Bosnia, where no group was a majority, the European Community brokered a power-sharing arrangement between Muslims, Serbs and Croats in the spring of 1992, promptly repudiated at US instigation by the first, who declared Bosnian independence, triggering a three-way civil war. When a UN force dispatched to protect lives and bring the parties peace failed to stop the killings, the worst committed by Serbs, the Clinton administration trained and armed a Croat counterattack in 1995 that cleansed the Krajina of its Serb population, and in conjunction with a NATO bombing campaign against Serb forces brought the war to an end, dividing Bosnia into three sub-statelets under a Euro-American proconsul. US actions marked two milestones. It was the first time the Security Council subcontracted a military operation to NATO, and the first time an aerial blitz was declared a humanitarian intervention.

Four years later, a far more massive NATO assault—36,000 combat missions and 23,000 bombs and missiles—was launched against what was still formally the remnant of Yugoslavia, in the name of stopping Serb genocide of the Albanian population in Kosovo. This was too much for the Yeltsin regime, facing widespread indignation at home, to countenance formally in the Security Council, so UN cover was lacking. But informally

Moscow played its part by inducing Milošević to surrender without putting up resistance on the ground, which was feared by Clinton. The war on Yugoslavia set three further benchmarks for the exercise of American power. NATO, a supposedly defensive alliance, had—newly enlarged—been employed for what was patently an attack on another state. The attack was a first demonstration of the 'revolution in military affairs' delivered by electronic advances in precision targeting and bombing from high altitudes: not a single casualty was incurred in combat by the US. Above all, it was legitimated in the name of a new doctrine. The cause of human rights, Clinton and Blair explained, overrode the principle of national sovereignty.

The final innovation of the Clinton presidency came in the Middle East. There, the survival of Saddam's dictatorship was a standing defiance of the US, which had to be brought to an end. When the rout of the Iraqi Army in the Gulf War was not followed, as expected, by the overthrow of the Baath regime from within, Washington pushed the most far-reaching sanctions on record through the Security Council, a blockade that Clinton's national security adviser Sandy Berger boasted was 'unprecedented for its severity in the whole of world history', banning all trade or financial transfers of any kind with the country, save in medicine and—in dire circumstances—foodstuffs. The levels of infant mortality, malnutrition, and excess mortality that this blockade inflicted on the population of Iraq remain contested,[7] but confronted with an estimate of half a million, Clinton's secretary of state declared that if that was the toll, it was worth it. When economic strangulation could not be achieved, Clinton signed the Iraq Liberation Act into law in

7 For a critical review of the evidence, see Michael Spagat, 'Truth and death in Iraq under sanctions', *Significance*, September 2010, pp. 116–20.

1998, making the political removal of Saddam's regime explicit US policy, and when stepped-up secret funding of operations to topple it were of no more avail, unloaded wave after wave of high explosives on the country. By the end of 1999, the same year as the war in Yugoslavia, in six thousand Anglo-American sorties some four hundred tons of ordnance had been dropped on Iraq.[8] Nothing quite like this had ever happened before. A new weapon had been added to the imperial arsenal: undeclared conventional war.

III

In a departure from the normal pattern, the second Bush campaigned for the White House calling for a less, not more, preceptorial American role in the world at large. In office, the initial priority of his defense secretary was a leaner rather than larger military establishment. The bolt from the blue of September 2001 transformed such postures into their opposite, the Republican administration becoming a byword for aggressive American self-assertion and armed force to impose American will. For the first time since Pearl Harbour, US soil had been violated. Retribution would leave the world in no doubt of the extent of American power. The enemy was terrorism, and war on it would be waged till it was rooted out, everywhere.

This was a nationwide reaction, from which there was virtually no dissent within the country, and little at first outside it. Apocalyptic commentary abounded on the deadly new epoch into which humanity was entering. The reality, of course, was that the *attentats* of 9/11 were an unrepeatable historical fluke, capable of catching the American state offguard only because

8   See Tariq Ali, 'Our Herods', *New Left Review* 5, Sept–Oct 2000, pp. 5–7.

their agents were so minimal a speck on the radar-screen of its strategic interests. In the larger scheme of things, Al Qaeda was a tiny organization of marginal consequence, magnified only by the wealth at the disposal of its leader. But though the outcome of its plan to attack symbolic buildings in New York and Washington was a matter of chance, its motivation was not. The episode was rooted in the geopolitical region where US policies had long been calculated to maximize popular hostility. In the Middle East, American support for dynastic Arab tyrannies of one stripe or another, so long as they accommodated US interests, was habitual. There was nothing exceptional in this, however—the pattern had historically been much the same in Latin America or Southeast Asia. What set the Middle East apart was the American bond with Israel. Everywhere else in the postwar world, the US had taken care never to be too closely identified with European colonial rule, even where it might for a spell have to be accepted as a dike against communism, aware that to be so would compromise its own prospects of control in the battlegrounds of the Cold War. The Free World could harbour dictators; it could not afford colonies. In the Middle East alone, this rule was broken. Israel was not a colony, but something still more incendiary—an expansionist settler state established, not in the eighteenth or nineteenth century, when European colonization was at its height across the world, but in the middle of the twentieth century, when decolonization was in full swing. Not only that: it was a state explicitly founded on religion, the Promised Land for the Chosen People—in a region where a far more populous rival religion, with memories of a much earlier confessional intrusion into the same territory and its successful expulsion, still held virtually untouched sway. A more combustible combination would be difficult to imagine.

American grand strategy, however construed, could have
no rational place for an organic—as distinct from occasional
—connection with a state offering such a provocation to an
environment so important to the US, as the world's major
source of petroleum.[9] Israeli military prowess could indeed
be of use to Washington. Counterproductive when allied to
Anglo-French colonialism in 1956, it had inflicted a welcome
humiliation on Soviet-leaning Arab nationalism in 1967,
helped to deliver Egypt to the United States in 1973, and crip-
pled the PLO in driving it from the Lebanon in 1982. But there
were limits to this functionality: the IDF had to be restrained
from occupying Beirut, and told to sit tight during the Gulf War.
Israeli firepower alone, of whose potential political costs in the
Arab world all American rulers were aware, offered no basis for
the extent of the US commitment to Israel over half a century.
Nor were the virtues of Israeli democracy amidst the deserts of
despotism, or the frontier spirit uniting the two nations, more
than ideological top dressing for the nature of the relationship between Tel Aviv and Washington. That stemmed from
the strength of the Jewish community within the American
political system, whose power was on display as early as 1947—
when Baruch and Frankfurter were to the fore in the bribes and
threats needed to lock down a majority at the UN for the partition of Palestine—and became decisive in the formation of
regional policy after 1967, installing a supervening interest at
odds with the calculus of national interest at large, warping the
rationality of its normal adjustments of means to ends.[10]

9   See 'Jottings on the Conjuncture', *New Left Review* 48, Nov–Dec 2007,
    pp. 15–18.
10 See 'Scurrying towards Bethlehem', *New Left Review* 10, July–Aug 2001,
    pp. 10–15 ff.

If the American connection with Israel was one factor setting the Middle East apart from any other zone of US power-projection abroad, there was another. Iraq remained unfinished business. The Baath state was not just any regime unsatisfactory to Washington, of which at one time or another there had been—indeed still were—many in the Third World. It was unique in postwar history as the first state whose overthrow was the object of a public law passed by Congress, countersigned by the White House, and prosecuted by years of unconcealed, if undeclared, conventional hostilities. During the Cold War, no Communist regime had ever been comparably outlawed. For Saddam's government to survive this legislation and the campaign of destruction it authorized would be a political-military defeat putting in question the credibility of American power. The second Bush had come to office promising a lower US profile at large, but never peace with Baghdad. From the start, his administration was filled with enthusiasts for the Iraq Liberation Act.

Finally, there was a third feature of the Middle Eastern scene that had no counterpart elsewhere. Over the course of the Cold War, the US had used a wide range of proxies to fight assorted enemies at a remove. French mercenaries, GMD drug lords, Cuban *gusanos*, Hmong tribesmen, South African regulars, Nicaraguan Contras, Vatican bankers—all in their time acted as vehicles of American will. None, however, received such massive support and to such spectacular effect as the *mujahedin* in Afghanistan. In the largest operation in its history, the CIA funnelled some $3 billion in arms and assistance, and orchestrated another $3 billion from Saudi Arabia, to the guerrillas who eventually drove the Russians out of the country. But beyond anti-communism, in this case unlike any other comparable

operation, there was virtually no common ideological denominator between metropolitan principal and local agent. The
Afghan resistance was not just tribal—Washington knew how
to handle that—but religious, fired by a faith as hostile to the
West as to the Soviet Union, and attracting volunteers from all
over the Muslim world. To the cultural barrier of Islam, impen-
etrable to American oversight, was added the political thicket
of Pakistan, through which aid had to pass, whose ISI enjoyed
far more direct control over the different *mujahedin* groups and
their camps in the Northwest Frontier than the CIA could ever
do. The result was to set loose forces that delivered the United
States its greatest single triumph in the Cold War, yet of which
it had least political understanding or mastery. When out of the
post-communist dispute for power in Kabul, the most rigorist
of all Islamist groups emerged the Afghan winner, flanked by
the most radical of Arab volunteers, the confidence and energy
released by a victorious *jihad* against one set of infidels turned,
logically enough, against the other, whose support had been
tactically accepted in the battle against the first, without any
belief that it was otherwise preferable.

Al Qaeda, formed in Afghanistan, but composed essentially
of Arabs, had its eyes fixed on the Middle East rather than
Central Asia. The first public manifesto of its leader explained
his cause. The fate of Palestine held pride of place. The outrages
of Israel in the region, and of its protector the United States,
called the devout to action: to the shelling of Beirut should
answer that of its perpetrators. Nor was this all. Since the Gulf
War against Iraq, American troops were stationed in Saudi
Arabia, violating the sanctity of the Holy Places. The Prophet
had expressly demanded *jihad* against any such intrusion. The
faithful had triumphed over one superpower in Afghanistan.

Their duty was now to expel the other and its offshoot, by carrying the war to the enemy. Behind 9/11 thus lay, in theological garb, a typical anti-imperialist backlash against the power that had long been an alien overlord in the region, from an organization resorting to terror—as nearly always—out of weakness rather than strength, in the absence of any mass basis of popular resistance to the occupier.[11]

The Bush administration's counterblow was rapid and sweeping. A combination of high-altitude bombing, small numbers of special forces, and purchase of Tajik warlords brought down the Taliban regime in a few weeks. There were seven American casualties. The US-led occupation acquired UN auspices, later transferred to NATO, and a pliant regime, headed by a former contractor for the CIA, in Kabul. Diplomatically, Operation Enduring Freedom was a complete success, blessed by all major powers and neighbouring states; if Pakistan at gunpoint, Russia not only of its own accord, but opening its airspace for Pentagon logistics, with the ex-Soviet republics of Central Asia competing with each other to offer bases to the US. Militarily, Taliban and Al Qaeda commanders might have escaped their pursuers, but high-technology war from the skies had done all that could be asked of it: the RMA was irresistible.

The speed and ease of the conquest of Afghanistan made delivery of a quietus to Iraq the obvious next step, premeditated in Washington as soon as 9/11 struck. Two difficulties lay in the way. Iraq was a much more developed society, whose regime possessed a substantial modern army that could not be dispersed with a few irregulars. A ground war, avoided in Yugoslavia, would be necessary to overthrow it. That meant

---

11 For a levelheaded discussion: Michael Mann, *Incoherent Empire*, London and New York 2003, pp. 113–5.

a risk of casualties unpopular with the American public, requiring a *casus belli* more specific than general loss of US credibility if the Baath regime lingered on. Casting about for what would be of most effect, the administration hit upon Iraqi possession of—nuclear or biological—weapons of mass destruction, presented as a threat to national security, as the most colourable pretext, though Saddam Hussein's trampling of human rights and the prospect of bringing democracy to Iraq were prominently invoked alongside it. That there were no more weapons of mass destruction in Iraq than there had been genocide in Kosovo hardly mattered. This was a portfolio of reasons sufficient to create a broad national consensus —Democrats and Republicans, print and electronic media, alike—behind an attack on Iraq.[12] European publics were

---

12 As at every stage of American imperial expansion, from the mid-nineteenth century onwards, there was a scattering of eloquent voices of domestic opposition, without echo in the political system. Strikingly, virtually every one of the most powerful critiques of the new course of empire came from writers of a conservative, not a radical, background. This pattern goes back to the Gulf War itself, of which Robert Tucker co-authored with David Hendrickson a firm rejection: the United States had taken on 'an imperial role without discharging the classic duties of imperial rule', one in which 'fear of American casualties accounts for the extraordinarily destructive character of the conflict', giving 'military force a position in our statecraft that is excessive and disproportionate', with 'the consent and even enthusiasm of the nation': *The Imperial Temptation: The New World Order and America's Purpose*, New York 1992, pp. 15–16, 162, 185, 195. Within a few weeks of the *attentats* of 11 September 2001, when such a reaction was unheard-of, the great historian Paul Schroeder published a prophetic warning of the likely consequences of a successful lunge into Afghanistan: 'The Risks of Victory', *The National Interest*, Winter 2001–2002, pp. 22–36. The three outstanding bodies of critical analysis of American foreign policy in the new century, each distinctive in its own way, share similar features. Chalmers Johnson, in his day an adviser to the CIA, published *Blowback* (2000), predicting that America would not enjoy impunity for its imperial intrusions around the world, followed by *The Sorrows of Empire* (2004) and *Nemesis*

more apprehensive, but most of their governments rallied to the cause.

The conquest of Iraq was as lightning as of Afghanistan: Baghdad fell in three weeks, where Kabul had required five. But the Baath regime, more long-standing than the Taliban, had a capillary structure that proved capable of ferocious resistance within days of the occupation of the country, detonating a Sunni *maquis* compounded by a rising among Shi'a radicals. The danger of a common front of opposition to occupiers was short-lived. Sectarian bombing of Shi'a mosques and processions by Salafi fanatics, and sectarian collaboration with the US by the top clerical authorities in Najaf as a stepping-stone to Shi'a domination, precipitated a civil war within Iraqi society that kept American forces in control, precariously at first, but eventually allowing them to split the Sunni community itself, and bring the insurgency to an end.

The third major ground war of the country since 1945 was, for the US, a relatively painless affair. Though its absolute cost in constant dollars was greater than the war in Korea or Vietnam—hi-tech weaponry was more expensive—as a

(2006), a trilogy packed with pungent detail, delivering an unsparing diagnosis of the contemporary Pax Americana. Andrew Bacevich, once a colonel in the US Army, brought out *American Empire* in 2002, followed by *The New American Militarism* (2005), and *The Limits of Power: The End of American Exceptionalism* (2008), in a series of works that recover the tradition of William Appleman Williams—to some extent also Beard—in lucid contemporary form, without being confined to it. Christopher Layne, holder of the Robert Gates Chair in Intelligence and National Security at the George Bush School of Government and Public Service at Texas A&M, has developed the most trenchant realist critique of the overall arc of American action from the Second World War into and after the Cold War, in the more theoretically conceived *The Peace of Illusions: American Grand Strategy from 1940 to the Present* (2006)—a fundamental work.

percentage of GDP it was lower, and its impact on the domestic economy much less. Over seven years, American casualties totalled 4,500—fewer than two months of car accidents in the US. Unpopular at home, after initial euphoria, the war in Iraq never aroused the extent of domestic opposition that met the war in Vietnam, or had the electoral impact of the war in Korea. Flurries of disquiet over torture or massacre by US forces soon passed. As in those earlier conflicts, the cost was borne by the country for whose freedom America ostensibly fought. It is possible that fewer Iraqis were killed by the invasion and occupation of their country than by the sanctions whose work they completed. But the number—at a conservative count, over 160,000—was still proportionately higher than total American casualties in World War Two.[13] To death was added flight—some two million refugees in neighbouring countries—ethnic cleansing and breakdown of essential services. Ten years later, over 60 per cent of the adult population is jobless, a quarter of families are below the poverty line, and Baghdad has no regular electricity.[14]

Militarily and politically, however, US objectives were achieved. There was no winter rout on the Yalu or helicopter scramble from Saigon. The Baath regime was destroyed, and American troops departed in good order, leaving behind a constitution crafted within the largest US embassy in the world, a leader picked on its premises by the US, and security forces totalling 1,200,000—nearly twice the size of Saddam's army—equipped with US weaponry. What made that legacy possible

---

13 For this figure, see the Iraq Body Count, which relies essentially on media-documented fatalities, for March 2013: civilian deaths 120–130,000.

14 'Iraq Ten Years On', *Economist*, 2 March 2013, p. 19.

was the support the American invasion received from the leaderships of the Shi'a and Kurdish communities that made up two-thirds of the population, each with longer histories of hostility to Saddam Hussein than Washington, and aims of replacing his rule. After the occupation was gone, the Iraq they divided between them, each with its own machinery of repression, remains a religious and ethnic minefield, racked by Sunni anger and traversed in opposite directions by manoeuvres from Turkey and Iran. But it has ceased to be an affront to the dignity of empire.[15]

Elsewhere too the Bush administration, distinct in rhetoric, was continuous in substance with its predecessor. Clinton had bonded with Yeltsin, a soft touch for the US. Bush did as well or better with Putin, a hard case, who yet granted Russian permission for American military overflights to Afghanistan, and put up with the extension of NATO to the Baltic states. China was no less supportive of the descent on Kabul, both powers fearing Islamic militancy within their own borders. The EU was cajoled into opening negotiations with Turkey for entry into the Union. If further deregulation of world trade with the Doha Round came to grief on India's refusal to expose its peasants to subsidized Euro-American grain exports, of much greater strategic significance was the lifting by Bush of the US embargo on nuclear technology to India, paving the way for

---

15 The underlying spirit of the American invasion was captured by Kennan when the PLA drove back MacArthur's troops from the Yalu in December 1950: 'The Chinese have now committed an affront of the greatest magnitude to the United States. They have done us something we cannot forget for years and the Chinese will have to worry about righting themselves with us not us with them. We owe China nothing but a lesson': *Foreign Relations of the United States*, vol. VII, pp. 1345–6. In his final years, Kennan had broken with this outlook and vigorously opposed the attack on Iraq.

closer relations with Delhi. Liberals wringing their hands over the reputational damage to America done by Iraq need not have worried. Among the powers that counted, the invasion was a Panama in the sands, leaving no discernible trace.

8

THE INCUMBENT

Democratic takeover of the White House in 2009 brought little alteration in American imperial policy. Continuity was signalled from the start by the retention or promotion of key personnel in the Republican war on terror: Gates, Brennan, Petraeus, McChrystal. Before entering the Senate, Obama had opposed the war in Iraq; in the Senate, he voted $360 billion for it. Campaigning for the presidency, he criticized the war in the name of another one. Not Iraq, but Afghanistan was where US firepower should be concentrated. Within a year of taking office, US troops had been doubled to 100,000 and Special Forces operations increased sixfold, in a bid to repeat the military success in Iraq, where Obama had merely to stick to his predecessor's schedule for a subsequent withdrawal. But Afghanistan was not Iraq, and no such laurels were in reach. The country was not only half as large again in size, but much of it mountainous, ideal guerrilla terrain. It abutted onto a still larger neighbour, forced to permit American operations across its soil, but more than willing to provide *sub rosa* cover and aid to resistance against the occupying forces across the border. Last but not least, American support in the country was confined to minority groups—Tajik, Hazara, Uzbek—while the Afghan resistance was based on the Pathan plurality, extending deep into the Northwest Frontier. Added to all these obstacles was the impact of the war in Iraq itself. In the Hindu Kush it mattered, as in Brussels, Moscow, Beijing, Delhi, it did not. The Iraqi resistance, divided and self-destructive, had been crushed. But it had taken five years and a quarter of a million troops to quell it, and by giving the Taliban breathing space to become fighters for something closer to a national war of liberation, allowed the Afghan guerrilla to regroup and strike back with increasing effect at the occupation.

Desperate to break this resistance, the Democratic administration escalated the war in Pakistan, where its predecessor had already been launching covert attacks with the latest missile-delivery system. The RMA had flourished since Kosovo, now producing unmanned aircraft capable of targeting individuals on the ground from altitudes of up to thirty thousand feet. Under Obama, drones became the weapon of choice for the White House, the Predators of 'Task Force Liberty' raining Hellfire missiles on suspect villages in the Northwest Frontier, wiping out women and children along with warriors in the ongoing battle against terrorism: seven times more covert strikes than launched by the Republican administration. Determined to show he could be as tough as Bush, Obama readied for war with Pakistan should it resist the US raid dispatched to kill Bin Laden in Abbottabad, for domestic purposes the leading trophy in his conduct of international affairs.[1] Assassinations by drone, initiated under his

1   'When confronted with various options during the preparations, Obama personally and repeatedly chose the riskiest ones. As a result, the plan that was carried out included contingencies for direct military conflict with Pakistan': James Mann, *The Obamians: The Struggle Inside the White*

predecessor, became the Nobel laureate's trademark. In his first term, Obama ordered one such execution every four days— over ten times the rate under Bush.

The War on Terror, now rebaptized at presidential instruction 'Overseas Contingency Operations'—a coinage to rank with the 'Enhanced Interrogation Techniques' of the Bush period—has proceeded unabated, at home and abroad. Torturers have been awarded impunity, while torture itself, officially disavowed and largely replaced by assassination, could still if necessary be outsourced to other intelligence services, above suspicion of maltreating captives rendered to them.[2] Guantánamo, its closure once promised, has continued as before. Within two years of his election in 2008, Obama's administration had created no less than sixty-three new counterterrorism agencies.[3]

Over all of this, the presidential mantle of secrecy has been drawn tighter than ever before, with a more relentless harassment and prosecution of anyone daring to break official *omertà* than its predecessor. War criminals are protected; revelation of war crimes punished—notoriously, in the case of Private

House to Redefine American Power, New York 2012, p. 303; 'There was no American war with Pakistan, but Obama had been willing to chance it in order to get Bin Laden'.

2   For the Obama administration, murder was preferable to torture: 'killing by remote control was the antithesis of the dirty, intimate work of interrogation. It somehow seemed cleaner, less personal', allowing the CIA, under fewer legal constraints than the Pentagon, 'to see its future: not as the long-term jailers of America's enemies but as a military organization that could erase them'—not to speak of anyone within range of them, like a sixteen-year-old American citizen in the Yemen not even regarded as a terrorist, destroyed by a drone launched on presidential instructions: Mark Mazzetti, *The Way of the Knife: The CIA, a Secret Army and a War at the Ends of the Earth*, New York 2013, pp. 121, 310–1.

3   Dana Priest and William Arkin, *Top Secret America: The Rise of the New American Security State*, New York 2011, p. 276.

Manning, with an unprecedented cruelty, sanctioned by the commander-in-chief himself. The motto of the administration's campaign of killings has been, in the words of one of its senior officials, 'precision, economy and deniability'.[4] Only the last is accurate; collateral damage covers the rest. Since the Second World War, presidential lawlessness has been the rule rather than the exception, and Obama has lived up to it. To get rid of another military regime disliked by the US, he launched missile and air attacks on Libya without congressional authorization, in violation both of the Constitution and the War Powers Resolution of 1973, claiming that this assault did not constitute 'hostilities', because no American troops were involved, but merely 'kinetic military action'.[5] With this corollary to Nixon's dictum that 'if the President does it, that means it is not illegal', a new benchmark for the exercise of imperial powers by the presidency has been set. The upshot, if less rousing at home, was more substantial than the raid on Abbottabad. The Libyan campaign, the easy destruction of a weak state at bay to a rising against it, refurbished the credentials of humanitarian intervention dimmed by the war in Iraq, and restored working military cooperation—as in Yugoslavia and Afghanistan—with Europe under the banner of NATO, Germany alone abstaining. An

4   David Sanger, *Confront and Conceal: Obama's Secret Wars and Surprising Use of American Power*, New York 2012, p. 246.

5   For this escalation in executive lawlessness, see the sober evaluation of Louis Fisher, 'Obama, Libya and War Powers', in *The Obama Presidency: A Preliminary Assessment*, Albany 2012, pp. 310–1, who comments that according to its reasoning, 'a nation with superior military force could pulverize another country and there would be neither hostilities nor war'. Or as James Mann puts it, 'Those drone and air attacks gave rise to another bizarre rationale: Obama administration officials took the position that since there were no American boots on the ground in Libya, the United States was not involved in the war. By that logic, a nuclear attack would not be a war': *The Obamians*, p. 296.

ideological and diplomatic success, Operation Odyssey Dawn offered a template for further defence of human rights in the Arab world, where these were not a domestic matter for friendly states.

A larger task remained. Gratified at the overthrow of two Sunni-based regimes by the US, Iran had colluded with the occupation of Afghanistan and of Iraq. But it had failed to make amends for the taking of the US embassy in Teheran, was not above meddling in Baghdad, and had long represented America as the Great Satan at large. These were ideological irritants. Much more serious was the clerical regime's commitment to a nuclear programme that could take it within reach of a strategic weapon. Enshrining an oligarchy of powers with sole rights to these, the NPT had been designed to preclude any such development. In practice, so long as a state was sufficiently accommodating to the US, Washington was prepared to overlook breaches in it: nothing was to be gained by punishing India or Pakistan. Iran was another matter. Its possession of a regional weapon would, of course, be no threat to the US itself. But, quite apart from the unsatisfactory nature of the Islamic Republic itself, there was another and overriding reason why it could not be allowed the same. In the Middle East, Israel had long amassed a large nuclear arsenal of two to three hundred bombs, complete with advanced missile delivery systems, while the entire West—the United States in the lead—maintained the polite fiction that it knew nothing of this. An Iranian bomb would break the Israeli nuclear monopoly in the region, which Israel—without, of course, ever admitting its own weapons— made clear it was determined to maintain, if necessary by attacking Iran before it could reach capability.

The American tie to Israel automatically made this an

imperative for the US too. But Washington could not simply rely on Tel Aviv to handle the danger, partly because Israel might not be able to knock out all underground installations in Iran, but mainly because such a blitz by the Jewish state risked uproar in the Arab world. If an attack had to be launched, it was safer that it be done by the superpower itself. Much ink had been spilled in the US and its allies over the Republican administration's grievous departure from the best American traditions in declaring its right to wage preventive war, often identified as the worst single error of its tenure. Pointlessly: the doctrine long predated Bush, and the Democratic administration has continued it, Obama openly threatening preventive war on Iran.[6] In the interim, just as Washington hoped to bring down the regime in Iraq by economic blockade and airwar, without having to resort to the ground invasion eventually rolled out, so now it hopes to bring the regime in Iran to its knees by economic blockade and cyber-war, without having to unleash a firestorm over the country. Sanctions have been steadily tightened, with the aim of weakening the social bases of the Islamic Republic by cutting off its trade and forcing up the price of necessities, hitting bazaari and popular classes alike, and confirming a middle-class and urban youth, on whose sympathies the West can count, in deep-rooted opposition to it.

Flanking this attack, while Israel has picked off Iranian scientists with a series of motorcycle and car-bomb assassinations, the administration has launched a massive joint US–Israeli

---

6　For long-standing American traditions of preventive war, see Gaddis's upbeat account in *Surprise, Security and the American Experience*. For Obama's continuance of these, see his declaration to the Israeli lobby AIPAC in the spring of 2011: 'My policy is not going to be one of containment. My policy is prevention of Iran obtaining nuclear weapons. When I say all options on the table, I mean it'.

assault on Iranian computer networks to cripple development of its nuclear programme. A blatant violation of what passes for international law, the projection of the Stuxnet virus was personally supervised by Obama—in the words of an admiring portrait, 'Perhaps not since Lyndon Johnson had sat in the same room, more than four decades before, had a president of the United States been so intimately involved in the step-by-step escalation of an attack on a foreign nation's infrastructure'.[7] Against Iraq, the US waged an undeclared conventional war for the better part of a decade, before proceeding to conclusions. Against Iran, an undeclared cyber-war is in train. As in Iraq, the logic of the escalation is clear. It allows for only two outcomes: surrender by Teheran, or shock and awe by Washington. The American calculation that it can force the Iranian regime to abandon its only prospect of a sure deterrent against an Iraqi or Libyan fate is not irrational. If the price of internal survival is to give way, the Islamic Republic will do so. Its factional divisions, and the arrival of an accommodating president, point in that direction. But should it not be endangered to such a point within, how likely is it to cast aside the most obvious protection against dangers without?

Happily for the US, a further lever lies to hand. In Syria, civil war has put Teheran's sole reliable ally in the region under threat of proximate extinction. There the Baath regime never provoked the US to the degree its counterpart in Iraq had done, even joining Operation Desert Storm as a local ally. But its hostility to Israel, and traditional links with Russia nonetheless made it an unwelcome presence in the region, on and off the list of rogue states to be terminated if the chance ever

---

7   Sanger, *Confront and Conceal*, p. x.

arose. The rising against the Assad dynasty presented just such an opportunity. Any prompt repetition of the NATO intervention in Libya was blocked by Russia and China, both—but especially Russia—angered by the way the West had manipulated the UN resolution on Libya to which they assented for the uncovenanted barrage of Odyssey Dawn. The regime in Damascus, moreover, was better armed and had more social support than that in Tripoli. There was also now less domestic enthusiasm for overseas adventures. The safer path was a proxy war, at two removes. The US would not intervene directly, nor even itself—for the time being—arm or train the Syrian rebels. It would rely instead on Qatar and Saudi Arabia to funnel weapons and funds to them, and Turkey and Jordan to host and organize them.

That this option was itself not without risks the Democratic administration, divided on the issue, was well aware. As the fighting in Syria wore on, it increasingly assumed the character of a sectarian conflict pitting Sunni against Alawite, in which the most effective warriors against the Assad regime became Salafist *jihadis* of just the sort that had wrought havoc among Shi'a in Iraq, not to speak of American forces themselves. Once triumphant, might they not turn on the West as the Taliban had done? But was not that a reason for intervening more directly, or at least supplying arms more openly and abundantly to the better elements in the Syrian rebellion, to avert such a prospect? Such tactical considerations are unlikely to affect the outcome. Syria is not Afghanistan: the social base for Sunni rigorism is far smaller, in a more developed, less tribal society, and playing the Islamist card safer for Washington—not least because Turkey, the very model of a staunchly capitalist, pro-Western Islamism, is virtually bound to be the overseeing power in any post-Baath order to emerge in Syria, that will inevitably be much weaker than its predecessor. To date, fierce Alawite loyalties, tepid Russian support, a precarious flow of weapons from Teheran and levies from Hizbollah have kept the Assad regime from falling. But the balance of forces is against it: not only Gulf and Western backing of the rebellion, but a pincer from Turkey and Israel, their longtime collusion in the region renewed at American insistence. For Israel, a golden opportunity looms: the chance of helping to knock out Damascus as a remaining adversary in the region, and neutralize or kill off Hizbollah in the Lebanon. For the US, the prize is a tightening of the noose around Iran.

Elsewhere in the region, the Arab Spring that caught the administration by surprise, stirring some initial disquiet, has so far yielded a crop of equally positive developments for the US. Even had they the will, incompetent Islamist governments in Egypt and Tunisia, stumbling about between repression and recession, were in no position to tinker with the compliant foreign policies of the police regimes they replaced, remaining at the mercy of the IMF and American good offices. Sisi's assumption of power in Cairo, once the temporary awkwardness of his path to it fades, promises a more congenial partner for Washington, with long-standing ties to the Pentagon. In the Yemen, a smooth succession from the previous tyrant has been engineered, averting the danger of a combustible popular upheaval by preserving much of the power of his family. In the only trouble spot in the Gulf, a timely Saudi intervention has restored order in Bahrain, headquarters of the US Fifth Fleet. For the Palestinians, masterly inactivity has long been taken as the best treatment. The Oslo Accords, written by Norwegian surrogates for Israel at American behest, have lost any credibility.

But time has taken its toll. The will of Palestinians to resist has visibly diminished, Hamas following down the same path of overtures to Qatar as earlier Fatah. With Arab support of any kind fast vanishing, could they not be left to rot more safely than ever before? If not, made to accept Jewish settlements on the West Bank and IDF units along the Jordan in perpetuity? Either way, Washington can reckon, they will eventually have to accept the facts on the ground, and a nominal statelet under Israeli guard.

A decade after the invasion of Iraq, the political landscape of the Middle East has undergone major changes. But though domestic support for its projection has declined, the relative position of American imperial power itself is not greatly altered in the region. One of its most trusted dictators has fallen—Obama thanking him for thirty years of service to his country—without producing any successor regime capable of more independence from Washington. Another, whom it distrusted, has been steadily weakened, sapped by proxy from the US. No strong government is on the horizon in either Egypt or Syria. Nor is Iraq, the Kurdish north virtually a breakaway state, any longer a force to be reckoned with. What the diminution of these populated centres of historic Arab civilization means for the balance of power in the region is a corresponding increase in the weight and influence of the oil-rich dynasties of the Arabian peninsula that have always been the staunchest supports of the American system in the Middle East.

Only where Arabic stops does Washington confront real difficulties. In Afghanistan, the good 'war of necessity' Obama upheld against the bad 'war of choice' in Iraq is likely to prove the worse of the two for the US, the battlefield where it faces raw defeat rather than bandaged victory.[8] Over Iran, the US, wagged by the Israeli tail, has left itself with as little room for manoeuvre as the regime it seeks to corner. Though it has good reason to hope that Teheran will give way, should it fail to suborn or break the will of the Islamic Republic, it risks paying a high price for executing its threat to it. But even with these caveats, the Greater Middle East offers no disastrous quicksand for the United States. Islam, though alien enough to God's Own Country, was never a monolithic faith, and much of its Salafist current less radical than anxious Westerners believed. The reality, long obvious, is that from the Nile Delta to the Gangetic plain, the Muslim world is divided between Sunni and Shi'a communities, whose antagonism today offers the US the same kind of leverage as the Sino-Soviet dispute in the Communist bloc of yesterday, allowing it to play one off against the other—backing Shi'a against Sunni in Iraq, backing Sunni against Shi'a in Syria—as tactical logic indicates. A united front of Islamic resistance is a dream from which American rulers have nothing to fear.

Strategically speaking, for all practical purposes the United States continues to have the Middle East largely to itself. Russia's relative economic recovery—till 2013 still growing at a faster clip than America—has not translated into much capacity for effective political initiative outside former Soviet territory, or significant return to a zone where it once rivalled the US in influence. Seeking to 'reset' relations with Moscow, Obama cancelled the missile defence system Bush planned to install in Eastern Europe, ostensibly to guard against the Iranian menace.

8   To avert this fate, the agreement signed between the US and the Karzai regime in 2012 ensures American bases, airpower, special forces and advisers in Afghanistan through to at least 2024, over a decade after exit from Iraq.

Perhaps as a quid pro quo, Russia did not oppose the UN resolution authorizing a no-fly zone over Libya, supposedly to protect
civilian life, quickly converted by the US and its EU allies into
a war with predictable loss of civilian life. Angered at this use
of its green light, Putin vetoed a not dissimilar resolution on
Syria, without offering notably greater support to the regime
in Damascus, and temporizing with the rebels. Weakened by
increasing opposition at home, he has since sought to make
an impact abroad with a scheme for UN inspection of chemi-
cal weapons in Syria to avert an American missile attack on it.
Intended to raise Moscow's status as an *interlocuteur valable* for
Washington, and afford a temporary respite to Damascus, the
result is unlikely to be very different from the upshot in Libya.
Born of the longing to be treated as a respectable partner by the
US, naivety and incompetence have been hallmarks of Russian
diplomacy in one episode after another since *perestroika*. Putin,
fooled as easily over Libya as Gorbachev over NATO, now risks
playing Yeltsin over Yugoslavia—thinking to offer weak help
to Assad, likely to end up sending him the way of Milošević.
Whether Obama, rescued from the embarrassment of a defeat
in Congress, will prove as grateful to his St Bernard as Clinton
was for escape from the need for a ground war, remains to be
seen. In the Security Council, Russia can continue to fumble
between collusion and obstruction. Its more significant relationship with the US unfolds elsewhere, along the supply-lines
it furnishes for the American war in Afghanistan. A foreign
policy as aqueous as this gives little reason for Washington to
pay over-much attention to relations with Moscow.

Europe, scarcely a diplomatic heavyweight, has required
more. France and Britain, once its leading imperial powers and
each anxious to demonstrate its continuing military relevance,

took the initiative in pressing for an intervention in Libya whose success depended on American drones and missiles. Paris and London have again been ahead of Washington in publicly urging delivery of Western arms to the rebels in Syria. Anglo-French belligerence in the Mediterranean has so far failed to carry the whole EU behind it, over German caution, and is hampered by lack of domestic support. But the Union has nevertheless played its role as the enforcer of sanctions against all three foes of peace and human rights, Libya, Syria and—crucially—Iran. Though benefiting from a general European wish to make up with Washington after differences over Iraq, and the Anglo-French desire to cut a figure once more on the world stage, the Obama administration can legitimately claim it an accomplishment that Europe is not only beside it in supervising the Arab world, but on occasion even notionally in front of it, providing the best of advertisements for its own moderation in the region.

II

As under the second Bush, the priorities of Obama's first term were set by the requirements of policing the less developed world. Lower down came the tasks of advancing the integration of the developed world. Chinese and later Russian entry into the WTO were certainly gains for the organization, but in each case the initiative was local, the negotiation a matter for bureaucratic adjustment, not major diplomacy, with no progress made on the Doha Round. With Obama's second term, international commerce has moved back up the agenda. To consolidate ties with Europe, a Trans-Atlantic Free Trade Agreement is now an official objective of the presidency. Since tariffs are already minimal across most goods between the US and EU, the creation of an economic NATO will make little material difference to either bloc—at most, perhaps, a yet greater share of Continental markets for American media companies, and entry of GM products into Europe. Its significance will be more symbolic: a reaffirmation, after passing squalls, of the unity of the West. The Trans-Pacific Partnership, launched by Washington somewhat earlier, is another matter. What it seeks to do is prise open the Japanese economy, protected by a maze of informal barriers that have frustrated decades of American attempts to penetrate local markets in retail, finance and manufactures, not to speak of farm products. Successful integration of Japan into the TPP would be a major US victory, ending the anomaly that its degree of commercial closure, conceded in a Cold War setting, has represented in the years since, and tying Japan, no longer even retaining its mercantilist autonomy, more firmly than ever into the American system of power. The willingness of the Abe government to accept this loss of the country's historic privilege reflects the fear in the Japanese political and industrial class at the rise of China, generating a more aggressive nationalist outlook that—given the disparity between the size of the two countries—requires US insurance.

Overshadowing these developments is the shift in response to the growing power of the PRC in America itself. While Obama was commanding successive overt and covert wars in the Greater Middle East, China was becoming the world's largest exporter (2010) and greatest manufacturing economy (2012). In the wake of the global financial crisis of 2008–2009, its stimulus package was proportionately three times larger than Obama's, at average growth rates nearly four times as fast.

Pulled to attention by the strategic implication of these changes, the administration let it be known that it would henceforward pivot to Asia, to check potential dangers in the ascent of China. The economies of the two powers are so interconnected that any open declaration of intent would be a breach of protocol, but the purpose of such a pivot is plain: to surround the PRC with a necklace of US allies and military installations, and—in particular—to maintain American naval predominance across the Pacific, up to and including the East China Sea. As elsewhere in the world, but more flagrantly, an undisguised asymmetry of pretensions belongs to the prerogatives of empire, the US regarding as natural a claim to rule the seas seven thousand miles from its shores, when it would never permit a foreign fleet in its own waters. Early on, Obama helped to bring down a hapless Hatoyama government in Tokyo for daring to contemplate a change in US bases in Okinawa, and has since added to its seven hundred-plus others in the world with a marine base in northern Australia,[9] while stepping up joint naval exercises with a newly complaisant India. The pivot is still in

---

9 Far the best analytic information on US bases is to be found in Chalmers Johnson's formidable trilogy: see the chapters on 'Okinawa, Asia's Last Colony' in *Blowback*, p. 36 ff; 'The Empire of Bases'—725 by an official Pentagon count, with others devoted to surveillance 'cloaked in secrecy'—in *The Sorrows of Empire*, pp. 151–86; and 'US Military Bases in Other Peoples' Countries' in *Nemesis*, taking the reader through the labyrinth of Main Operating Bases, Forward Location Sites and Cooperative Security Locations ('lily pads', supposedly pioneered in the Gulf): pp. 137–70. Current revelations of the nature and scale of NSA interception of communications worldwide find their trailer here. Unsurprisingly, given the closeness of cooperation between the two military and surveillance establishments, former British defence official Sandars, in his survey of American bases, concludes with satisfaction that 'the United States has emerged with credit and honour from the unique experience of policing the world, not by imposing garrisons on occupied territory, but by agreement with her friends and allies': *America's Overseas Garrisons*, p. 331.

its early days, and its meaning is as much diplomatic as military. The higher US hope is to convert China, in the language of the State Department, into a responsible stakeholder in the international system—that is, not a presumptuous upstart, let alone menacing outsider, but a loyal second in the hierarchy of global capitalist power. Such will be the leading objectives of the grand strategy to come.

How distinct has Obama's rule been, as a phase in the American empire? Over the course of the Cold War, the US presidency has amassed steadily more unaccountable power. Between the time of Truman and of Reagan, staff in the White House grew tenfold. The NSC today—over two hundred strong—is nearly four times as large as it was under Nixon, Carter, or even the elder Bush. The CIA, whose size remains a secret, though it has grown exponentially since it was established in 1949, and whose budget has increased over tenfold since the days of Kennedy—$4 billion in 1963, $44 billion in 2005 at constant prices—is in effect a private army at the disposal of the president. So-called signing statements now allow the presidency to void legislation passed by Congress, but disliked by the White House. Executive acts in defiance of the law are regularly upheld by the Office of Legal Counsel in the Justice Department, which furnished memoranda on the legality of torture, but even its degree of subservience has been insufficient for the Oval Office, which has acquired its own White House Counsel as a still more unconditional rubber stamp for whatever it chooses to do.[10] Obama inherited this system of arbitrary power and violence, and like most of his predecessors, has extended it. Odyssey Dawn, Stuxnet, Targeted Killing,

---

10 For this development, see Bruce Ackerman, *The Decline and Fall of the American Republic,* Cambridge, MA 2010, pp. 87–115.

Prism have been the coinages of his tenure: war that does not even amount to hostilities, electronic assault by long-distance virus, assassination of US citizens, along with foreign nationals, wholesale surveillance of domestic, along with foreign, communications. The executioner-in-chief has even been reluctant to forego the ability to order the killing without trial of an American on native soil. No one would accuse this incumbent of want of humane feeling: tears for the death of schoolchildren in New England have moved the nation, and appeals for gun control converted not a few. If a great many more children, most without even schools, have died at his own hands in Ghazni or Waziristan, that is no reason for loss of presidential sleep. Predators are more accurate than automatic rifles, and the Pentagon can always express an occasional regret. The logic of empire, not the unction of the ruler, sets the moral standard.

The principal constraint on the exercise of imperial force by the United States has traditionally lain in the volatility of domestic opinion, repeatedly content to start but quick to tire of foreign engagements should these involve significant American casualties, for which public tolerance has dropped over time, despite the abolition of the draft—even the very low loss of American life in Iraq soon becoming unpopular. The main practical adjustments in US policy under Obama have been designed to avert this difficulty. The official term for these in the administration is rebalancing, though rebranding would do as well. What this watchword actually signifies are three changes. To reduce American casualties to an absolute minimum—in principle, and in some cases in practice, zero—there has been ever increasing reliance on the long-distance technologies of the RMA to obliterate the enemy from afar, without risking any battlefield contact. Where ground combat is unavoidable, proxies equipped with clandestine funds and arms are preferable to American regulars; where US troops have to be employed, the detachments to use are the secretive units of the Joint Special Operations Command, in charge of covert warfare.

Lastly, reputable allies from the First World should be sought, not spurned, for any major, or even minor, undertaking: whatever their military value, necessarily variable, they provide a political buffer against criticism of the wisdom or justice of any overseas action, giving it the ultimate seal of legitimacy—approval by the 'international community'. A more multilateral approach to issues of global security is in no way a contradiction of the mission of the nation to govern the world. The immovable lodestone remains US primacy, now little short of an attribute of national identity itself.[11] In the words of Obama's stripling speechwriter Benjamin Rhodes, now deputy national security advisor: 'What we're trying to do is to get America another fifty years as leader'. The president himself is not willing to settle for half a loaf. In over thirty pronouncements, he has explained that all of this, like the last, will be the American Century.[12]

---

11 As David Calleo wrote in 2009: 'It is tempting to believe that America's recent misadventures will discredit and suppress our hegemonic longings and that, following the presidential election of 2008, a new administration will abandon them. But so long as our identity as a nation is intimately bound up with seeing ourselves as the world's most powerful country, at the heart of a global system, hegemony is likely to remain the recurring obsession of our official imagination, the *idée fixe* of our foreign policy': *Follies of Power: America's Unipolar Fantasy*, Cambridge 2009, p. 4.

12 Rhodes: *The Obamians*, p. 72; Obama: Bacevich, ed., *The Short American Century*, p. 249.

III

Seventy years after Roosevelt's planners conceived the outline of a Pax Americana, what is the balance sheet? From the beginning, duality defined the structure of US strategy: the universal and the particular were always intertwined. The original vision postulated a liberal-capitalist order of free trade stretching around the world, in which the United States would automatically —by virtue of its economic power and example—hold first place. The outbreak of the Cold War deflected this scheme. The defeat of communism became an overriding priority, relegating the construction of a liberal ecumene to a second-order concern, whose principles would have to be tempered or set aside to secure victory over an enemy that threatened capitalism of any kind, free trade or protectionist, laissez-faire or dirigiste, democratic or dictatorial. In this mortal conflict, America came to play an even more commanding role, on a still wider stage, than the projections of Bretton Woods and Dumbarton Oaks had envisaged, as the uncontested leader of the Free World. In the course of four decades of unremitting struggle, a military and political order was constructed that transformed what had once been a merely hemispheric hegemony into a global empire, remoulding the form of the US state itself.

In the Cold War, triumph was in the end complete. But the empire created to win it did not dissolve back into the liberal ecumene out of whose ideological vision it had emerged. The institutions and acquisitions, ideologies and reflexes bequeathed by the battle against communism now constituted a massive historical complex with its own dynamics, no longer needing to be driven by the threat from the Soviet Union. Special forces in over a hundred countries round the world; a military budget larger than that of all other major powers combined; tentacular apparatuses of infiltration, espionage and surveillance; ramifying national security personnel; and last but not least, an intellectual establishment devoted to revising, refining, amplifying and updating the tasks of grand strategy, of a higher quality and productivity than any counterpart concerned with domestic affairs—how could all this be expected to shrink once again to the slender maxims of 1945? The Cold War was over, but a gendarme's day is never done. More armed expeditions followed than ever before; more advanced weapons were rolled out; more bases were added to the chain; more far-reaching doctrines of intervention developed. There could be no looking back.

But beside the inertial momentum of a victorious empire, another pressure was at work in the trajectory of the now sole superpower. The liberal-capitalist order it set out to create had started, before it had even cleared the field of its historic antagonist, to escape the designs of its architect. The restoration of Germany and Japan had not proved of unambiguous benefit to the United States after all, the system of Bretton Woods capsizing under the pressure of their competition: power that had once exceeded interest, permitting its conversion into hegemony, had begun to inflict costs on it. Out of that setback emerged a more radical free-market model at home, which when the Cold War was won could be exported without inhibition as the norm of a neoliberal order. But against the gains to the US of globalized deregulation came further, more radical losses, as its trade deficit and the borrowing needed to cover it steadily mounted. With the emergence of China—capitalist in its fashion, certainly, but far from liberal, indeed still ruled by a Communist party—as an economic power not only of superior dynamism but of soon comparable magnitude, on whose financial reserves its own public credit had come to depend, the logic of long-term American grand strategy threatened to turn against itself. Its premise had always been the harmony of the universal and the particular—the general interests of capital secured by the national supremacy of the United States. To solder the two into a single system, a global empire was built. But though the empire has survived, it is becoming disarticulated from the order it sought to extend. American primacy is no longer the automatic capstone of the civilization of capital. A liberal international order with the United States at its head risks becoming something else, less congenial to the Land of the Free. A reconciliation, never perfect, of the universal with the particular was a constitutive condition of American hegemony. Today they are drifting apart. Can they be reconjugated? If so, how? Around these two questions, the discourse of empire now revolves, its strategists divide.

CONSILIUM

In the American intellectual landscape, the literature of grand strategy forms a domain of its own, distinct from diplomatic history or political science, though it may occasionally draw on these. Its sources lie in the country's security elite, which extends across the bureaucracy and the academy to foundations, think tanks and the media. In this milieu, with its emplacements in the Council on Foreign Relations, the Kennedy School in Harvard, the Woodrow Wilson Center in Princeton, the Nitze School at Johns Hopkins, the Naval War College, Georgetown University, the Brookings and Carnegie Foundations, the Departments of State and of Defense, not to speak of the National Security Council and the CIA, positions are readily interchangeable, individuals moving seamlessly back and forth between university chairs or think tanks and government offices, in general regardless of the party in control of the administration.

This amphibious environment sets output on foreign policy apart from the scholarship of domestic politics, more tightly confined within the bounds of a professional discipline and peer-review machinery, where it speaks mainly to itself. The requirements of proficiency in the discourse of foreign policy are not the same, because of a twofold difference of audience: officeholders on the one hand, an educated public on the other. This body of writing is constitutively advisory, in a sense stretching back to the Renaissance—counsels to the Prince. Rulers tolerate no pedants: what advice they receive should be crisp and uncluttered. In contemporary America, they have a relay below them which values an accessible éclat for reasons of its own. Think tanks, of central importance in this world, dispense their fellows from teaching; in exchange, they expect a certain public impact—columns, op-eds, talk-shows, bestsellers— from them: not on the population as a whole, but among the small, well-off minority that takes an interest in such matters. The effect of this dual calling is to produce a literature that is less scholarly, but freer and more imaginative—less costive— than its domestic counterpart.

The contrast is also rooted in their fields of operation. Domestic politics is of far greater interest, to many more Americans, than diplomacy. But the political system at home is subject only to slow changes over time, amid repeated institutional deadlock of one kind or another. It is a scene of much frustration, rare excitement. The American imperial system, by contrast, is a theatre of continual drama—coups, crises, insurgencies, wars, emergencies of every kind; and there, short of treaties which have to pass the legislature, no decision is ever deadlocked. The executive can do as it pleases, so long as the masses—a rare event: eventually Korea or Vietnam; marginally Iraq—are not startled awake by some unpopular setback.[1]

1   In the words of a representative insider: 'In the United States, as in other countries, foreign policy is the preoccupation of only a small part of the population. But carrying out any American foreign policy requires the support of the wider public. Whereas for the foreign-policy elite, the need

In this enormous zone of potential action, the advisory imagination can roam—run riot, even—with a liberty impossible at home. Whatever the results, naturally various, there is no mistaking the greater intellectual energy that foreign policy attracts in the thought-world of the Beltway and its penumbra.

---

for American leadership in the world is a matter of settled conviction, in the general public the commitment to global leadership is weaker. This is not surprising. That commitment depends on a view of its effects on the rest of the world and the likely consequences of its absence. These are views for which most Americans, like most people in most countries, lack the relevant information because they are not ordinarily interested enough to gather it. The politics of American foreign policy thus resembles a firm in which the management—the foreign-policy elite—has to persuade the shareholders—the public—to authorize expenditures': Michael Mandelbaum, 'The Inadequacy of American Power', *Foreign Affairs*, Sept–Oct 2002, p. 67. It is enough to ask how many firms consult shareholders over their expenditures—in this case, of course, military— to see the pertinence of the analogy.

9

NATIVE TRADITIONS

On the threshold of the attacks on the World Trade Center and the Pentagon, there appeared a confident portmanteau of the native resources that for two centuries ensured that American foreign policy had 'won all the prizes'. Walter Russell Mead's *Special Providence: American Foreign Policy and How It Changed the World* (2001) can be taken as a baseline for the subsequent literature. Continental European traditions of geopolitical realism, Mead argued, had always been alien to the United States.[1] Morality and economics, not geopolitics, were the essential guidelines of the nation's role in the world. These did not preclude the use of force for right ends—in twentieth-century warfare, America had been more disproportionately destructive of its enemies than Nazi Germany.[2] But the policies

---

1   Walter Russell Mead, *Special Providence: American Foreign Policy and How It Changed the World*, New York 2001, pp. 34–9 ff. Rejection of Kissinger's brand of realism as un-American in *Special Providence* was no bar to Mead's appointment as Kissinger Senior Fellow at the Council on Foreign Relations in the wake of its success, before taking a chair at Bard.

2   'In the last five months of World War II, American bombing raids killed more than 900,000 Japanese civilians, not counting the casualties from

determining these ends were the product of a unique democratic synthesis: Hamiltonian pursuit of commercial advantage
for American enterprise abroad; Wilsonian duty to extend the
values of liberty across the world; Jeffersonian concern to preserve the virtues of the republic from foreign temptations; and
Jacksonian valour in any challenge to the honour or security of
the country. If the first two were elite creeds, and the third an
inclination among intellectuals, the fourth was the folk ethos of
the majority of the American people. But out of the competition between these—the outlook of merchants, of missionaries,
of constitutional lawyers and of frontiersmen—had emerged,
as in the invisible hand of the market, the best of all foreign
policies.[3] Combining hard and soft power in ways at once flexible, pragmatic and idealistic, America's conduct of world affairs
derived from the complementary diversity of its inspirations a
homeostatic stability and wisdom.

Descriptively, the tally of native traditions laid out in this
construction is often vivid and ingenious, assorted with many
acute observations, however roseate the retrospect in which
they issue. Analytically, however, it rests on the *non sequitur*
of an equivalence between them, as so many contributors to
a common upshot. A glance at the personifications offered
of each undoes any such idea. The long list of Hamiltonian
statesmen at the helm of the State Department or ensconced
in the White House—Clay, Webster, Hay, Lodge, TR, Hull,

---

the atomic strikes against Hiroshima and Nagasaki. This is more than
twice the number of combat deaths (441,513) that the United States has
suffered in all its foreign wars combined', while the ratio of civilian to
combat deaths in the American wars in Korea and Vietnam was higher
even than in the German invasion of Russia. Naturally, Mead assures his
readers, no moral parallel is implied: *Special Providence*, pp. 218–9.

3   Mead, *Special Providence*, pp. 95–6, 311–2.

Acheson, the first Bush are mentioned—can find a Wilsonian counterpart only by appealing to the regularity of mixtures since the Second World War—FDR, Truman, Kennedy and the rest; while of Jeffersonian rulers or chancellors there are virtually none—even the eponym himself scarcely exemplifying abstinence from external ambition and aggrandisement,[4] leaving as illustration only a forlorn train of isolates and outsiders, in a declension down to Borah, Lippman, Fulbright. As for Jacksonians, aside from a subsequent string of undistinguished military veterans in the nineteenth century, Polk and the second Bush could be counted among their number, but most of the recent instances cited in *Special Providence*— Patton, MacArthur, McCain: Wallace might be added—were burst bullfrogs. Popular support for American wars, Mead correctly notes, requires galvanization of Jacksonian truculence in the social depths of the country. But the foreign policy that determines them is set elsewhere. The reality is that of the four traditions, only two have had consistent weight since the Spanish–American conflict; the others furnish little more than sporadic supplies of cassandrism and cannon fodder.

In that sense, the more conventional dichotomy with which Kissinger—identified by Mead as the practitioner of a European-style *Realpolitik* with no roots in America—opened his treatise *Diplomacy* some years earlier, can be taken as read. In Kissinger's version, the two legacies that matter are lines that descend respectively from Theodore Roosevelt and Wilson: the first, a realist resolve to maintain a balance of power in the

---

4   For the actual record of the architect of Montebello, see Robert W. Tucker and David C. Hendrickson, *Empire of Liberty: The Statecraft of Thomas Jefferson*, New York 1990.

world; the second, an idealist commitment to put an end to arbitrary powers everywhere. Though discredited at the time, Wilson's ideas had in the long run prevailed over Roosevelt's. American foreign policy would come to conjugate the two, but the Wilsonian strain would be dominant. 'A universal grouping of largely democratic nations would act as the "trustee" of peace and replace the old balance-of-power and alliance systems. Such exalted sentiments had never before been put forward by any nation, let alone implemented. Nevertheless, in the hands of American idealism they were turned into the common currency of national thinking of foreign policy', Kissinger declared. Nixon himself had hung a portrait of the Man of Peace as inspiration to him in the Oval Office: 'In all this time, Wilson's principles have remained the bedrock of American foreign-policy thinking.'[5]

II

The authorship of the dictum is enough to indicate the need to invert it. Since the Second World War, the ideology of American foreign policy has always been predominantly Wilsonian in register—'making the world safe for democracy' segueing into a 'collective security' that would in due course become the outer buckler of 'national security'. In substance, its reality has been unswervingly Hamiltonian—the pursuit of American supremacy, in a world made safe for capital.[6] But with rare exceptions

---

5   Once 'the post-war world became largely America's creation', the US would 'play the role Wilson had envisioned for it—as a beacon to follow, and a hope to attain': Kissinger, *Diplomacy*, New York 1994, pp. 52, 55.

6   As Wilson himself intimated in 1923. 'The world has been made safe for democracy', he wrote. 'But democracy has not yet made the world

like Kissinger, the ideology has been a credulous rather than a cynical adornment of the exercise of American power, whose holders—Bush and Obama are only the latest—have always believed that there is no conflict between American values and American interests. That US paramountcy is at once a national prize and a universal good is taken for granted by policy-makers and their counsellors, across the party-political board. Terminologically, in this universe, 'primacy' is still preferable to empire, but in its more theoretical reaches, 'hegemony' is now acceptable to virtually all. The contemporary editors of *To Lead the World*, a symposium of eminences from every quarter, remark that all of them agree 'the United States should be a leader in the international system', accept Clinton's description of it as 'the indispensable nation', and concur that the country should retain its military predominance: 'none of the contributors proposes to reduce military spending significantly or wants to allow US superiority to erode'.[7]

safe against irrational revolution. That supreme task, which is nothing less than the salvation of civilization, now faces democracy, insistent, imperative. There is no escaping it, unless everything we have built up is presently to fall in ruin about us; and the United States, as the greatest of democracies, must undertake it'. For these reflections, see 'The Road Away from Revolution', c. 8 April 1923, *The Papers of Woodrow Wilson*, vol. 68, Princeton 1993, p. 323.

7   Melvyn Leffler and Jeffrey Legro, eds, *To Lead the World: American Strategy after the Bush Doctrine*, New York 2008, pp. 250–2. The contributors include Francis Fukuyama, Charles Maier, John Ikenberry, James Kurth, David Kennedy, Barry Eichengreen, Robert Kagan, Niall Ferguson and Samantha Power, Obama's ambassador to the UN. Leffler has himself elsewhere explained that if 'the community that came into existence after the Second World War' is to survive, 'the hegemonic role of the United States must be relegitimized', or—as Wilson put it—'peace must be secured by the organized moral force of mankind'. Leffler, '9/11 and The Past and Future of American Foreign Policy', *International Affairs*, October 2003, pp. 1062–3.

That it should even be necessary to say so, marks the period since 2001 as a new phase in the discourse, if not the practice, of empire. Here the vicissitudes of the last dozen years—the *attentats* of 2001, the invasion of Iraq in 2003, the financial crisis of 2008, the continuing war in Afghanistan—have generated an all but universal problematic. Is American power in global decline? If so, what are the reasons? What are the remedies?

Common *leitmotifs* run through many of the answers. Few fail to include a list of the domestic reforms needed to restore the competitive superiority of American economy and society. All calculate the risks of a renewal of Great Power rivalry— China figuring most prominently, but not exclusively—that could endanger American primacy, and contemplate the dangers of terrorism in the Middle East, threatening American security. The fortunes of capitalism and the future of democracy are rarely out of mind. Each construction differs in some significant ways from the next, offering a spectrum of variations that can be taken as a proxy for the current repertoire—partly ongoing, partly prospective—of US grand strategy in the new century.

The core of the community producing these is composed of thinkers whose careers have moved across appointments in government, universities and foundations. In this milieu, unlike that of diplomatic historians, direct dispute or polemical engagement are rare, not only because of the extent of common assumptions, but also because writing is often shaped with an eye to official preferment, where intellectual pugilism is not favoured, though divergences of outlook are still plain enough. Individual quirks ensure that no selection of strategists will be fully representative.

But a number of the most conspicuous contributions are readily identified.[8]

---

8   Excluded in what follows are figures whose careers have only been within the media or the academy. Prominent among the former are the journalists Fareed Zakaria of *Newsweek* and Peter Beinart of *Time*, authors respectively of *The Post-American World* (2008) and *The Icarus Syndrome* (2010). For the second, see Anders Stephanson, 'The Toughness Crew', *New Left Review* 82, July–Aug 2013. In the academy, the field of international relations or 'security studies' includes a literature as dedicated to the technicalities of game theory and rational choice as any domestic political science, alembications precluding a wider audience; but also theorists of distinction whose independence of mind has saved them from temptations of office. John Mearsheimer of Chicago is an outstanding example, for whose *Tragedy of Great Power Politics* (2001), see Peter Gowan's essay, 'A Calculus of Power', *New Left Review* 16, July–Aug 2002; but there are not a few others. Of leading in-and-outers passed over below, Joseph Nye—Harvard Kennedy School; undersecretary of state in the Carter administration and chairman of the NSC under Clinton; author of *Bound to Lead* (1990) and *The Paradox of American Power* (2002)—is insufficiently original, with little more than the banalities of soft power to his name, to warrant consideration. Philip Bobbitt—currently Director of the National Security Center at Columbia; service on the CIA under Carter, NSC under Clinton and for the State Department under the second Bush; author of *The Shield of Achilles* (2003) and *Terror and Consent* (2008)—is far from banal, but has been discussed in depth by Gopal Balakrishnan, 'Algorithms of War', *New Left Review* 23, Sept–Oct 2003.

10

CRUSADERS

They can start with the protean figure of Mead himself. His first work *Mortal Splendor*, published in 1987 at the height of the Iran–Contra debacle, chronicled the failures in turn of Nixon, of Carter and of Reagan to restore the American empire—bluntly described as such—to its lustre. Criticizing the archaism, involution and corruption of the Constitution, Mead lamented falling popular living standards and escalating budgetary deficits, ending with a call to Democrats to put an end to a decaying 'bureaucratic and oligarchic order' with the creation of a 'fourth republic', recasting the New Deal with a more populist and radical drive, and projecting it outwards as a programme for the world at large.[1] Fourteen years later, his standpoint had somersaulted. A virtual pallbearer of empire in *Mortal Splendor*, by the time of *Special Providence* he had become its trumpeter, though the term itself now disappeared, the US featuring for the most part simply as 'the central power

---

[1] 'The reforms must go far beyond those of the Roosevelt period', Mead insisted. 'The next wave will have a more socialist and less liberal coloration than the first one': *Mortal Splendor: The American Empire in Transition*, New York 1987, pp. 336–8.

in a world-wide system of finance, communications and trade', and 'gyroscope of world order'. International hegemony, it was true, the nation did enjoy. But Americans were insufficiently reflective of its meanings and purposes, about which more debate between their national traditions of foreign policy was now needed. His own inclinations, Mead explained, were Jeffersonian.[2]

These did not last long. Mead's response to the attacks of 2001, a few months after the appearance of *Special Providence*, set its taxonomy to work with a difference. *Power, Terror, Peace and War* (2004) set out a robust programme to meet the challenges now confronting the 'American project' of domestic security and a peaceful world, whose failure would be a disaster for humanity. Fortunately, the US continued to combine the three forms of power that had hitherto assured its hegemony: 'sharp'—the military force to prevent the Middle East becoming a 'theocratic terror camp'; 'sticky'—the economic interdependence that tied China to America through trade and debt; and 'sweet'—the cultural attractions of American popular movies and music, universities, feminism, multinationals, immigration, charities. But the socioeconomic terrain on which these should now be deployed had shifted. After the Second World War, Fordism had provided a firm ground for US ascendancy, combining mass production and mass consumption in a way of life that became the envy of the world. With the end of the Cold War, the American example appeared to promise a future in which free markets and free government could henceforward spread everywhere, under a protective canopy of US might.[3]

But that was to forget that capitalism is a dynamic system,

2   Mead, *Special Providence*, pp. 323–4, 333–4.

3   Mead, *Power, Terror, Peace and War*, New York, 2004, pp. 26–55.

again and again destroying what it has created, to give birth to new forms of itself. The bureaucratized, full employment, manufacturing economy of Fordism was now a thing of the past in America, as elsewhere. What had replaced it was a 'millennial capitalism' of more freewheeling competition and individual risk-taking, corporate downsizing and hi-tech venturing, shorn of the props and protections of an earlier epoch: a force feared by all those—governments, elites or masses—who had benefited from Fordism and still clung to its ways. Restless and disruptive, it was the arrival of this millennial capitalism that underlay the revolution in American foreign policy in the new century. Its champions were now at the helm, remaking Hamiltonian conceptions of business, reviving Wilsonian values of liberty, and updating a Jacksonian bent for preemptive action.[4] The Bush administration might have offered too thin a version of the rich case for attacking Iraq, since weapons of mass destruction were less important than a blow to regional fascism and the prospect of the first Arab democracy in Baghdad. But this was no time for Jeffersonian misgivings. Strategically, the Republican administration had made most of the right choices. If its execution of them had been somewhat choppy, TR and Wilson had on occasion stumbled at the start of their revolutions too. With US troops on the Tigris, the correct strategy for dealing with Arab fascists and terrorists, indeed all other enemies of freedom, was moving

4   Mead, *Power, Terror, Peace and War*, pp. 73–103. By this time, Kissinger himself—another supporter of the invasion of Iraq—had adopted Mead's taxonomy for the purposes of criticizing American conduct of the Cold War prior to the Nixon administration and his own assumption of office, as an overly rigid blend of Wilsonism and Jacksonism, forgetful of Hamiltonian principles. See *Does America Need a Foreign Policy?*, New York 2002, pp. 245–56, a volume whose intellectual quality rarely rises much above the level of its title.

ahead: 'forward containment', complete where necessary with preventive strikes at the adversary.

Three years later, *God and Gold: Britain, America and the Making of the Modern World* encased these themes in a vaster world-historical theodicy. Behind the rise of the United States to global hegemony lay the prior ascendancy of Britain, in a relation not of mere sequence but organic connexion, that across five hundred years had given the Anglo-American powers a succession of unbroken victories over illiberal enemies—Habsburg Spain, Bourbon and Napoleonic France, Wilhelmine and Nazi Germany, Imperial Japan, Soviet Russia. The secret of this continuous triumph lay in a culture uniquely favourable to the titanic forces of capitalism, crossing Anglican religion and its offshoots with the Enlightenments of Newton and Smith, Madison and Darwin—a form of Christianity reconciling reason, revelation and tradition, allied to a 'golden meme' of secular conceptions of order arising out of the free play of natural forces, and their evolution. In due course, out of the combination of an Abrahamic faith committed to change— not a static, but a dynamic religion in the sense described by Bergson—and the explosion of human potential released by capitalism, came the Whig narrative of overarching historical progress.

Such was the cultural environment that nurtured the monumental creativity of Anglo-American finance, first in London and then New York, the core of capitalist efficiency as a system of rational allocation of resources, with its ingenuity in developing ever-new devices in banking, trading, stockjobbing, insurance, all the way to the credit cards and mortgage-backed securities of contemporary prosperity. The power of mass consumption, in turn, harnessed by flexible markets to the economic interests of the talented—'perhaps the most revolutionary discovery in human history since the taming of fire'—generated the cascade of inventions in which Britain and America took the lead: white goods, railways, department stores, automobiles, telephones, popular culture at large. It was little wonder these two countries proved invincible on the world stage.

But the very success of Anglo-America bred its own illusions—a persistent belief that the rest of the world must of its own accord follow, if not sooner then later, the path to liberty, diversity and prosperity where it had led the way. Capitalism, however, could emerge smoothly and gradually into the world only within the privilege of its Anglican–Whig setting. Everywhere else, its arrival was harsher—more sudden and disruptive of old ways; typically infected, too, with resentment at the prowess of the first-comers, and the rough justice others had reason to feel these meted out to them—a ruthlessness draped with many a pious expression of regret or rectitude, in the spirit of the Walrus and the Carpenter. That kind of resentment had been true of successive continental powers in the Europe of the past, and remained widespread in the extra-European world today, from the Russian bear licking its wounds to the Chinese dragon puffing its envious fire, not to speak of assorted Arab scorpions in the Middle East.

After the end of the Cold War, dangerous forces were still afoot. In confronting them, the United States should show tact where other cultures were concerned, whose sensibilities required the finesse of a 'diplomacy of civilizations'. But it had no reason for doubt or despondency. Command of the seas remained the key to global power, and there US supremacy remained unchallenged: the maritime system that had assured Anglo-American triumph over every foe, from the time of Elizabeth I and Philip II onwards, held as firmly as ever. Europe, united and free, was an ally; Russia, much weakened; China could be balanced by Japan and India. In the Middle East, Islam as a faith belonged to the conversation of the world, in which all peoples and cultures were entitled to their collective recognition, even as the ghost dancers of Arab terror were crushed. The *Pax Americana* would persist, for it was wrong to think that all empires must inevitably decline or disappear. Rather, as the example of China showed, they may wax and wane over millennia.

By this time, the invasion of Iraq had 'proved to be an unnecessary and poorly planned war', after all. But US engagement in the Middle East would have to deepen, and Mead looked forward to the arrival of centrist Democrats for a course correction. Imbued with the tragic sense of history and American responsibility bequeathed by Niebuhr, and sustained by the awakening of a new Evangelical moderation, the nation could recover the dynamism of that 'deep and apparently in-built human belief that through change we encounter the transcendent and the divine'. Capitalism was taking us into a future of accelerating change, and there lay the country's opportunity. For the American project was not simply to bring personal freedom and material abundance for all. It had a higher meaning. In leading the world on a 'voyage of exploration into unknown waters', that is 'both our destiny and duty', its maritime order would be sailing towards an as yet unimagined horizon: there, where 'the end of history is the peace of God'.[5]

The extravagance of this mystico-commercial construction might seem, on the face of it, to remove its author from

---

5   Mead, *God and Gold: Britain, America and the Making of the Modern World*, New York 2007, pp. 378, 387–402, 409, 411, 412.

mainstream discourse on foreign policy, and it is true that unlike most of his peers, Mead has never worked in government. But if he nevertheless remains central as a mind within the field, that is due not so much to the brutal energy of his style and restless ingenuity of his imagination, but to the indivisible fashion in which he has embodied in extreme form two opposite strains of American nationalism, each usually expressed more temperately: the economic and political realism of the tradition represented by the first Roosevelt, and the preceptorial and religious moralism consecrated by Wilson. Drumming out the blunt verities of capitalism, without flinching at—even rubbing in—the misdeeds of Anglo-American expansion, on the one hand; sublimating liberal democracy and higher productivity into a *parousia* of the Lord, on the other. The flamboyance of the combination has not meant marginalization. As he had foreseen, a Democrat was soon in the White House again, intoning the wisdom of Niebuhr, as Mead had wished, in a speech to the Nobel Committee he could have scripted. When Francis Fukuyama broke with the journal that had made him famous, *The National Interest*, on the grounds that it was tilting too far towards Nixonian *Realpolitik*, forgetting the salve of Wilsonian idealism that ought to be its complement, it was Mead who joined him in creating a new forum, *The American Interest*, to restore the balance of a true Liberal Realism.[6]

---

6   After coming to the conclusion that most of his fellow neoconservatives had been too warmly Wilsonian in their enthusiasm for bringing democracy to Iraq, Fukuyama then decided that others were becoming too coldly Kissingerian in a calculus of power detached from the values of democracy. Getting the ideological temperature right is no easy task, but on it the good health of America's relations with the world depends. I have not included Fukuyama in the literature considered here, though his work *America at the Crossroads* (2006) is an eminent example of it, having written about that earlier: see the annexe below. Fukuyama and

II

More typical of the field than this ecstatic hybrid are thinkers who belong without ambiguity to a particular tradition
within the external repertory of the American state. There,
as noted, the dominant has since the mid-forties always been
Wilsonian—never more so than under the last three presidencies, all of which have proclaimed their devotion to the goals of
the Peacemaker more vocally than any of their predecessors.
The leading theorists within this camp, Michael Mandelbaum
and John Ikenberry, each with a spell in the State Department,
offer alternative versions of this outlook, substantially overlapping in intellectual framework, if diverging at significant points
in political upshot.[7] Mandelbaum is the more prominent and
prolific, producing five widely applauded books in less than
a decade, beginning with a trio whose titles speak for themselves: *The Ideas that Conquered the World* (2002), *The Case for
Goliath* (2005) and *Democracy's Good Name* (2007).

For Mandelbaum, the story of the twentieth century was 'a
Whig history with a vengeance': the triumph of the Wilsonian
triad of peace, democracy and free markets. These were the
ideas that finished off the Soviet Union, bringing the Cold
War to a victorious end as its rulers succumbed to their attrac-
tive force. In part this was an outcome comparable to natural

---

Mead keep up a running commentary on questions of the hour, national
and international, in the *American Interest*, which bills itself as having
broader concerns—notably in 'religion, identity, ethnicity and demo-
graphics'—than the *National Interest*, under a former editor of the latter.

7   Mandelbaum worked under Eagleburger and Shultz in the first Reagan
administration; Ikenberry under Baker in the Bush Senior administration. Characteristically of such 'in-and-outers', partisan affiliations were
not involved, the personal links of both men being Democrat rather than
Republican.

selection, eliminating the economically unfit. But it was also an effect of the moral revelation wrought by a superior creed, comparable to the religious conversion that in late antiquity transformed pagans into Christians—Gorbachev, even Deng Xiaoping, had become latter-day Constantines. The result could be seen after the outrage of 2001. Every significant government in the world declared its solidarity with America, for all 'supported the market-dominated world order that had come under attack and of which the United States served as the linchpin', to which there was no viable alternative. To be sure, the full Wilsonian triad was not yet universally entrenched. The free market was now the most widely accepted idea in world history. But peace and democracy were not secure to quite the same extent. The foreign polices of Moscow and Beijing were less than completely pacific, their economies were insufficiently marketized, their political systems only incipiently democratic. The highest objective of the West must now be to transform and incorporate Russia and China fully into the liberal world order, as the earlier illiberal powers of Germany and Japan were made over from challengers into pillars of the system, after the war.

In that task, leadership fell to one nation, because it is more than a nation. The United States was not simply a benign Goliath among states, the sun around whom the solar system turns. It was 'the World's Government', for it alone provided the services of international security and economic stability to humanity, its role accepted because of the twenty-first century consensus around the Wilsonian triad. American contributions to the maintenance of peace and the spread of free markets were generally acknowledged. But the importance of the United States in the diffusion of democracy was scarcely less. Historically, the ideas of liberty and of popular sovereignty—how to govern, and who governs—were analytically and chronologically distinct. The former predated the latter, which arrived only with the French Revolution, but then spread much more rapidly, often at the expense of liberty. Democracy, when it came, would be the improbable fusion of the two. Its rise in the twentieth century was due in good part to the dynamism of free markets in generating social prosperity and civil society. But it also required the magnetic attraction of the power and wealth of the two great Anglophone democracies, Great Britain and—now overwhelmingly—the United States. Without their supremacy, the best form of rule would never have taken root so widely. It was they who made it 'the leading brand' that so many others would want to acquire.

In this construction, Wilsonian devotion presents an apotheosis of the United States in some ways more pristine even than the syncretic version in Mead, with its jaunty allowance of a dark side to the history of American expansionism. Not that the World's Government was infallible. Mandelbaum, who had counselled Clinton in his campaign for the presidency, had a disagreeable surprise when he was elected: the new national security adviser to the White House was Anthony Lake, rather than himself. Three years later, taking direct aim at Lake, he published a withering critique of the international performance of the Clinton regime, 'Foreign Policy as Social Work', dismissing its interventions in Haiti and Bosnia as futile attempts to play Mother Teresa abroad, and attacking its expansion of NATO to the east as a foolish provocation of Russia, jeopardizing its integration into a consensual ecumene after the Cold War.[8]

---

8 'Foreign Policy as Social Work', *Foreign Affairs*, Jan–Feb 1996; followed by *The Dawn of Peace in Europe*, New York 1996, pp. 61–3: 'NATO expansion

Nor, as time went on, was all well at home. A decade into the new century, *The Frugal Superpower* (2010) warned of widening inequality and escalating welfare entitlements amid continuing fiscal improvidence—Medicare potentially worse than Social Security, Keynesian deficits compounded by Lafferesque tax-cuts—and the need for the country to adjust its overseas ends to its domestic means. *That Used to Be Us* (2011), co-authored with Thomas Friedman, extended the bill of anxieties. America's secondary education was in crisis; its infrastructure was collapsing; it was spending too little on R&D; it had no coherent energy policy; its welcome to immigrants had become grudging. Many individuals offered inspiring examples of altruism and enterprise, but the nation needed to pull itself collectively together with a set of public–private partnerships to regain the economic success and social harmony of old. For that to be possible, shock therapy was needed to shake up partisan deadlock in the political system—a third-party presidential candidate upholding the banner of a 'radical centrism'.

The urgency of such reforms spells no disaffection with America or retraction of its guardian role in the world. 'We, the authors of this book, don't want simply to restore American solvency. We want to maintain American greatness. We're not green-eyeshade guys. We're Fourth of July guys', they explain, in Friedman's inimitable tones.[9] What follows from the tonics they propose? Mandelbaum's cool view of Clinton precluded

---

is, in the eyes of Russians in the 1990s, what the war guilt clause was for Germans in the 1930s: it reneges on the terms on which they believe the conflict in the West ended. It is a betrayal of the understanding they thought they had with their former enemies', which could 'produce the worst nightmare of the post-Cold War era: Weimar Russia'.

9   Thomas Friedman and Michael Mandelbaum, *That Used To Be Us: What Went Wrong with America—and How It Can Come Back*, New York 2011, p. 10.

conventional contrasts with Bush. In substance the foreign policy of the two had been much the same. Humanitarian intervention and preventive war were twins, not opposites. The occupation of Iraq, hailed in an afterword to *Ideas That Conquered the World* as a mission to bring the Wilsonian triad— 'the establishment, where they had never previously existed, of peace, democracy and free markets'—to the Middle East, had four years later shrunk in *Democracy's Good Name* to a quest for peace—depriving the regime in Baghdad of weapons of mass destruction—rather than democracy. By the time of *The Frugal Superpower,* it had 'nothing to do with democracy', and stood condemned as a bungled operation.[10] Still, though the immediate costs of Bush's invasion of Iraq were higher, Clinton's expansion of NATO was a much more lasting and graver blunder: not attempting, if failing, to solve a real problem, but creating a problem where none had otherwise existed. The US should eschew military attempts at nation-building, and seek international cooperation for its endeavours wherever possible. But major allies were not always reliable; if the West was faltering in Afghanistan, it was due to underperformance by a fragmented Europe, rather than to an overbearing, unilateral America. In the Middle East, war might still have to be waged against Iran. There closer cooperation was required with 'the only democratic and reliably pro-American country' in the

10 Mandelbaum, *The Ideas That Conquered the World,* New York 2002, p. 412; and *Democracy's Good Name,* New York 2007, p. 231 (where he reflects that if the US had taken hold of Iraq in the nineteenth century, it could eventually have created the institutions and values needed for a democracy as the British did in India, producing a local equivalent of Nehru); *The Frugal Superpower,* New York 2010, pp. 76–7, 153 (which continues to hope that 'the American efforts in Iraq might someday come to be considered successful'). The modulation is not specific to Mandelbaum; it is widely distributed in the field.

region, one with 'a legitimate government, a cohesive society, and formidable military forces: the state of Israel'.[11]

III

Mandelbaum's writing is the most strident version of a Wilsonian creed since the end of the Cold War, but in two respects it is not the purest. Of its nature, this is the tradition with the highest quotient of edulcoration—the most unequivocally apologetic—in the canon of American foreign policy, and by the same token, as the closest to ideology *tout court*, the most central to officialdom. Mandelbaum's edges are too sharp for either requirement, as his relations with the Clinton administration showed. Their perfect embodiment is to be found in Ikenberry, 'the poet laureate of liberal internationalism', from whom the dead centre of the establishment can draw on a more even unction. In 2006, the Princeton Project on National Security unveiled the Final Paper he co-authored with Anne-Marie Slaughter, after some four hundred scholars and thinkers had contributed to the endeavour under their direction.[12] With a bipartisan preface co-signed by Lake and Shultz, and the benefit of 'candid conversations with Zbigniew Brzezinski and Madeleine Albright', not to speak of the 'wisdom and insight of Henry Kissinger', *Forging a World of Liberty under Law: US National Security in the 21st Century* sought, Ikenberry and

---

11 Mandelbaum, *Frugal Superpower*, pp. 98, 189–90.

12 Slaughter, author of *A New World Order* (2004) and *The Idea that is America: Keeping Faith with Our Values in a Dangerous World* (2007), can be regarded as a runner-up in the stakes won by Ikenberry. Director of policy planning (2009–11) under Clinton at the State Department, she has, however, been ahead of the field in clamouring for interventions in Libya and Syria.

Slaughter explained, to offer nothing less than 'a collective X article' that would provide the nation with the kind of guidance in a new era that Kennan had supplied at the dawn of the Cold War—though NSC–68, too, remained an abiding inspiration.

How was a world of liberty under law to be brought about? Amid much familiar counsel, half a dozen more pointed proposals stand out. Across the planet, the United States would have to 'bring governments up to PAR'—that is, seek to make them 'popular, accountable and rights-regarding'. At the United Nations, the Security Council should be cleansed of the power of any member to veto actions of collective security, and the 'responsibility to protect' made obligatory on all member states. The Non-Proliferation Treaty needed to be tightened, by cutting down leeway for civilian development of nuclear power. In the interests of peace, the US had the right where necessary to launch preventive strikes against terrorists, and should be willing to 'take considerable risks' to stop Iran acquiring nuclear capability. Last but not least, a worldwide Concert of Democracies should be formed as an alternative seat of legitimacy for military interventions thwarted in the UN, capable of bypassing it.

Ikenberry's subsequent theoretical offering, *Liberal Leviathan* (2011), revolves around the idea that since the American world order of its subtitle 'reconciles power and hierarchy with cooperation and legitimacy', it is—emphatically —a 'liberal hegemony, not empire'. For what it rests on is a consensual 'bargain', in which the US obtains the cooperation of other states for American ends, in exchange for a system of rules that restrains American autonomy. Such was the genius of the multilateral Western alliance enshrined in NATO, and in bilateral form, of the Security Pact with Japan, during the Cold

War. In the backward outskirts of the world, no doubt, the US on occasion dealt in more imperious fashion with states that were clients rather than partners, but these were accessories without weight in the overall structure of international consent it enjoyed.[13] Today, however, American hegemony was under pressure. A 'crisis of authority' had developed, not out of its failure, but from its very success. For with the extinction of the USSR, the US had become a unipolar power, tempted to act not by common rules it observed, but simply by relationships it established, leaving its traditional allies with less motive to defer to it just as new transnational fevers and forces— conspicuously terrorism—required a new set of responses. The Bush administration had sought to meet the crisis with uni- lateral demonstrations of American will, in a regression to a conservative nationalism that was counterproductive. The solution to the crisis lay rather in a renewal of liberal interna- tionalism, capable of renegotiating the hegemonic bargain of an earlier time to accommodate contemporary realities.

That meant, first and foremost, a return to multilateralism: the updating and refitting of a liberal democratic order, as 'open, friendly, stable' as of old, but with a wider range of powers included within it.[14] The expansion of NATO, the launching of

13 A discreet footnote informs us that 'this study focuses primarily on the international order created by the United States and the other great powers. It does not fully illuminate the wider features of the world order that include America's relations with weaker, less developed and peripheral states': Ikenberry, *Liberal Leviathan: The Origins, Crisis and Transformation of the American World Order*, Princeton 2011, p. 27.

14 In the kind of metaphor that comes readily to anyone's mind: 'If the old post-war hegemonic order were a business enterprise, it would have been called American Inc. It was an order that, in important respects, was owned and operated by the United States. The crisis today is really over ownership of that company. In effect, it is a transition from a semi- private company to one that is publicly owned and operated—with an

NAFTA and the creation of the WTO were admirable examples. So too were humanitarian interventions, provided they won the assent of allies. Westphalian principles were outdated: the liberal international order now had to be more concerned with the internal condition of states than in the past. Once it had recovered its multilateral nerve, America could face the future confidently. Certainly, other powers were rising. But duly rene-gotiated, the system that served it so well in the past could 'slow down and mute the consequences of a return to multi-polarity'. The far-flung order of American hegemony, arguably the most successful in world history, was 'easy to join and hard to overturn'.[15] If the swing state of China were to sign up to its rules properly, it would become irresistible. A wise regional strategy in East Asia needs to be developed to that end. But it can be counted on: 'The good news is that the US is fabulously good at pursuing a milieu-based grand strategy'.[16]

At a global level, of course, there was bound to be some tension between the exigencies of continued American lead-ership and the norms of democratic community. The roles of liberal hegemon and traditional great power do not always coincide, and should they conflict too sharply, the grand bargain on which the peace and prosperity of the world rest would be at risk. For hegemony itself, admittedly, is not dem-ocratic.[17] But who is to complain if its outcome has been so beneficent? No irony is intended in the oxymoron of the book's

---

expanding array of shareholders and new members on the board of directors': Ikenberry, *Liberal Leviathan*, p. 335. Like the metamorphosis of News Corp, one might say.

15   Ikenberry, *Liberal Leviathan*, p. xi; 'Liberal Order Building', in Leffler and Legro, eds, *To Lead the World*, p. 103.

16   Ikenberry, *Liberal Leviathan*, pp. 343–4 ff; 'Liberal Order Building', p. 105.

17   Ikenberry, *Liberal Leviathan*, p. 299.

title. For Hobbes, a liberal Leviathan—liberal in this pious usage—would have been matter for grim humour.

IV

Within the same ideological bandwidth, an alternative prospectus can be found in the work of Charles Kupchan, once a co-author with Ikenberry, who has since drifted somewhat apart. On the policy planning staff of the State Department under Baker, during the last year of the first Bush presidency; promoted to director of European Affairs on the National Security Council under Clinton; currently holder of a chair in the School of Foreign Service and Government at Georgetown and senior fellowship at the Council on Foreign Relations, Kupchan feared for liberal internationalism as the second Bush presidency neared its end. During the Cold War, it had been the great tradition of American statecraft, combining a heavy investment in military force with a strong commitment to international institutions—power and partnership held in a balance that commanded a bipartisan consensus. Now, amid increasing polarization in Congress and public opinion, broad agreement on American foreign policy had faded, and the compact on which it was based had broken apart. For under the second Bush, power had overridden partnership, in a conservative turn whose fallout had greatly damaged the nation abroad. A new grand strategy was needed to repair the balance between the two, adapted to the changed circumstances in which the country now found itself.[18]

18 Charles Kupchan and Peter Trubowitz, 'The Illusion of Liberal Internationalism's Revival', *International Security*, Summer 2010, arguing against complacency: it was wrong to maintain that liberal internationalism was in good shape in America. A vigorous new programme was needed to restore it to health.

Chief among these was the predictable loss of the absolute global predominance the United States had enjoyed at the conclusion of the Cold War. As early as 2002, Kupchan had sought to come to terms with this in *The End of the American Era*, arguing that while the US still enjoyed a unipolar predominance, power was becoming more diffused internationally, and the American public more inward-looking. Speculative excesses on Wall Street, moreover, were troubling.[19] So far the European Union, a huge success to date, was the only major competitor on the horizon. But the US would be prudent to meet the challenge of a more plural world in advance, lending it form with the creation of a 'global directorate', comprising Russia, China and Japan as well, and perhaps states from other parts of the earth too. That would involve 'a conscious effort to insulate foreign policy and its domestic roots from partisan politics', where regional cultures and interests were unfortunately diverging. A 'self-conscious political ceasefire' was required if liberal internationalism was to be revived.[20]

A decade later, the diagnosis of *No One's World* (2012) was more radical. Economically, educationally and technologically, not only were other major powers closing the gap with the United States, but some—China foremost—would in due

---

19 Kupchan's awareness that a financial bubble had developed under Clinton did not prevent him gushing that: 'The economic side of the house could not have been in better hands. Rubin will go down in history as one of the most distinguished and talented individuals to grace the Treasury since Alexander Hamilton': *The End of the America Era: US Foreign Policy and the Geopolitics of the Twenty-First Century*, New York 2002, p. 25.

20 Kupchan, *End of the American Era*, pp. 296, 244. Kupchan's confidence in the political credentials of his country for global leadership remained unimpaired. Since it was 'not an imperial state with predatory intent', he informed his readers (in 2002) that 'the United States is certainly more wanted than resented in most regions of the world, including the Middle East': p. 228.

course overtake it in various measures. The result was going to be an interdependent world, with no single guardian or centre of gravity, in which the West could not, as Ikenberry implied, simply corral others into the institutional order it had created after the war. Rather, Kupchan argued, they would seek to revise it in accordance with their own interests and values, and the West would have to partner them in doing so. That would mean dropping the demand that they all be accredited democracies before being admitted to the shaping of a new system of international rules and conduct. Modernization was taking many different paths around the world, and there could be no dictating its forms elsewhere.

Three types of autocracy were salient in this emergent universe: communal, as in China; paternal, as in Russia; and tribal, as in the Gulf. Theocrats in Iran, strongmen in Africa, populists in Latin America, 'democracies with attitude' (less than friends of the US) like India, added to the brew. The United States, which had always stood for tolerance, pluralism and diversity at home, must extend the same multicultural respect for the variety of governments, doctrines and values abroad, and it could afford to do so. Since 'capitalism had shown its universal draw', there were few grounds for anxiety on that score. There was no need to insist on reproduction of Western forms of it. It was not liberal democracy that should be the standard for acceptance as a stakeholder in the global order to come, but 'responsible governance', enjoying legitimacy by local standards.[21]

Meanwhile, the task was to restore the cohesion and vitality of the West, threatened by re-nationalization of politics in the

---

21 Kupchan, *No One's World: The West, the Rising Rest and the Coming Global Turn*, New York 2012, p. 189.

European Union and polarization of them in the United States. At home Americans were confronted with economic distress and increasing inequality, in a political system paralysed by special interests and costly campaign finance. To overcome partisan deadlock and revitalize the economy, centrists should seek to muster a progressive populism that—without abandoning Western principles—would accept a measure of planning, 'combining strategic guidance with the dynamism that comes from market competition'. To strengthen the cohesion of the Atlantic community, NATO must not only continue to be employed for out-of-area operations, as in the Balkans or Afghanistan, but converted into 'the West's main venue for coordinating engagement with rising powers'—an endeavour in which, if it could be drawn into NATO, Moscow might in due time play a sterling role.[22]

The emerging multipolar landscape abroad, and the need to restore solvency at home, imposed a modest retrenchment of American commitments overseas. To husband resources, more reliance should be put on regional allies and a few bases might be closed. In compensation, Europe should step up its military spending. Kupchan ends his case with a general admonition: 'The United States still aspires to a level of global dominion for which it has insufficient resources and political will. American elites continue to embrace a national narrative consistent with this policy—"indispensable nation", "the American century", "America's moment"—these and other catchphrases like them still infuse political debate about US strategy. They crowd out considered debate about the more diverse global order that lies ahead.'[23]

---

22 Ibid., pp. 171, 111; 'NATO's Final Frontier: Why Russia Should Join the Atlantic Alliance', *Foreign Affairs*, May–June 2010.

23 Ibid., p. 204.

Ostensibly, in such declarations, *No One's World* marks a break with the axiomatic insistence on American primacy as the condition of international stability and progress that lies at the core of the foreign-policy consensus in the United States. Kupchan's intention, however, is not to bid farewell to the 'liberal internationalism' that served the country so staunchly during the Cold War, but to modernize it. Partnership needs to be brought back into balance with power. But the putative partners have changed and there is no point scrupling over assorted shortfalls from the norms of the Atlantic community, since all are *en route* to one form or other of capitalist modernity. Refurbishing partnership does not, however, entail relinquishing power. In the necessary work of constructing a new global consensus, 'the US must take the lead'. The purpose of a 'judicious and selective retrenchment' is not to wind down American influence at large, but 'to rebuild the bipartisan foundations for a steady and sustainable brand of US leadership'. In that task, 'American military primacy is a precious national asset', whose reconfiguration need not impair 'America's ability to project power on a global basis'.[24]

Nor, in admitting responsible autocracies to the counsels of the world, need America forsake its historic commitments to democracy and human rights. The 'responsibility to protect' was entirely consistent with it. Rogue states like Iran, the DRPK or Sudan must be confronted, and tyranny eradicated, where

---

24 Ibid., pp. 7, 179, 203; 'Grand Strategy: The Four Pillars of the Future', *Democracy—A Journal of Ideas*, Winter 2012, pp. 13–24, where Kupchan observes that the US 'must guard against doing too little', especially in the Persian Gulf and East Asia, where 'retrenchment must be accompanied by words and deeds that reassure allies of America's staying power'; while in general, since 'there is no substitute for the use of force in dealing with imminent threats', the US needs to 'refurbish its armed forces and remain ready for the full spectrum of possible missions'.

necessary by preventive intervention—optimally multilateral, as in NATO's exemplary action in Libya, but in all cases humanitarian. Empires, like individuals, have their moments of false modesty. The kind of retrenchment envisaged by Kupchan belongs to them. Between the lines, its motto is an old one: *reculer pour mieux sauter*.

REALIST IDEALS

In apparently diametric contrast has been the output of the most influential thinker commonly identified with neo-conservatism, Robert Kagan. At Policy Planning and then the Inter-American Affairs desk in the State Department under Shultz and Baker, Kagan had a controlling part in the Contra campaign of the Reagan administration, of which he later wrote the authoritative history, *A Twilight Struggle: American Power and Nicaragua, 1977–1990*. A vigorous champion of the strategy of the second Bush for recasting the world, he was foreign-policy adviser to McCain during his run for the presidency. But, like most in-and-outers, he has readily crossed party lines, supporting Clinton in 1992 and counselling his wife at the State Department during the first Obama administration. His fame dates from the book he published in 2003, *Of Paradise and Power*, during a season in Brussels as husband of the US deputy ambassador to NATO.[1] Appearing

---

1   Victoria Nuland: successively chief of staff to Strobe Talbott in the Clinton administration; deputy foreign policy adviser to Cheney and later envoy to Brussels in the Bush administration; currently assistant secretary for European affairs in the Obama administration.

at the height of transatlantic tensions over the impending invasion of Iraq, it proposed an explanation of them that
made short work of liberal bewailing of the rift in the Atlantic
community.

Europe and America were divided, not as conventionally
held, by subjective contrasts in culture or politics (the 'social
model' of the Old World), but by differing objective situations,
determining opposite outlooks. If the EU stood for law, in a
Kantian world of patience and peaceful persuasion, and the
US for power, in a Hobbesian world of vigilance and force, that
was a function of their respective military capacities: weakness
and strength. When this distribution was reversed, so were
concomitant stances: in the nineteenth century, Americans
typically appealed to international law and the values of peaceful commerce, denouncing power politics as Europeans do
today, while Europeans practised—and preached—the necessities of *Realpolitik*, and the inherently agonistic character of
an inter-state system whose ultimate resort was violence. In the
twentieth century, with the change in the correlation of forces,
there was an inversion of attitudes.[2]

The inversion was not completely symmetrical, because
above and beyond the objective 'power gap' of each epoch, there
was the particularity of the history of each side. Traumatized
by the internecine wars to which power politics in the Old
World had led, Europe after 1945 accepted for fifty years complete strategic dependence on America in the battle against
Communism. Then, once the Soviet Union had collapsed,
Europe was effectively released from any such concerns.
That did not mean, however, that it was capable of building a

2   Kagan, *Of Paradise and Power: America and Europe in the New World
    Order*, New York 2003, pp. 7–11.

counterpower to the United States, or stepping again onto the world stage as a major actor. For European integration itself was such a complex, unprecedented process that it allowed for little consistent focus on anything external to it, while at the same time weakening—with enlargement of the EU—any capacity for unitary action. Contrary to the dreams of its enthusiasts, integration was the enemy of global power projection, not the condition of it. The result was very low military spending, no sign of any increase of it, and little strategic cooperation even within the EU itself.

The American experience was entirely different. Originally, the US too had been a 'protected' republic, guarded not only by two oceans but British naval power. But even when still a comparatively weak state by the standards of the time, it had always been expansionist—from Indian clearances to Mexican annexations, the seizure of Hawaii to the conquest of the Philippines—and no American statesman had ever doubted the future of the US as a great power and the superiority of American values to all others. Thereafter, the country knew no invasion or occupation, and only limited casualties in the two World Wars, emerging after 1945 as a global power in the Cold War. In turn, the end of the Cold War had led to no retraction of US might, or withdrawal to the homeland, but on the contrary to a further expansion of American power projection, first under Clinton and then under Bush, with a giant leap forward after the attacks of 9/11. For just as Pearl Harbour had led to the occupation of Japan and the transformation of the US into an East Asian power, so the Twin Towers was going to make the US a Middle Eastern power *in situ*.[3] A new era of American hegemony was just beginning.

---

3   Kagan, *Paradise and Power*, pp. 95–6.

Under its protective mantle, Europe had entered a post-historical paradise, cultivating the arts of peace, prosperity and civilized living. Who could blame them? Americans, who stood guard against the threats in the Hobbesian world beyond this Kantian precinct, could not enter that Eden, and proud of their might, had no wish to do so. They had helped create the European Union and should cherish it, taking greater diplomatic care with its susceptibilities, just as Europeans should learn to value and adjust to the new level of American paramountcy, in a world where the triumph of capitalism made the cohesion of the West less pressing, and the remaining enemy of Muslim fundamentalism posed no serious ideological challenge to liberalism. In Washington multilateralism had always been instrumental, practised in the interests of the US, rather than as an ideal in itself. There was less need for that now, and if it had to act alone, no reason for America to be shackled by European inhibitions. The pleasures of Venus were to be respected; the obligations of Mars lay elsewhere.

Expanding the thumbnail sketch of the American past in *Paradise and Power* to a full-length survey with *Dangerous Nation* (2006), Kagan took direct aim at the self-image of the US as historically an inward-looking society, venturing only reluctantly and sporadically into the outside world. From the outset, it had on the contrary been an aggressive, expansionist force, founded on ethnic cleansing, land speculation and slave labour, unabashed heir to the ruthless legacy of British colonialism in the New World. In a detailed narrative demystifying one episode after another, from the Seven Years War to the Spanish–American War—with most of which, apart from the scant role accorded ideals of a Christian Commonwealth, William Appleman Williams would have found little to disagree—Kagan emphasized the central importance of the Civil War as the model, not only for the American use of unrestrained power with divine approval—as Lincoln put it, 'the judgements of the Lord are true and righteous altogether'—but as the template for future enterprises in ideological conquest and nation-building.[4]

Two years later, *The Return of History and the End of Dreams* made good a weak joint in the argument of *Paradise and Power*. If, after Communism, Muslim fundamentalism was left as the only ideological alternative to liberalism, yet was too archaic to pose any serious challenge to it, the conflict with it could only be a sideshow, with no resemblance to the Cold War. But in that case where were the menacing dangers from which Mars had to protect Venus? Correcting aim, Kagan now explained that the liberal international order extolled by Mandelbaum and Ikenberry had not, as they imagined, superseded great-power conflicts of old. These were re-emerging in the new century with the rise of China and recovery of Russia—vast autocracies anti-thetical by their nature to the democracies of the West, whose rulers were not mere kleptocrats lolling in wealth and power for their own sake, but leaders who believed that in bringing order and prosperity to their nations, and restoring their global influence and prestige, they were serving a higher cause. Well aware that the democracies would like to overthrow them, they were unlikely to be softened to the West, as often hoped, by mere commercial ties and economic interdependence. Historically, trade had rarely trumped the emotional forces of national pride and political competition.[5] It was a delusion to believe

4   Kagan, *Dangerous Nation: America and the World 1600–1900*, London 2006, pp. 269–70.

5   Kagan, *The Return of History and the End of Dreams*, New York 2008, pp. 78–80. This depiction of the great autocracies is just where Kupchan would later take issue with Kagan.

that a peaceful, consensual ecumene was around the corner. The time for dreams was over. The great powers shared few common values; the autocracies were antagonists. A League of Democracies was needed to prevail over them.

The World America Made (2012) brought reassurance in this struggle. Threatening though China and Russia might be, the United States was more than capable of seeing them off. Like that of Rome in its day, or for millennia imperial China, the American order of the twentieth century had established norms of conduct, shaped ideas and beliefs, determined legitimacies of rule, around itself. Peace and democracy had spread under its carapace. But these were not the fruit of American culture, wisdom or ideals. They were effects of the attraction exercised by American power, without which they could not have arrived. That power—for all the excesses or failures of which, like any predecessor, it has never been exempt—remains, exceptionally, accepted and abetted by others. In a historically unique pattern, no coalition has attempted to balance against it.

That is not because American power has always been used sparingly, or in accordance with international law, or after consultation with allies, or simply because of the benefits its liberal order confers at large. Crucial is also the fact the United States alone is not contiguous with any other great power, as are Europe, Russia, China, India and Japan, all of whom have more reason to fear their immediate neighbours than distant America. On this stage there can be no 'democratic peace', because Russia and China are not democracies; and what peace there is remains too brief an experience—since 1945, only twenty years longer than 1870–1914—to rely on nuclear weapons to keep indefinitely. The only reliable guarantee of peace continues to be US predominance. Should that fade, the world would be at risk. But happily America is not in decline. Its world-historical position is like that of Britain in 1870, not later. Domestic economic problems there are, which need to be fixed. The country is not omnipotent. But it suffers no over-stretch in troops or cash, military spending remaining a modest percentage of GDP. Its hegemony is essentially unimpaired, and will remain so, for as long as Americans harken to Theodore Roosevelt's call: 'Let us base a wise and practical international-ism on a sound and intense nationalism.'[6]

The authority of the first Roosevelt indicates the distance of this body of writing from the pedigree descending from Wilson, at its most pronounced in *Paradise and Power* and *Dangerous Nation*. But the adage itself speaks to the underlying invariant of the ideology of American foreign policy since the Second World War, which had its equivalent in imperial China: *ru biao, fa li*—decoratively Confucian, substantively Legalist.[7] Liberal internationalism is the obligatory idiom of American imperial power. Realism, in risking a closer correspondence to its prac-tice, remains facultative and subordinate. The first can declare itself as such, and regularly achieve virtually pure expression. The second must pay tribute to the first, and offer an articula-tion of the two. So it is with Kagan. In 2007, he joined forces with Ivo Daalder—a perennial Democratic stand-by, in charge of Bosnian affairs on Clinton's National Security Council, later Obama's ambassador to NATO—to advocate a League of Democracies virtually identical to the Concert of Democracies proposed a year earlier by Ikenberry and Slaughter as a way

---

6   Kagan, *The World America Made*, New York 2012, p. 98.
7   Literally: 'Confucianism on the outside, Legalism on the inside'—Legalism in Ancient China representing rule by force, Confucianism by sanctimony of benevolence.

of firming up support for humanitarian interventions.[8]
Reaffirmed in *The Return of History* and adopted as a platform
by McCain in 2008, with Kagan at his side, this conception was
Wilsonism cubed, alarming even many a *bona fide* liberal. It
was soon shot down as unwelcome to America's allies in Europe
and provocative to its adversaries in Russia and China, who
were better coaxed tactfully into the ranks of free nations than
stigmatized *ab initio* as strangers to them. *The World America
Made* had better luck. Its case captivated Obama, who confided
his enthusiasm for it on the eve of his State of the Union address
in 2012, in which he proclaimed 'America is back'.[9] Kagan would
return the compliment, crediting Obama not only with 'a very
smart policy in Asia'—the opening of a new base in Australia
'a powerful symbol of America's enduring strategic presence in
the region'—but a welcome return to 'a pro-democracy posture
not only in the Middle East, but also in Russia and Asia'. If
the record was marred by failure to secure agreement from
Baghdad to continuing US troops in Iraq, it was star-spangled

---

8 The first version of this notion was the 'Community of Democracies'
   launched by Albright in 2000—among invitees: Mubarak's Egypt, Aliyev's
   Azerbaijan and the Khalifa dynasty in Bahrain. The leading manifesto
   for a more muscular League of Democracies came from Ivo Daalder and
   James Lindsay, 'Democracies of the World, Unite', *The American Interest*,
   Jan–Feb 2007 (elder statesmen on its proposed Advisory Board to include
   Fischer, Menem, Koizumi and Singh), followed by Daalder and Kagan,
   'The Next Intervention', *Washington Post*, 6 August 2007, and Kagan, 'The
   Case for a League of Democracies', *Financial Times*, 13 May 2008.

9 'In an off-the-record meeting with leading news anchors', *Foreign Policy*
   reported, 'Obama drove home that argument using an article written
   in the *New Republic* by Kagan titled "The Myth of American Decline".
   Obama liked Kagan's article so much that he spent more than 10 minutes
   talking about it in the meeting, going over its arguments paragraph
   by paragraph, National Security Council spokesman Tommy Vietor
   confirmed.' The article was a pre-publication excerpt from *The World
   America Made*.

by the intervention in Libya. The terms of Kagan's praise speak for themselves: 'Obama placed himself in a great tradition of American presidents who have understood America's special role in the world. He thoroughly rejected the so-called realist approach, extolled American exceptionalism, spoke of universal values and insisted that American power should be used, when appropriate, on behalf of those values.'[10]

II

Realism comes, without such disavowals, in a more unusual amalgam in the outlook of a thinker with Cold War credentials superior even to those of Kagan. Responsible, as Carter's national security adviser, for the American operation arming and bankrolling the Islamist revolt against Afghan communism and subsequent war to drive the Red Army out of the country, Zbigniew Brzezinski is the highest former officeholder in the gallery of contemporary US strategists. From a Polish *szlachta* background, his European origins offer a misleading comparison with Kissinger.[11] The contrast in formation and outlook is marked. Where Kissinger fancied himself as the heir to balance-of-power statesmen of the Old World, Brzezinski comes from the later, and quite distinct, line of geopolitics. This is a filiation more radically distant from the Wilsonian pieties to which Kissinger has always paid nominal tribute. But in this case the harder-edged realism to which it tends, free from liturgies of democracy and the market, comes combined with a *Kulturkritik* of classically minatory stamp, whose genesis lies

---

10 *Weekly Standard*, 28 March 2011.
11 Brzezinski did not arrive in North America as a refugee in 1938, but as an offspring of the Polish Consul-General in Canada.

in the rhetoric of malaise associated with Carter's presidency. Brzezinki's tenure in power, cut short when Reagan was elected in 1980, was only half Kissinger's, leaving him with a greater drive to make his mark during subsequent administrations, with a succession of five books timed around electoral calendars: *Out of Control* (1993) as Clinton took office; *The Grand Chessboard* (1997) as he started his second term; *The Choice* (2004) as Kerry battled Bush for the White House; *Second Chance* (2007), as the prospect for Democratic recapture of it loomed; *Strategic Vision* (2012), as Obama approached a second term.[12]

Brzezinski laid out his general vision in the first of these works, which he dedicated to Carter. Far from victory in the Cold War ushering in a new world order of international tranquillity, security and common prosperity, the United States was faced with an era of global turmoil, of which the country was itself one of the chief causes. For while the Soviet Union might have gone, there were no grounds for domestic complacency. American society was not just pockmarked with high levels of indebtedness, trade deficits, low savings and investment, sluggish productivity growth, inadequate health care, inferior secondary education, deteriorating infrastructure, greedy rich and homeless poor, racism and crime, political gridlock—ills

---

12 As could be surmised from this scheduling, Brzezinski's ties to the Democratic Party have been closer than Kissinger's to the Republican, without being exclusive: see his amicable dialogue with Brent Scowcroft, national security adviser to the elder Bush, in *America and the World: Conversations on the Future of American Foreign Policy*, New York 2008. His comments on Obama have been generally laudatory—'a genuine sense of strategic direction and a solid grasp of what today's world is all about'—while urging the president to be more intrepid: 'From Hope to Audacity: Appraising Obama's Foreign Policy', *Foreign Affairs*, Jan–Feb 2010.

enumerated by Brzezinski long before they became a standard list in buck-up literature along Friedman–Mandelbaum
lines. It was more deeply corroded by a culture of hedonistic
self-indulgence and demoralized individualism. A 'permissive cornucopia' had bred massive drug use, sexual license,
visual-media corruption, declining civic pride and spiritual
emptiness. Yet at the same time, in the attractions of its material wealth and seductions of its popular culture, the US was a
destabilizing force everywhere in the less advanced zones of the
world, disrupting traditional ways of life and tempting unpre-
pared populations into the same 'dynamic escalation of desire'
that was undoing America.

Such effects were all the more incendiary in that across most
of the—still poor and underdeveloped—earth, turmoil was in
store as the youth bulge unleashed by population explosion
interacted with the growth of literacy and electronic communications systems to detonate a 'global political awakening'.
As this got under way, newly activated masses were prone to
primitive, escapist and manichean fantasies, of an ethnically
narrow and often anti-Western bent, insensible of the needs
for pluralism and compromise. The export of an American
lack of self-restraint could only add fuel to the fire. Politically,
the United States was the guardian of order in the world; culturally, it was a force sowing disorder. This was an extremely
dangerous contradiction. To resolve it, America would have
to put its own house in order. 'Unless there is some deliber-
ate effort to re-establish the centrality of some moral criteria
for the exercise of self-control over gratification as an end in
itself, the phase of American predominance may not last long',
Brzezinski warned: it was unlikely that a 'global power that
is not guided by a globally relevant set of values can for long

exercise its predominance'.[13] A new respect for nature must ultimately be part of this, even if rich and poor societies might not share the same ecological priorities. At home economic and social problems, however acute, were less intractable than metaphysical problems of common purpose and meaning. What America needed above all—Brzezinski disavowed any particular prescriptions for reform—was cultural revaluation and philosophical self-examination, not to be achieved overnight.

Meanwhile, the affairs of the world could not wait. American hegemony might be at risk from American dissolution, but the only alternative to it was global anarchy—regional wars, economic hostilities, social upheavals, ethnic conflicts. For all its faults, the United States continued to enjoy an absolute superiority in all four key dimensions of power—military, economic, technological, cultural; and it was a benign hegemon, whose dominance, though in some ways reminiscent of earlier empires, relied more than its predecessors on co-option of dependent elites rather than outright subjugation. Huntington was right that sustained American primacy was central to the future of freedom, security, open markets and peaceful relations worldwide. To preserve these, the US required 'an integrated, comprehensive and long-term geopolitical strategy' for the great central landmass of the earth, on whose fate the pattern of global power depended: 'For America, the chief geopolitical prize is Eurasia.'[14]

From *The Grand Chessboard* (1997) onwards, this would be the object of Brzezinski's work, with a more detailed set of prescriptions than any of his peers has offered. Since the

---

13 Brzezinski, *Out of Control*, New York 1993, p. xii.

14 Brzezinski, *The Grand Chessboard*, New York 1997, p. 29.

end of the Cold War, his construction begins, a non-Eurasian power was for the first time in history preeminent in Eurasia. America's global primacy depended on its ability to sustain that preponderance. How was it to do so? In the struggle against communism, the US had entrenched itself at the western and eastern peripheries of the mega-continent, in Europe and Japan, and along its southern rim, in the Gulf. Now, however, the Soviet Union had vanished and the Russia that succeeded it had become a huge black hole across the middle of Eurasia, of top strategic concern for the United States. It was illusory to think that democracy and a market economy could take root swiftly, let alone together, in this geopolitical void. Traditions for the former were lacking, and shock therapy to introduce the latter had been folly.

The Russian elites were resentful of the historic reduction of their territory, and potentially vengeful; there existed the makings of a Russian fascism. The biggest single blow for them was the independence of Ukraine, to which they were not resigned. To check any temptations of revanchism in Moscow, the US should build a barrier encompassing Ukraine, Azerbaijan and Uzbekistan to the south, and—crucially—extending NATO to the east. For Brzezinski, expansion of the Atlantic Alliance to the borders of Russia was the most important single priority of the post-Cold War era. Pushed through by his former pupil Albright at the State Department—a son was also closely involved at the National Security Council—its realization was a huge achievement. For with Europe serving as a springboard for the progressive expansion of democracy deeper into Eurasia, the arrival of NATO at their frontiers might in due course persuade Russians that it was to good relations with the EU that they should turn for their future, abandoning any nostalgia for an imperial past, even perhaps—why not?—breaking up into three more modest states, one west of the Urals, one in Siberia and a third in the Far East, or a loose confederation between them.

The EU, for its part, sharing a common civilizational heritage with the US, no doubt pointed the way to larger forms of post-national organization: 'But first of all, Europe is America's essential geopolitical bridgehead on the Eurasian continent.' Regrettably, it was not itself in the pink of condition, suffering from a pervasive decline in internal vitality and loss of creative momentum, with symptoms of escapism and lack of nerves in the Balkans. Germany was helpful in the expansion of NATO, and France could balance it with Poland. Britain was an irrelevance. But as to their common status, Brzezinski did not mince words: 'The brutal fact is that Western Europe, and increasingly Central Europe, remains largely an American protectorate, with its allied states reminiscent of ancient vassals and tributaries.'[15] This was not a healthy situation. Nor, on the other hand, was the prospect of Europe becoming a great power capable of competing with the United States, in such regions of vital interest to it as the Middle East or Latin America, desirable. Any such rivalry would be destructive to both sides. Each had their own diplomatic traditions. But 'an essentially multilateralist Europe and a somewhat unilateralist America make for a perfect marriage of convenience. Acting separately, America can be preponderant but not omnipotent; Europe can be rich but impotent. Acting together, America and Europe are in effect globally omnipotent.'[16]

This last was an uncharacteristic flourish. At the other end

---

15 Ibid., p. 58.
16 Brzezinski, *The Choice*, New York 2004, pp. 91, 96.

of Eurasia, Brzezinski was more prudent. There, for want of any collective security system, Japan could not play the same kind of role as Germany in Europe. It remained, however, an American bastion, which could be encouraged to play the role of an Asian Canada—wealthy, harmless, respected, phil-anthropic. But what of China? Proud of his role under Carter in negotiating diplomatic relations with Beijing as a counter-weight to Moscow, Brzezinski—like Kissinger, for the same reasons—has consistently warned against any policies that could be construed as building a coalition against China, which was inevitably going to become the dominant regional—though not yet a global—power. The best course would clearly be 'to co-opt a democratizing and free-marketing China into a larger Asian regional framework of cooperation'. Even short of such a happy outcome, however, 'China should become America's Far Eastern anchor in the more traditional domain of power politics', serving as 'a vitally important geostrategic asset—in that regard coequally important with Europe and more weighty than Japan—in assuring Eurasia's stability'.[17] Still, a thorny question remained: 'To put it very directly, how large a Chinese sphere of influence, and where, should America be prepared to accept as part of a policy of successfully co-opting China into world affairs? What areas now outside of China's political radius might have to be conceded to the realm of the reemerging Celestial Empire?'[18] To resolve that ticklish issue, a strategic consensus between Washington and Beijing was required, but it did not have to be settled immediately. For the moment, it would be important to invite China to join the G7.

17 Brzezinski, *Grand Chessboard*, pp. 54, 193, 207.
18 Ibid., p. 54.

Western and eastern flanks of Eurasia secured, there remained the southern front. There, some thirty lesser states comprised an 'oblong of violence' stretching from Suez to Xinjiang that could best be described as a Global Balkans—a zone rife with ethnic and religious hatreds, weak governments, a menacing youth bulge, not to speak of dangers of nuclear proliferation, but rich in oil, gas and gold. The US was too distant from Central Asia to be able to dominate it, but could block Russian attempts to restore its hold on the area. In the Middle East, on the other hand, the US had since the Gulf War enjoyed an exclusive preponderance. But this was a brittle dominion, Brzezinski warned, lacking political or cultural roots in the region, too reliant on corrupt local elites to do its bidding. After the attack on the Twin Towers and the Pentagon, he was critical of the War on Terror as an overreaction that mistook a tactic—age-old among the weak—for an enemy, refusing to see the political problems in the Arab world that lay behind it, in which the US had played a part. Nor was it any good trying to foist democracy on the region as a solution. Patience was needed in the Middle East, where gradual social modernization was the best way forward, not artificial democratization. The US and EU should spell out the terms of a peace treaty between Israelis and Palestinians, on which there was an international consensus: mutual adjustment of the 1967 borders, merely symbolic return of refugees and demilitarization of any future Palestine.

In Brzezinski's later works, many of these themes were radicalized. *Second Chance* (2007) offered a scathing retrospect of the foreign-policy performance of Bush I, Clinton and Bush II. The first, though handling the end of the Cold War skillfully enough (if unable to see the importance of backing Ukrainian independence and breaking up the Soviet Union), bungled the unsatisfactory outcome of the Gulf War, which might have been avoided by exchanging forcible exile for Saddam against preservation of the Iraqi Army, and missed the unique chance it gave the White House of imposing a peace settlement on Israel and the Palestinians in the wake of it. There was no real substance to his talk of a new world order, which in its absence could only look like a relapse to the 'old imperial order'. Clinton had one great accomplishment to his credit, expansion of NATO; another of some moment, in the creation of the WTO; and had at least restored fiscal balance at home. But he too had failed to get a peace settlement in the Middle East, bringing Israelis and Palestinians together at Camp David too late, and then favouring the former too much. His faith in the vapid mantra of globalization had bred a complacent economic determinism, resulting in a casual and opportunist conduct of foreign affairs.

Worse still were the neoconservative doctrines that replaced it, which without 9/11 would have remained a fringe phenomenon. Under the second Bush, these had led to a war in Iraq whose costs far outweighed its benefits, not only diverting resources from the struggle in Afghanistan, but causing a grievous loss of American standing in the world. This dismal record was compounded by failure of the Doha Round, and an ill-starred nuclear deal with India, risking Chinese ire.[19]

19 Brzezinski would later criticize Obama's sale of advanced weaponry to India too, and on the same grounds warn against advocates of a closer bond with Delhi. Prominent among the latter has been Fareed Zakaria, who enthuses that it is all but inevitable that the US will develop more than a merely strategic relationship with India. For not only are Indians perhaps the most pro-American nation on earth, but the two peoples are so alike—'Indians understand America. It is a noisy, open society with a chaotic democratic system, like theirs. Its capitalism looks distinctly like America's free-for-all', just as 'Americans understand India', having had

Virtually everywhere, major geopolitical trends had moved against the United States. 'Fifteen years after its coronation as global leader, America is becoming a fearful and lonely democracy in a politically antagonistic world'.[20] Nor was the situation better at home. Of the fourteen out of twenty maladies of the country he had listed in 1993 that were measurable, nine had worsened since. The US was in bad need of a cultural revolution and regime change of its own.

Yet, *Strategic Vision* insists five years later, American decline would be a disaster for the world, which more than ever is in want of responsible American leadership. Though still skirting obsolescence at home and looking out of touch abroad, the US retained great strengths, along with its weaknesses. These it should put to work in a grand strategy for Eurasia that could now be updated. Its objectives ought to be two. The West should be enlarged by the integration of Turkey and Russia fully within its framework, extending its frontiers to Van and Vladivostok, and all but reaching Japan. European youth could re-populate and dynamize Siberia. In East Asia, the imperative was to create a balance between the different powers of the region. Without prejudice to that aim, China could be invited to form a G2 with the United States. But China should remember that, if it gave way to nationalist temptations, it could find itself rapidly isolated, for 'unlike America's favourable geographical

such 'a positive experience with Indians in America'. The ties between the two countries, Zakaria predicts, will be like those of the US with Britain or Israel: 'broad and deep, going well beyond government officials and diplomatic negotiations': *The Post-American World*, New York 2008, pp. 150–2, a work of which Christopher Layne has remarked that it would more appropriately be entitled *The Now and Forever American World*. See Sean Clark and Sabrina Hoque, eds, *Debating a Post-American World: What Lies Ahead?*, New York 2012, p. 42.

20 Brzezinski, *Second Chance*, New York 2007, p. 181.

location, China is potentially vulnerable to a strategic encircle-ment. Japan stands in the way of China's access to the Pacific Ocean, Russia separates China from Europe, and India towers over an ocean named after itself that serves as China's main access to the Middle East.' A map repairs the tactful omission of the US from this ring of powers.[21]

Geopolitically then, 'America must adopt a dual role. It must be the *promoter* and *guarantor* of greater and broader unity in the West, and it must be the *balancer* and *conciliator* between the major powers in the East.'[22] But it should never forget that, as Raymond Aron once wrote, 'the strength of a great power is diminished if it ceases to serve an idea'. The higher purpose of American hegemony, which would not last forever, was the creation of a stable framework to contain potential turmoil, based on a community of shared values that alone could over-come 'the global crisis of the spirit'. Democracy, the demand for which had been overrated even in the fall of communism, in which many other longings were involved, was not the indi-cated answer.[23] That lay in another ideal: 'Only by identifying itself with the idea of universal human dignity—with its basic requirement of respect for culturally diverse political, social and religious emanations—can America overcome the risk that the global political awakening will turn against it.'[24]

In its peculiar register, Brzezinski's overall construction—part geopolitical, part metacultural—does not escape, but

---

21 Brzezinski, *Strategic Vision*, New York 2012, pp. 85–6.

22 Ibid., p. 185.

23 Brzezinski, *Out of Control*, pp. 54, 60–1. In fact, democracy had become since the fall of communism a dubiously uniform ideology, 'most govern-ments and most political actors paying lip-service to the same verities and relying on the same clichés'.

24 Brzezinski, *Second Chance*, p. 204.

replicates, the dualism of the American ideology for foreign service since 1945.[25] In his formulation: 'idealistic internationalism is the common-sense dictate of hard-nosed realism'. But in his latter-day version of the combinatory, both components have a markedly European inflection: a *Realpolitik* based on a geographical calculus descending from Mackinder, and a *Kulturkritik* of contemporary mores descending from Arnold or Nietzsche. As a tradition, *Kulturkritik* has always tended to a pessimism at radical variance with the optimism of the American Creed, as Myrdal classically depicted it. In Brzezinski's case, the late absence of that national note has no doubt also been a function of his fortunes, the coolness of his view of post-Cold War euphoria due in part to displeasure that credit for the collapse of communism was so widely ascribed to the Reagan rather than Carter or earlier administrations, and the acerbity of his judgement of subsequent presidencies to his failure to return to high office—a sharpness of tongue at once cause and effect of lack of preferment. In his capacity to deliver blunt truths about his adopted country and its allies—the United States with its 'hegemonic elite' of 'imperial bureaucrats', a Europe of 'protectorates' and 'vassals' dependent on them—Brzezinski breaks ranks with his fellows. Emollience is not among his failings.

In its departures from the American norm, the substance, as well as style, of his output bears the marks of his European origins. Above all, in the relentless Russophobia, outlasting the fall of communism and the disappearance of the Soviet foe, that is a product of centuries of Polish history. For two

---

25 For 'metaculture' and *Kulturkritik* as a subspecies of it, see Francis Mulhern, *Culture/Metaculture*, London 2000, and 'Beyond Metaculture', *New Left Review* 16, July–Aug 2002.

decades his Eurasian strategies would revolve around the spectre of a possible restoration of Russian power. China, by contrast, he continued to view, not only out of personal invest- ment in his past, but anachronistic fixation on the conjuncture of his achievement, as America's ally against a common enemy in Moscow. When it finally dawned on him that China had become a much greater potential threat to the global hegem- ony of the United States, he simply switched pieces on the chessboard of his imaginary, now conceiving Russia as the geopolitical arm of an elongated West linking Europe to Japan, to encircle China, rather than China as the American anchor in the east against Russia. In their detachment from reality, these schemes—culminating at one point in a Trans-Eurasian Security system stretching from Tokyo to Dublin—belong with the American self-projections from which Brzezinski's think- ing otherwise departs: where tough-minded realism becomes rosy-eyed ideation.

III

Tighter and more dispassionate, the writing of Robert Art, occupying a position further away from the Wilsonian centre of the spectrum, offers a pointed contrast. Analytic precision, closely reasoned argument and lucid moderation of judgement are its hallmarks, producing a realism at higher resolution.[26] The difference begins with Art's definition of his object. 'Grand strategy differs from foreign policy'. The latter covers all the ways the interests of a state may be conceived, and the instruments

---

26 Art's three role models, he explains, are Spykman, Lippman and Tucker, authors of 'perhaps the best books written on American grand strategy in the last half century', whose geopolitical tradition he has sought to follow: *A Grand Strategy for America*, New York 2003, p. xv.

with which they may be pursued. The former refers more narrowly to the ways a state employs its military power to support its national interests: 'Foreign policy deals with all the goals and all the instruments of statecraft; grand strategy deals with all the goals but only one instrument.'[27] It is the role of armed force in America's conduct in the world that is the unswerving focus of Art's concern. Less visible to the public eye than others, with no bestseller to his name, from his chair at Brandeis he has served more discreetly as a consultant to the Pentagon— Long-Range Planning Staff under Weinberger—and the CIA.

Art's starting point is the fungibility—not unlimited, but substantial—of military power: the different ways in which it can be cashed out politically or economically. Coercive diplomacy, using the threat of force to compel another state to do the bidding of a stronger one—tried by Washington, he notes, over a dozen times between 1990 and 2006—is rarely a conspicuous success: among its failures to date, attempts to oblige Iran or the DPRK to abandon their nuclear programmes. Nuclear weapons, on the other hand, are more useful than is often supposed, not only as deterrence against potential attack, but for the wide margin of safety they afford for diplomatic manoeuvre; the advantages to be extracted from states to which their protection may extend; and the resources which the cost-efficiency of the security they provide releases for other purposes. More generally, so long as anarchy obtains between states, force not only remains the final arbiter of disputes among them, but affects the ways these may be settled short of force.

Of that there is no more positive example than the role of US military power in binding together the nations of the free world after 1945, by creating the political conditions for the

---

27 Art, *America's Grand Strategy and World Politics*, New York 2008, p. 1.

evolutionary intertwining of their economies: 'Force cannot be irrelevant as a tool of policy for America's economic relations with her great power allies: America's military preeminence politically pervades these relations. It is the cement of economic interdependence.'[28] The Japanese and West Europeans could grow and prosper together under the safety of a US nuclear umbrella whose price was submission to American monetary and diplomatic arrangements. For 'it would be odd indeed if this dependence were not exploited by the United States on political and economic matters of interest to it'. So it has been—Washington first obliging its ally Britain, even before the arrival of the A-bomb, to accept fixed exchange rates at Bretton Woods, and then cutting the link of the dollar to gold in 1971, not only without consulting its allies, but for twenty years thereafter confronting them with unpleasant choices between inflation and recession. Without its military pre-eminence, as well as its industrial strength, the US could never have acted as it did: 'America used her military power politically to cope with her dollar devaluation problem.' We are a long way from the placebo of the nation of nations.

Since the end of the Cold War, what are the purposes the armed forces of the US should serve? Atypically, Art ranks them in an explicit hierarchy, distinguishing between interests that are actually vital and those that are only desirable, in an updated geopolitics. Vital include, in order of importance: security of the homeland against weapons of mass destruction, prevention of great power conflicts in Eurasia, a steady flow of oil from Arabia. Desirable, in order of importance, are: preservation of an open international economic order, fostering of democracy and defence of human rights, protection of the

28 Ibid., p. 132.

global environment. The course Art recommends for pursuing these goals is 'selective engagement': a strategy that gives priority to America's vital interests, but 'holds out hope that the desirable interests can be partially realized', striking a balance between trying to use force to do too much and to do too little.[29] Operationally, selective engagement is a strategy of forward defence, allowing a reduction of overall American troop levels, but requiring the maintenance of US military bases overseas, where they serve not only as guardians of political stability, but also checks on economic nationalism.

In the same way, the expansion of the Atlantic Alliance to the east—a top-down project of the Clinton administration from the start—was designed not just to fill a security vacuum or give NATO a new lease of life, but to preserve American hegemony in Europe. In the Middle East, policy in the Gulf should be to 'divide, not conquer', pitting the various oil-rich rulers against each other without attempting closer management of them. In Afghanistan, the US had to stay the course. On the other hand, it would be folly to attack Iran. The security of Israel was an essential American interest. But a settlement of the Palestinian problem would be the most important single step in undercutting support for anti-American terrorism. The path to achieving it lay in a formal defence treaty with Israel, stationing US forces on its territory and obliging it to disgorge the occupied territories. In East Asia, the security of South Korea was also an essential American interest. But the goal of American policy should be the denuclearization and unification of the peninsula. Should China gain preponderant influence in Korea thereafter, that could be accepted. The US alliance with Korea was expendable, as the alliance with

29 Ibid., p. 235.

Japan—the bedrock of American presence, and condition of its maritime supremacy, in East Asia—was not.

Looming over the region was the rise of China. How should the United States respond to it? Not by treating the PRC as a potential danger comparable to the USSR of old. The Soviet Union had been a geopolitical menace to both Europe and the Gulf. China was neither. If it eventually came to dominate much of Southeast Asia, as it might Korea, so what? Provided the US held naval bases in Singapore, the Philippines or Indonesia, while Europe, the Gulf, India, Russia and Japan remained independent or tied to the US, Chinese hegemony on land in East and Southeast Asia would not tip the global balance of power. The PRC could never be the same kind of threat to American influence that the Soviet Union, straddling the vast expanse of Eurasia, had once represented. Friction over Taiwan aside— resolvable in due course either by reduction of the island to a dependency of the mainland through economic leverage, or political reunification with it if the mainland democratized— there was no basis for war between America and China. Beijing would build up a powerful navy, but it would not be one capable of challenging US command of the Pacific. In fact, China needed to acquire a sea-based nuclear deterrent if mutually assured destruction was to work, and the US should not oppose it doing so.

The role of force endured, as it must. American political and economic statecraft could not be successful without the projection of military power abroad to shape events, not just to react to them; to mould an environment, not merely to survive in one. That did not mean it should be employed recklessly or indiscriminately. Art, unlike so many who supported it at the time and dissociated themselves from it later, was a prominent opponent of the war on Iraq six months before it began,[30] and once underway condemned it as a disaster. 'Muscular Wilsonism' had led to disgrace and loss of legitimacy. Even selective engagement was not immune from the inherent temptations of an imperial power—for such was the United States—to attempt too much, rather than too little. Its global primacy would last only a few more decades. Thereafter, the future probably lay in the transition to 'an international system suspended for a long time between a US-dominated and a regionally based, decentralized one'.[31] The country would do well to prepare for that time, and meanwhile put its economic house in order.

As a theorist of national security, Art remains within the bounds of the foreign-policy establishment, sharing its unquestioned assumption of the need for American primacy in the world, if disorder is not to supervene.[32] But within its

---

30 See 'War with Iraq is *Not* in America's National Interest', *New York Times*, 26 September 2002, an advertisement signed by some thirty 'scholars of international security affairs': among others, Robert Jervis, John Mearsheimer, Robert Pape, Barry Posen, Richard Rosecrance, Thomas Schelling, Stephen Van Evera, Stephen Walt and Kenneth Waltz.

31 Art, *America's Grand Strategy*, p. 387.

32 Art seeks to distinguish 'dominion' from 'primacy'. The former would indeed 'create a global American imperium' allowing the US to 'impose its dictates on others' and, he concedes, while 'the US has never pursued a full-fledged policy of dominion', since 1945 'semblances of it have appeared four times': at the outset of the Cold War (undeclared rollback); under Reagan; after the end of the Gulf War (the Defense Planning Guidance of 1992); and under the second Bush. 'Dominion is a powerful temptation for a nation as strong as the United States.' But it is impossible to achieve and any whiff of it is self-defeating. Primacy, on the other hand, is 'superior influence', not 'absolute rule'. Nor is it a grand strategy, but simply that margin of extra military strength which makes the state that enjoys it the most influential actor at large: *A Grand Strategy*, pp. 87–92. But since, as Samuel Huntington once observed, there is by definition no such thing as absolute power in an inter-state system, the

literature, the intellectual quality of his work stands out, not only for its lack of rhetorical pathos, but the calmness and respect with which other, less conventional, positions are considered, and certain orthodox taboos broken. Opposition from the outset to the war on Iraq, impatience with obduracy from Israel, acceptance of regional ascendancy for China, can be found in Brzezinski too. But not only utterly dissimilar styles separate them. Art is not obsessed with Russia—its absence is striking in his recent reflections—and his proposals for Tel Aviv and Beijing have more edge: forcing an unwelcome treaty on the one; conceding an extended hegemony on land, and a strike capacity at sea, to the other. In all this, the spirit of the neorealism, in its technical sense, to which Art belongs—whose foremost representative Kenneth Waltz could advocate proliferation of nuclear weapons as favourable to peace—is plain.

But neorealism as pure theory, a paradigm in the study of international relations, is one thing; the ideological discourse of American foreign policy, another. Through those portals, it cannot enter unaccompanied. Art does not escape this rule. Selective engagement, he explains, is a '*Realpolitik* plus' strategy. What is the plus? The night in which all cows are black: 'realism cum liberalism'. The first aims to 'keep the United States secure and prosperous'; the second to 'nudge the world towards the values the nation holds dear—democracy, free markets, human rights and international openness'.[33] The distinction between them corresponds to the hierarchy of America's interests: realism secures what is vital,

---

power of any state always being relative to that of others, the distinction between the two terms is inevitably porous.

33 Art, *America's Grand Strategy*, p. 235.

liberalism pursues what is only desirable. The latter is an add-on: Art's writing is overwhelmingly concerned with the former. But it is not mere adornment, without incidence on the structure of his conception as a whole. For the line between the vital and the desirable is inherently blurred, Art's own listings of the two fluctuating over time. 'International economic openness', the classic Open Door, is—realistically, one might say—ranked second out of (then) five top American interests in 'A Defensible Defense' (1991), only to be downgraded to fourth out of six in 'Geopolitics Updated' (1998), on the grounds that 90 per cent of US GDP is produced at home. In *A Grand Strategy for America* (2003), there is only one vital interest: defence of the homeland, and two highly important ones—peace in Eurasia and Gulf oil.[34] War should not be waged to further the promotion of democracy or protection of human rights (ranked without supporting reasons above global climate change)—but there will be exceptions, where military intervention to create democracy or restrain slaughter is required. Art admits, candidly enough, that selective engagement has its 'pitfalls', since unless care is taken, 'commitments can become open-ended', while himself falling in with the perfect example of just that—'staying the course' (to where?) in Afghanistan.[35] What is selective about a requirement for 'permanent forward operating bases' in East and Southeast Asia, Europe, the Persian Gulf and Central Asia, eschewing 'in general' only South America and Africa?[36] The telltale formula, repeated more than once in explaining the merits of this version of grand strategy, informs Americans that US power-projection can 'shape events' and 'mould the

---

34 Art, *A Grand Strategy*, p. 46; *America's Grand Strategy*, pp. 190, 235, 237.
35 Art, *America's Grand Strategy*, pp. 254, 379.
36 Ibid., p. 374.

environment' to 'make them more congenial to US interests.'[37] In the vagueness and vastness of this ambition, open-ended with a vengeance, realism dissolves itself into a potentially all-purpose justification of any of the adventures conducted in the name of liberalism.

---

37 Ibid., pp. 373, 235.

ECONOMY FIRST

Are there any significant constructions in the discourse of American foreign policy that escape its mandatory dyad? Perhaps, in its way, one. In background and aim Thomas P. M. Barnett belongs in the company of grand strategists, but in outlook is at an angle to them. Trained as a Sovietologist at Harvard, he taught at the Naval War College, worked in the Office of Force Transformation set up by Rumsfeld at the Pentagon, voted for Kerry and now directs a consultancy offering technical and financial connexions to the outside world in regions like Iraqi Kurdistan. *Great Powers: America and the World After Bush*, the product of this trajectory, is unlike anything else in the literature, in manner and in substance. In the breezy style of a salesman with an inexhaustible store of snappy slogans, it lays out a eupeptic, yet far from conventional, vision of globalization as the master narrative for grasping the nature and future of US planetary power—one calculated to disconcert equally the *bien-pensant* platitudes of Clintonism, and their condemnation by critics like Brzezinski, in a triumphalism so confident it dispenses with a good many of its customary accoutrements.

America, Barnett's argument runs, has no cause for doubt or despondency in the aftermath of a war in Iraq that was well-intentioned, but hopelessly mismanaged. Its position is not slipping: 'This is still America's world.' For as the earth's first and most successful free-market economy and multiethnic political union, whose evolution prefigures that of humanity at large, 'we are modern globalization's source code—its DNA.' The implication? 'The United States isn't coming to a bad end but a good beginning—our American system successfully projected upon the world.'[1] That projection, properly understood, neither involves nor requires US promotion of democracy at large. For Barnett, who declares himself without inhibition an economic determinist, it is capitalism that is the real revolutionary force spawned by America, whose expansion renders unnecessary attempts to introduce parliaments and elections around the world. The Cold War was won by using US military strength to buy time for Western economic superiority over the Soviet Union to do its work. So too in the post-Cold War era, peace comes before justice: if the US is willing to go slow in its political demands on regions that neither know nor accept liberal democracy, while getting its way on economic demands of them, it will see the realization of its ideals within them in due course. 'America needs to ask itself: is it more important to make globalization truly global, while retaining great-power peace and defeating whatever anti-globalization insurgencies may appear in the decades ahead? Or do we tether our support for globalization's advance to the upfront demand that the world first resembles us politically?'[2]

---

1   Thomas P. M. Barnett, *Great Powers: America and the World After Bush*, New York 2009, pp. 1–2, 4.

2   Ibid., p. 30.

So today it is not a league of democracies that is called for, but a league of capitalist powers, committed to making the order of capital workable on a world stage, rebranded along Lincoln lines as a 'team of rivals' comprising China and Russia along with Japan, Europe, India, Brazil. Americans have no reason to baulk at the inclusion of either of their former adversaries in the Cold War. It took the United States half a century after its revolution to develop a popular multi-party democracy, even then excluding women and slaves, and it protected its industries for another century beyond that. China is closing the distance between it and America with the methods of Hamilton and Clay, though it now needs regulatory reforms like those of the Progressive Era (as does contemporary Wall Street). Its nationalist foreign policy already resembles that of the first Roosevelt. As for Russia, with its economic brutalism and crude materialism, its mixture of raw individualism and collective chauvinism, it is in its Gilded Age—and there will be plenty of other versions of its younger self America is going to bump up against, who may not take it at its own estimation: 'Moscow pragmatically sees America for what it truly is right now: militarily overextended, financially overdrawn and ideologically overwrought.' But its anti-Americanism is largely for show. In view of Russia's past, the US could scarcely ask for a better partner than Putin, whose regime is nationalist, like that of China, but not expansionist. 'Neither represents a systemic threat, because each supports globalization's advance, and so regards the world's dangers much as we do', with no desire to challenge the dominant liberal trade order, merely to extract maximum selfish benefit from it.[3] The varieties of capitalism these and other rising contenders represent are one of its assets

3   Ibid., pp. 184–5, 227–31.

as a system, allowing experiments and offsets in its forms that can only strengthen it.

Between the advanced core and the more backward zones of the world, a historic gap remains to be overcome. But a capitalist domino effect is already at work. In that sense, 'Africa will be a knock-off of India, which is a knock-off of China, which is a knock-off of South Korea, which is a knock-off of Japan, which half a century ago was developed by us as a knock-off of the United States. Call it globalization's "six degrees of replication".[4] But if economically speaking, 'history really has "ended"', transition across the gap is going to generate unprecedented social turmoil, as traditional populations are uprooted and customary ways of life destroyed before middle-class prosperity arrives. Religion will always be the most important bridge across the gap, as a way of coping with that tumult, and as globalization spreads, it is logical that there should be the greatest single religious awakening in history, because it is bringing the most sweeping changes in economic conditions ever known. In this churning, the more mixed and multicultural societies become, the more individuals, in the absence of a common culture, cling to their religious identity. There too, America in its multicultural patterns of faith is the leading edge of a universal process.

What of the war zone where Barnett himself has been involved? For all the spurious pretexts advanced for it, the decision to invade Iraq was not irrational: however mismanaged, it has shaken up the stagnation of the Middle East, and begun to reconnect the region with the pull of globalization. By contrast, the war in Afghanistan is a dead end, only threatening further trouble with Pakistan. Bush's greatest failure was that he got

4　Ibid., *Great Powers*, p. 248.

nothing from Iran for toppling its two Sunni enemies, Saddam and the Taliban, and persisted—in deference to Saudi and Israeli pressure—in trying to contain rather than co-opt it. So it is no surprise that the mullahs have concluded nuclear weapons would keep them safe from US attempts to topple them too. In that they are absolutely right. Iran should be admitted to the nuclear club, since the only way to stop it acquiring a capability would be to use nuclear weapons against it—conventional bombing would not do the trick. Needed in the Middle East is not a futile attack on Iran by Israel or America, but a regional security system which the big Asian powers, China and India, both more dependent on Gulf oil than America, cooperate with the US to enforce, and Iran—the only country in the region where governments can be voted out of office—plays the part to which its size and culture entitle it.[5]

For the rest, by raising the bar so high against great power wars, US military force has been a huge gift to humanity. But the latter-day Pentagon needs to cut its overseas troop strength by at least a quarter and possibly a third. For Barnett, who lectured to Petraeus and Schoomaker, the future of counter-insurgency lies in the novel model of AFRICOM, which unlike the Pentagon's other area commands—Central, Pacific, European, Northern, Southern—maintains a light-footprint network of 'contingency operating locations' in Africa, combining military vigilance with civilian assistance: 'imperialism to some, but nothing more than a pistol-packing Peace Corps to me'.[6] Chinese investment will do more to help close the gap in the Dark Continent, but AFRICOM is playing its part too.

In the larger scene, American obsessions with terrorism,

5   Ibid., pp. 10–11, 26–7.

6   Ibid., pp. 286–9.

democracy and nuclear weapons are all irrelevances. What matters is the vast unfolding of a globalization that resembles the internet as defined by one of its founders: 'Nobody owns it, everybody uses it, and anybody can add services to it'. The two now form a single process. Just as globalization becomes 'a virtual Helsinki Accords for everyone who logs on', so WikiLeaks is—this from a planner fresh from the Defense Department—'the Radio Free Europe of the surveillance age'.[7] To join up, there is no requirement that a society be an electoral democracy, reduce its carbon emissions or desist from sensible protection of its industries. The rules for membership are simply: '*come as you are* and *come when you can*'. As the middle class swells to half the world's population by 2020, America need have no fear of losing its preeminence. So long as it remains the global economy's leading risk-taker, 'there will never be a post-American world. Just a post-Caucasian one'.[8]

Topped and tailed with a poem by Lermontov as epigraph and a tribute to H. G. Wells for envoi, as an exercise in grand strategy *Great Powers* is, in its way, no less exotic than *God and Gold*. The two can be taken as bookends to the field. Where Mead's construction marries realism and idealism *à l'americaine* in a paroxysmic union, Barnett sidesteps their embrace, without arriving—at least formally—at very different conclusions. In his conception of American power in the new century, though he tips his hat to the president, the Wilsonian strain is close to zero. Even the 'liberal international order' is more a token than a touchstone, since in his usage it makes no case of economic protection. If, in their local meanings, idealism is all but absent, elements of realism are more visible. Theodore Roosevelt—not

7   Ibid., pp. 301, 318.
8   Ibid., pp. 413, 251.

only the youngest, but 'the most broadly accomplished and experienced individual ever to serve as president'—is singled out as the great transformer of American politics, both at home and abroad, and Kagan's *Dangerous Nation* saluted as the work that set Barnett thinking of ways in which he could connect Americans to globalization through their own history. But the cheerful welcome *Great Powers* extends to the autocracies of China and Russia as younger versions of the United States itself is at the antipodes of Kagan. Treatment of Putin is enough to make Brzezinski's hair stand on end. Ready acceptance of Iranian nuclear weapons crosses a red line for Art.

Such iconoclasm is not simply a matter of temperament, though it is clearly also that—it is no surprise the Naval War College felt it could do without Barnett's services. It is because the underlying problematic has so little to do with the role of military force, where the realist tradition has principally focused, or even economic expansion, as a nationalist drive. The twist that takes it out of conventional accounts of American exceptionalism, while delivering a maximized version of it, is its reduction of the country's importance in the world to the pure principle of capitalism—supplier of the genetic code of a globalization that does not depend on, nor require, the Fourteen Points or the Atlantic Charter, but simply the power of the market and of mass consumption, with a modicum of force to put down such opponents as it may arouse. In its unfazed economic determinism, the result is not unlike a materialist variant, from the other side of the barricades, of the vision of America in Hardt and Negri's *Empire*. That empire in its more traditional sense, which they repudiate, has not entirely fled the scene in *Great Powers*, its paean to the Africa Command makes plain. There, the footprints are ever more frequent. Created only in 2007,

AFRICOM now deploys US military effectives in 49 out of 55 countries of the continent.[9] Not America rules the world—the world becomes America. Such is the message, taken straight, of *Great Powers*. In the interim, there is less distinction between the two than the prospectus suggests.

II

An alternative economic vision, at once antithesis and coda, more traditional in outlook yet more *à la page* in the second Obama administration, is since available. *The Resurgence of the West* (2013) by Richard Rosecrance—Harvard Kennedy School, tour of duty on the Policy Planning Staff of the State Department—takes as its starting point American economic decline relative to the rise of China or India. These are societies still benefiting from the transfer of labour from agriculture to industry or services and the import of foreign technology, which permit very fast growth. The US, like every other mature economy with a middle-class population, cannot hope to sustain comparable rates. But by forging a transatlantic union with Europe, it could compensate spatially for what it is losing temporally, with the creation of a market more than twice the size of the US, commanding over half of global GDP—an enlargement unleashing higher investment and growth, and creating an incomparable economic force in the world. For though tariffs between the US and EU are now low, there are plenty of non-tariff barriers—above all, in services and food-stuffs—whose abolition would dynamize both. Moreover a customs union, with linkage of the two currencies, would have

---

9   See the striking documentation by Nick Turse, 'The Pivot to Africa', *TomDispatch.com*, 5 September 2013.

as chastening an effect on other powers as Nixon's freeing of the dollar from gold once had, in the days of Treasury Secretary Connally.[10]

Outsourcing to low-wage Asian countries—satisfactory enough to US corporations today, but not to the US state, which cannot lay off citizens as they can workers, and risks punishment if jobs disappear—would dwindle, and the inbuilt advantage of the West's high-technology and scientific clusters would come fully into their own. China, more dependent than any other great power on raw materials and markets abroad, with a manufacturing base largely consisting of links in production chains beginning and ending elsewhere, would be in no position to challenge such a transatlantic giant—possibly transpacific too, were Japan to join it. Nor would the benefits of a Western Union be confined to the United States and Europe. Historically, hegemonic transitions always carried the risks of wars between ascending and descending powers, and today many are fearful that China could prove a Wilhelmine Germany to America's Edwardian England. But the lesson of history is also that peace is best assured, not by a precarious balance of power—it was that which led to the First World War—but by an overbalance of power, deterring all prospect of challenging it, attracting instead others to join it. Rejuvenating the West, a Euro-American compact would create just that: 'The possibility of an enduring overbalance of power lies before us. It needs only to be seized upon.' Moreover, once in place, 'overweening power can act as a magnet'.[11] Indeed, who is to say that China

---

10 Richard Rosecrance, *The Resurgence of the West: How a Transatlantic Union Can Prevent War and Restore the United States and Europe*, New Haven 2013, p. 79.

11 Ibid., pp. 108, 163, 173, 175.

could itself not one day join a TAFTA, assuring everlasting peace?

With a low view of European economic and demographic health, the vision of any kind of TAFTA as an open sesame to restoration of American fortunes is an object for derision in *Great Powers*: 'Whenever I hear an American politician proclaim the need to strengthen the Western alliance, I know that leader promises to steer by our historical wake instead of crafting a forward-looking strategy. Recapturing past glory is not recapturing our youth but denying our parentage of this world we inhabit so uneasily today.'[12] Europeans are pensioners in it. It would be wrong to reject them, but pointless to look to them. After all, Barnett remarks kindly, on the freeway of globalization grandad can come along for the ride, whoever is sitting in the front seat next to the driver.

---

12 Barnett, *Great Powers*, p. 369.

OUTSIDE THE CASTLE

The driver remains American. The discourses of foreign policy since the time of Clinton return to a common set of themes confronting the nation: the disorders of the homeland, the menace of terrorism, the rise of powers in the East. Diagnoses of the degree of danger these represent for the United States vary—Mead or Kagan sanguine, Mandelbaum or Kupchan concerned, Brzezinski alarmist. What does not change, though its expressions vary, is the axiomatic value of American leadership. The hegemony of the United States continues to serve both the particular interests of the nation and the universal interests of humanity. Certainly, it needs adjustment to the hour, and on occasion has been mishandled. But of its benefits to the world there can be no serious question. The American Way of Life, it is true, can no longer be held up for imitation with the confidence of Henry Luce seventy years ago. Ailments at home and missteps abroad have made it less persuasive. But if the classic affirmative versions of the blessings of American power now have to be qualified, without being abandoned, its negative legitimation is propounded ever more strenuously. The primacy of the US may at times grate on others, even with cause, but who could doubt the alternative to it would be far worse? Without American hegemony, global disorder—war, genocide, depression, famine—would fatally ensue. In the last resort, the peace and security of the planet depend on it. Admiration of it is no longer necessary; simply, acceptance *um schlimmeres zu vermeiden*.

That, in one way or another, it is in need of repair is the premise of virtually all this literature. The bill of particulars for internal reform is repeated with relentless regularity in one writer after another: inequality has got out of hand, the school system is failing, health care is too expensive, infrastructure is out of date, energy is wasted, R&D is insufficient, labour is under-skilled, finance is under-regulated, entitlements are out of control, the budget is in the red, the political system is overly polarized. Needed, all but invariably, is a 'centrist' agenda: increasing investment in science and human capital, improvements in transport and communications, cost control in health care, fiscal restraint, more realistic claims on social security, energy conservation, urban renewal, and so forth. The menu may be ignored—it largely is by Kagan or Barnett—but rarely, if ever, is it outright rejected.

Remedies for external setbacks or oncoming hazards are more divisive. The Republican administration of 2000–2008, more controversial than its predecessor, enjoyed the support of Kagan throughout, Mead and Barnett at first, while incurring criticism, much of it vehement, from Ikenberry and Kupchan, Art and Brzezinski. In the wake of it, the refrain is universal that in the interests of American primacy itself, more consideration should be given to the feelings of allies and aliens than Bush and Cheney were willing to show, if legitimacy is to be restored. Multilateralism is the magic word for Wilsonians, but after their fashion harder cases pay their respects to the same requirement—Kagan calls for greater tact in handling Europeans, Mead for a 'diplomacy of civilizations' in dealing with Islam, Art wants American hegemony to 'look more benign', Fukuyama urges 'at least a rhetorical concern for the poor and the excluded'.[1]

Democracy, on the other hand, its spread till yesterday an irrenounceable goal of any self-respecting diplomacy, is now on the back burner. Openly discarded as a guideline by Kupchan, Barnett and Brzezinski, downgraded by Art, matter for horticulture rather than engineering for Mandelbaum, only Ikenberry and Kagan look wistfully for a league of democracies to right the world. The zone where America sought most recently to introduce it has been discouraging. But while few express much satisfaction with US performance in the Middle East, none proposes any significant change of American dispositions in it. For all, without exception, military control of the Gulf is a *sine qua non* of US global power. Ties with Israel remain a crucial 'national interest' even for Art; Brzezinski alone permitting himself a discreet grumble at the excessive leverage of Tel Aviv in Washington. The most daring solution for resolving the Palestinian question is to iron-clad the bantustans on offer under Clinton—demilitarized fragments of a quarter of the former Mandate, leaving all major Jewish settlements in place—with American troops to back up the IDF, and signature of a formal defence treaty with Israel. If Iran refuses to obey Western instructions to halt its nuclear programme, it

1 Mead: *God and Gold*, pp. 378 ff. Art: 'The task for US leaders is a tough one: to make the United States look more benign and yet at the same time advance America's national interests by employing the considerable power the nation wields', *America's Grand Strategy*, p. 381. Fukuyama: 'Soft Talk, Big Stick', in Leffler and Legro, eds, *To Lead the World*, p. 215.

will—no one, of course welcomes the prospect—*in extremis* have to be attacked, hopefully with a helping hand or a friendly wink from Moscow and Beijing. Only Barnett breaks the taboo that protects the Israeli nuclear monopoly in the name of nonproliferation.

How is American domination to be preserved in the arena of *Weltpolitik* proper—the domain of the great powers and their conflicts, actual or potential? The European Union is the least contentious of these since it evidently poses no threat to US hegemony. Ikenberry and Kupchan piously, Art impassively, Brzezinski and Kagan contemptuously, underline or recall the need for Western cohesion, for which Rosecrance proposes a sweeping institutional form. Japan still safely a ward of the US and India not yet a leading player, it is Russia and China that are the major apples of discord. In each case, the field divides between advocates of containment and apostles of co-option. Brzezinski would not only pinion Russia between one American castellation in Europe, and another in China, but ideally break the country up altogether. For Mandelbaum, on the other hand, the expansion of NATO to Russia's borders is a gratuitous provocation that can only rebound against the West, while Kupchan hopes to embrace Russia itself within NATO. For Kagan, China and Russia alike are hostile regimes, well aware of Western hopes to turn or undermine them, that can only be dealt with by demonstration of superior strength. For Mandelbaum and Ikenberry, on the contrary, China is the great prize whose adhesion to the liberal international order is increasingly plausible, and will render it irreversible, while for Barnett, with his more relaxed conception of such an order, the PRC is to all intents and purposes already in the bag. Art is willing to concede it a swathe of predominance from Northeast to Southeast Asia—provided the US continues to rule the waves in the Pacific. Brzezinski, after first imagining China as, *par pouvoir interposé*, a forward base of America to encircle Russia from the east, now envisages Russia encircling China from the north.

II

In such counsels of the time, three features are most striking. For all the attention they now pay to domestic woes, quite new in a discourse of foreign policy, salience of concern never transcends superficiality of treatment. On the underlying causes of the long slowdown in the growth of output, median income and productivity, and concomitant rise of public, corporate and household debt, not only in the US but across the advanced capitalist world, there is not a line of enquiry or reflection. In this community, the work of those who have explored them—Brenner, Duncan, Duménil and Levy, Aglietta—is a closed book. No doubt it would be unreasonable to expect specialists in international relations to be familiar with the work of economic historians. In ignorance of them, however, the roots of the decline so many deplore and seek to remedy remain invisible.

These are internal affairs. The external counsels, naturally far more copious and ambitious, are of a different order. There professional commitment is far from barren. To the task of redressing the present position of the country at large, and imagining the future of the world, passion and ingenuity continue to be brought. Arresting, however, is the fantastical nature of the constructions to which these again and again give rise. Gigantic rearrangements of the chessboard of Eurasia, vast countries moved like so many castles or pawns across it; elongations of NATO to the Bering Straits; the PLA patrolling the derricks of Aramco; Leagues of Democracy sporting Mubarak and Ben Ali; a *Zollverein* from Moldova to Oregon, if not to Kobe; the End of History as the Peace of God. In the all but complete detachment from reality of so many of these—even the most prosaic, the Western Union of US and EU, lacking so much as a line on the political means of its realization—it is difficult not to see a strain of unconscious desperation, as if the only way to restore American leadership to the plenitude of its merits and powers in this world, for however finite a span of time, is to imagine another one altogether.

Finally, and most decisively, to the luxuriance of schemes for the transmogrification of its foes and friends alike corresponds the dearth of any significant ideas for a retraction of the imperium itself. Not withdrawal, but adjustment, is the common bottom line. Of the adjustments under way—further tentacles in Africa, Central Asia and Australia; assassinations from the air at presidential will; universal surveillance; cyber-warfare—little is ever said. Those who speak of them belong elsewhere. 'In international politics', Christopher Layne has written, 'benevolent hegemons are like unicorns—there is no such animal. Hegemons love themselves, but others mistrust and fear them—and for good reason.'[2] The tradition of foreign-policy dissent in the US that he represents is alive and well. Like its counterpart in imperial Britain of old, it remains, as it has always been, marginal in national debate, and invisible in the affairs of the state, but no less penetrating for that. It is there that genuine realism, understood not as a stance in inter-state relations, or a theory about them, but as an ability to look

2   Layne, *Peace of Illusions*, p. 142.

at realities without self-deception, and describe them without euphemism, is to be found. The names of Johnson, Bacevich, Layne, Calleo, not to speak of Kolko or Chomsky, are those to honour. The title of Chalmers Johnson's last book, which calls for the closing down of the CIA and the myriad bases of the Pentagon, can stand for the sense of their work, and an hour as distant as ever: *Dismantling the Empire*.

ANNEXE

Three years into the war in Iraq, with no end in sight, soul-searching has broken out in the foreign policy establishment. Second thoughts about the invasion are now a library. Among these, few have received wider coverage than Francis Fukuyama's. The fame of the author of *The End of History and the Last Man* is, of course, one reason. The frisson of an illustrious defection from the ranks of neoconservatism is another, no doubt more immediate one. But to take *America at the Crossroads* simply as a political straw in the wind is to diminish its intellectual interest. This lies essentially in its relation to the work that made Fukuyama's name.

The argument of *America at the Crossroads* falls into three parts. In the first, Fukuyama retraces the origins of contemporary neoconservatism. His story begins with a cohort of New York intellectuals, mostly Jewish, who were socialists in their youth, but rallied to the cause of democracy in the Cold War, and then stood firm against the New Left when the nation was fighting communism in Vietnam. In due course, out of their ranks came a social agenda, too: the critique of welfare liberalism developed in *The Public Interest*, edited by Irving Kristol and Daniel Bell. Meanwhile, moral reaction against the laxness of the sixties was being lent philosophical depth by Leo Strauss in Chicago and cultural zip by his pupil Allan Bloom. Military understanding and technical expertise were provided by nuclear strategist Albert Wohlstetter, theorist of counter-force missile capacity and prophet of electronic warfare. Fukuyama explains that in one way or another he was personally involved in all of these enterprises. But his account of them is calm and balanced, and if anything understates the potency of the political cocktail they represented. His emphasis falls rather on their ultimate confluence with broader and more popular currents of conservatism—belief in small government, religious piety, nationalism—in the base of the Republican party. Together, this was the political torrent that powered the turn of the Reagan presidency.

But the greatest triumph of the conservative ascendancy—victory in the Cold War—contained, he goes on, the seeds of what would become the undoing of neoconservatism. For the fall of the Soviet Union bred overconfidence in the ability of America to reshape the world at large. Exaggerating the role of US economic and military pressure in the sudden collapse of the USSR, which in reality was decaying within, a younger levy of thinkers—William Kristol and Robert Kagan are singled out—came to believe that tyranny could be felled and liberty planted with comparable speed elsewhere. It was this illusion, according to Fukuyama, which led to the attack on Iraq. Ignoring not only the quite different political landscape of the Middle East, but the warnings of the original neoconservatives against overly voluntarist schemes of social reconstruction, the projectors of the invasion have saddled the US with a disaster from which it will take years to recover. Needless resort to a unilateral force has isolated America from world opinion, above all that of its European allies, weakening rather than strengthening the US position in the world. Fukuyama devotes the rest of his book to the outline of an alternative foreign policy that would restore America to its rightful place in the world. A 'realistic Wilsonianism', tempering the best of neoconservative convictions with a more informed sense of the intractability of other cultures and the limits of American power, would retain the need for preemptive war as a last resort, and the promotion of democracy across the globe as a permanent goal. But it would confer with allies, rely more often on soft than hard power, undertake state-building in the light of social science, and encourage the spread of new, overlapping forms of multilateralism, bypassing the deadlocks of the United Nations. 'The most important way that American power can be exercised', Fukuyama concludes, 'is not through the exercise of military power but the ability of the United States to shape international institutions.' For what they can do is 'reduce the transaction costs of achieving consent' to US actions. [1]

In the tripartite structure of *America at the Crossroads*—capsule history of neoconservatism; critique of the way it went awry in Iraq; proposals for a rectified version—the crux of the argument lies in the middle section. Fukuyama's account of the milieu to which he belonged, and its role in the run-up to the war, is level-headed and informative. But it is a view from within that contains a revealing optical illusion. Everything happens as if neoconservatives were the basic driving force behind the march to Baghdad, and it is their ideas that must be cured if America is

---

1   *America at the Crossroads: Democracy, Power and the Neoconservative Legacy*, New York 2006, pp. 190–1.

to get back on track. In reality, the front of opinion that pressed for an assault on Iraq was far broader than a particular Republican faction. It included many a liberal and a Democrat. Much the most detailed case for attacking Saddam Hussein was made by Kenneth Pollack, a functionary of the Clinton administration. What remains by a long way the most sweeping theorization of a programme for American military intervention to destroy rogue regimes and uphold human rights round the world is the work of Philip Bobbitt, nephew of Lyndon Johnson and another and more senior ornament of Clinton's national security apparatus. Beside the six hundred pages of his magnum opus, *The Shield of Achilles*, a work of vast historical ambition that ends with a series of dramatic scenarios of the coming wars for which America must prepare, the writers of the *Weekly Standard* are thin fare. No neoconservative has produced anything remotely comparable. Nor was there any shortage of lesser trumpeters on the liberal end of the spectrum for an expedition to the Middle East—the Ignatieffs and Bermans. There was no illogic in that. The Democrats' war in the Balkans, dismissing national sovereignty as an anachronism, was a precondition and proving-ground of the Republicans' war in Mesopotamia—genocide in Kosovo only a little less overstated than weapons of mass of destruction in Iraq. The operations of what Fukuyama at one point allows himself, in a rare lapsus, to call 'America's overseas empire'[2] have historically been bipartisan, and continue to be so.

In the Republican camp itself, moreover, neoconservative intellectuals were only one, and not the most significant, element in the constellation that propelled the Bush administration into Iraq. Of the six 'Vulcans' in James Mann's authoritative study of those who paved the road to war, Paul Wolfowitz alone—in

2   Ibid., p. 30.

origin a Democrat—belongs to Fukuyama's retrospect. None of the three leading figures in the design and justification of the attack, Rumsfeld, Cheney and Rice, had any particular neo-conservative attachments. Fukuyama is aware of this, but offers no explanation, merely remarking that 'we do not at this point know the origin of their views'.[3] What, then, of his own location within the galaxy he describes? Here—it must be said that this is uncharacteristic—he smoothes out the record. With a misleadingly casual air, he says that while he started out 'fairly hawkish on Iraq',[4] at a time when no invasion was ever envisaged, when one was later launched, he was against it.

In this his memory has failed him. In June 1997 Fukuyama was a founder, alongside Rumsfeld, Cheney, Quayle, Wolfowitz, Scooter Libby, Zalmay Khalilzad, Norman Podhoretz, Elliott Abrams and Jeb Bush, of the Project for a New American Century, whose statement of principles called for 'a Reaganite policy of military strength and moral clarity' to 'promote the cause of political and economic freedom abroad'. In January 1998 (revealingly, he misdates this) he was one of the sixteen signatories of an open letter from the Project to Clinton insisting on the need for 'willingness to undertake military action' to secure 'the removal of Saddam Hussein's regime from power', and declaring that 'the US has the authority under existing UN resolutions to take the necessary steps' to do so. Four months later, he was among those denouncing lack of such action as a 'capitulation to Saddam' and an 'incalculable blow to American leadership and credibility', and spelling out just what measures against the Ba'ath regime were required: 'We should help establish and support (with economic, political and military means)

3   Ibid., p. 4.
4   Ibid., p. x.

a provisional, representative and free government' in 'liberated areas in northern and southern Iraq', under the 'protection of US and allied military power'. In other words: an invasion to set up a Chalabi regime in Basra or Najaf, and topple Saddam from this base.

Under Bush, the Project—its ranks now swollen by such Democratic stalwarts as Stephen Solarz and Marshall Wittmann—returned to the attack, and Fukuyama was again to the fore in pressing for an onslaught on Iraq. On the 20 September 2001, within little more than a week of 9/11, he appended his signature to a blunt demand for war that waved aside any relevance of links to Al Qaeda, and did not even bother to raise the spectre of WMD:

> It may be that the Iraqi government provided assistance in some form to the recent attack on the United States. But even if evidence does not link Iraq directly to the attack, any strategy aiming at the eradication of terrorism and its sponsors must include a determined effort to remove Saddam Hussein from power in Iraq. Failure to undertake such an effort will constitute an early and perhaps decisive surrender in the war on international terrorism. The United States must therefore provide full military and financial support to the Iraqi opposition. American military force should be used to provide a 'safe zone' in Iraq from which the opposition can operate. And American forces must be prepared to back up our commitment to the Iraqi opposition by all necessary means.

For good measure, the signatories added that 'any war on terrorism must target Hezbollah' and prepare for 'appropriate measures of retaliation' against Syria and Iran as its sponsors.

To recall this campaign for blood and steel in the Middle East is not to single Fukuyama out for especial incrimination.

Congress, after all, would give the green light for war on Iraq with virtually complete bipartisan unanimity. The question posed by Fukuyama's deeper implication in the drive to Baghdad than he now suggests lies elsewhere. It is this. Why, if he was originally so committed to the adventure in Iraq, did he later break so sharply with his fellow thinkers over it? The disasters of the occupation are, of course, the most obvious reason—all kinds of creatures, large and small, jumping off the ship as it tilts lower in the waters. But this cannot be the principal explanation of Fukuyama's change of mind. He himself says he had lost belief in an invasion before the war started, and there is no reason to doubt him. Moreover, disillusion with the lack of practical success in an enterprise regarded as commendable in principle has been common enough among conservatives without leading to the kind of historical critique and dissociation Fukuyama has embarked upon. It would have been quite possible to say Operation Iraqi Freedom has gone wrong, even that in retrospect it was a mistake from the beginning, without writing an obituary of neoconservatism. What suddenly put such distance between Fukuyama and his fellow spirits?

Two factors of division can be deduced from *America at the Crossroads*, and the essay on 'The Neoconservative Moment' in *The National Interest* which preceded it. Fukuyama did not share the same degree of commitment to Israel as his Jewish colleagues. In *The National Interest* he complained—not of actual subordination of American to Israeli objectives in the Middle East—but rather of a mimesis of the Israeli outlook on the Arab world among too many of his companions. Applying a mailed fist to the region might well be rational for Tel Aviv, he remarked, but was not necessarily so for Washington. His criticism was tactful enough, but it met with a vehement response. Replying, Charles Krauthammer charged Fukuyama with inventing a 'novel way of Judaizing neoconservatism', less crude than the slanders of Pat Buchanan and Mahathir Muhammad, but equally ridiculous—moving Fukuyama in turn to object to imputations of anti-Semitism. Evidently burnt by this exchange, and aware of the general delicacy of the topic, Fukuyama does not revert to it in *America at the Crossroads*, explaining that the mind-set he had criticized, 'while true of certain individuals, cannot be attributed to neoconservatives more broadly', and offering the olive branch of general support for the administration's policies towards Palestine. Behind the politesse, it is doubtful if his reservations have disappeared.

Another consideration, however, has certainly been more important. It was a trip to Europe in late 2003, Fukuyama has explained, that opened his eyes to the dismay felt by many of even America's staunchest admirers at the unilateralism of the Bush presidency. The disappointment expressed by such a pillar of Atlanticism as the editor of the *Financial Times* was sobering. Could a foreign policy that so alienated our closest allies be really worth it? Unlike Israel, which after his initial disclaimer, scarcely figures at all in *America at the Crossroads*, Europe looms large. Fukuyama voices the utmost alarm about its reactions to the Bush administration. The rift caused by the war in Iraq is no mere passing quarrel, he believes. It is a 'tectonic shift' in the Western alliance. With thousands on the streets, 'Europe had never before appeared as spontaneously unified around a single issue as this one, which is why former French finance minister Dominique Strauss-Kahn labelled the demonstrations the "birth of the European nation".[5] Anti-Americanism is

5   Ibid., pp. 100–1.

rampaging across the Atlantic, and the unity of the West at risk.

Though such fears are now widespread, they bear little relation to reality. European hostility to the war is broad, but not deep. The invasion was widely opposed, but once consummated has not given rise to much further protest. Demonstrations against the occupation have been few and far between—it is enough to compare it to the war in Vietnam. The British government that joined in the American attack has not been punished at the polls. The German government that opposed the invasion was soon helping out behind the scenes, providing information on targets in Baghdad and assistance with CIA renditions. The French government, taxed by Fukuyama with double-crossing the US in the Security Council, in fact told the White House to go ahead without a new resolution, and has worked closely with Washington to install suitable regimes in Haiti and the Lebanon. All stand united on Iran. European hostility to the current presidency is more pique than conniption. What has grated is indifference to diplomatic niceties and insufficient homage of acceptable vice to ostensible virtue. Elites and masses alike are attached to the veils that have traditionally draped compliance with American will, and resent a government that has discarded them. Grievances of this kind, a matter of style rather than substance, will pass with a return to decorum. A Clinton restoration would no doubt see a swift and rapt reunion of the Old World with the New.

Here Krauthammer was more clear-eyed than his critic. Dismissing Fukuyama's anxiety that US foreign policy is in jeopardy because it has lost international legitimacy, he remarked with justice that what threatens it is not any lack of EU certificates or UN resolutions—it has plenty of such rubber stamps, as he notes—but the Iraqi insurgency. It is the will of the resistance that threatens the Bush Doctrine. The rest is weak ripple effect. Without the *maquis*, European opinion would be no more troubled by the seizure of Iraq than it was by that of Panama.

Fukuyama's misreading of European sentiments is now conventional. His view of Islamic fundamentalism, on the other hand, is refreshingly unconventional, at variance with both his own milieu and mainstream wisdom. Compared with the great historic antagonists of capitalist democracy, fascism and communism, Al Qaeda and its affiliates are a miniscule force. Other than by somehow getting hold of weapons of mass destruction, they have no chance of inflicting serious damage on American society, let alone becoming a global threat to liberal civilization. Proclaiming a generalized 'war against terrorism' is a pointless inflation of the punctual operations needed to stamp out the handful of fanatics who dream of a new caliphate. Panicking over this relatively minor threat risks major miscalculations and is to be avoided, above all by Americans, who since 9/11 risk further *attentats* less than do Europeans, with their larger enclaves of Muslim immigrants.

This is a belated lucidity, after so much crying of havoc in the open letters, but it is one more typical of the note struck in Fukuyama's writing, whose tone is generally cool and unruffled. Its judgement takes us back to the logic of his larger work as a whole. The celebrated argument of *The End of History and the Last Man* was that with the defeat of communism, following that of fascism, no improvement on liberal capitalism as a form of society was any longer imaginable. The world was still full of conflicts, which would continue to generate unexpected events, but they would not alter this verdict. There was no guarantee of a rapid voyage of humanity from every corner of the earth to the destination of a prosperous, peaceful democracy, based on private property, free markets and regular elections, but these institutions were the terminus of historical development. The closure of social evolution now in view could not be regarded as altogether a blessing. For with it would inevitably come a lowering of ideal tension, perhaps even a certain *tedium vitae*. Nostalgia for more hazardous and heroic times could be foreseen.

The philosophical basis of this construction came, as Fukuyama explained, from the reworking of Hegel's dialectic of recognition by a Russian exile in France, Alexandre Kojève, for whom centuries of struggles between masters and slaves—social classes—were on the brink of issuing into a definitive condition of equality, a 'universal and homogeneous state', that would bring history to a halt: a conception he identified with socialism, and later with capitalism, if always with an inscrutable irony. Fukuyama took over this narrative structure, but grounded it in an ontology of human nature, quite alien to Kojève, that was derived from Plato and came—along with a much more conservative outlook—from his Straussian formation. Kojève and Strauss had valued each other as interlocutors and shared many intellectual reference points, but politically—as well as metaphysically—they were very distant. Strauss, an unyielding thinker of the right, had no time for Hegel, let alone Marx. In his eyes, Kojève's deduction from their conceptions of liberty and equality could only presage a levelling, planetary tyranny. He believed in particular regimes and natural hierarchy.

So there was always a tension in Fukuyama's synthesis of his two sources. In the final years of the Cold War, when his joining of them took shape, this could remain hidden, because the universal interests of democratic capitalism were consensually guarded, without significant strain, by a Pax Americana: there was no significant contradiction between the Free World and US hegemony. But once communism had been eradicated in Russia, and neutered in China, a new situation arose. On the one hand, there was no longer a common enemy to compel other capitalist states to disciplined acceptance of US command. But at the same time, the disappearance of the USSR increased the global reach of the American state enormously. Thus just when the hegemon was objectively less essential for the system as a whole, subjectively it was bound to become more ambitious than ever before, as now the world's single superpower. In these conditions, it was inevitable that the general requirements of the system would at some point diverge from the operations of the singular nation-state at its head. This is the context in which *America at the Crossroads* should be understood. For Fukuyama's break with neoconservatism has occurred at the fault line between the two. At the centre of the book is an extended attack on American 'exceptionalism', by which he means the doctrine that 'the United States is different from other countries and can be trusted to use its military power justly and wisely in ways that other powers cannot'. This is the delusion broadcast by Kristol and Kagan, he argues, that has antagonized allies and led to the overweening errors of the war in Iraq.

Politically, Fukuyama's loyalties were formed in a Straussian matrix. But intellectually, the imprint of Kojève went deeper, supplying his master narrative. Forced by alterations of the strategic landscape to choose between the logic of the two, his head has prevailed over his heart. If Fukuyama has taken leave of the company of neoconservatives, it is because the war in

Iraq has exposed a genealogical difference between them. In origin, his leading ideas were European, as theirs never were. Kojève indeed regarded the creation of a supranational Europe as the decisive reason why a globalizing capitalism, rather than a still nationally cramped bureaucratic socialism, had turned out, contrary to his original expectations, to be the common destination of humanity. For Strauss, on the other hand, whose earliest allegiance was to Zionism, every regime was by nature particular: he was impervious to universal schemes. Though himself no great admirer of American society, he respected the Founders and seeded an ardently nationalist school of constitutional thinkers. The options of the different neoconservative heirs reflect their respective ancestries.

Not that either side repudiates the preoccupations of the other, which remain common to both. Rather it is the way these are combined—the balance struck between them—which sets the two apart. Kristol or Krauthammer may be American patriots, but they are second to none in their commitment to the spread of capitalist democracy around the world: in that respect, few universalisms are as aggressive as theirs. Vice versa, Fukuyama may criticize US exceptionalism, but he has certainly not relinquished the national portion of his inheritance. His new journal is not called *The American Interest* for nothing. Krauthammer calls his outlook 'Democratic Realism'; Fukuyama terms his 'Realistic Wilsonianism'. A distinction without a difference? Not exactly—rather an inversion in which the nouns indicate the primary, and the adjectives the secondary, allegiances. For the neoconservative core, American power is the engine of the world's liberty: there neither is, nor can be, any discrepancy between them. For Fukuyama, the coincidence is not automatic. The two may drift away from each other—and nothing is more likely to force them apart than to declare they cannot do so, in the name of a unique American virtue unlikely to persuade anyone else. As he puts it:

> The idea that the United States behaves disinterestedly on the world stage is not widely believed because for the most part it is not true and, indeed, could not be true if American leaders fulfill their responsibilities to the American people. The United States is capable of acting generously in its provision of global public goods, and has been most generous when its ideas and its interests have coincided. But the United States is also a great power with interests not related to global public goods.[6]

Denial of this obvious truth leads to policies that damage American interests and do not deliver global goods: see Baghdad.

How are these then best reconciled? Fukuyama remains fully committed to the American mission of spreading democracy round the world, and the use of all effective means at the disposal of Washington to do so. His criticism of the Bush administration is that its policies in the Middle East have been not only ineffective, but counterproductive. The promotion of internal regime change by the right mixture of economic and political pressures is one thing. Military action to enforce it externally is another, conducive to misfortune. In reality, of course, there is no sharp dividing line between the two in the imperial repertoire. Fukuyama forgets the successful overthrow of the Sandinistas in Nicaragua, of which Robert Kagan is the major historian—a triumph of political will we can be sure he applauded at the time. Today, in the wake of Iraq, he is concerned to distance himself from such forms of activism.

---

6   Ibid., p. 111.

He now explains there is no universal craving for freedom that ensures democracy will emerge wherever a society is liberated from tyranny. Modern liberty typically requires certain levels of economic and social development for the habits needed to sustain it. These cannot be created overnight, but must be carefully nurtured over many years. Nor will neoliberal recipes relying on market incentives alone bring the necessary order and prosperity. For these a strong state capable of 'good governance' is the essential condition, and a sensible American policy will often give precedence to fostering such state-ness over building democracy in the more dangerous parts of the world.

In the service of this revision, Fukuyama disfigures his original construction. *The End of History and the Last Man*, he assures us, was actually an exercise in modernization theory. All he said was that a desire for higher living standards—not liberty—was universal, and that this created a middle class which tended to seek political participation, with democracy eventually emerging as a by-product of this process. This banalization of a complex argument in the philosophy of history is not just an effort to simplify its message for a wider audience. It has a bowdlerizing impulse. In the work that made Fukuyama's name, the quest for recognition and the promptings of desire— driving respectively the struggle for equality and the advance of science—were the two motors of history. The concatenation between them was never quite pulled off in the theory, generating significant disjunctures towards the end of the story.[7] But in the structure of the narrative as a whole, Fukuyama's assignment of their respective significance was unequivocal;

7   For reflections on the character of Fukuyama's argument as a whole, and its place in the line of theorists of historical closure, see 'The Ends of History', *A Zone of Engagement*, London 1992, pp. 279–375.

the 'desire behind the desire' of economic man was 'a totally non-economic drive, *the struggle for recognition*'. It was the political dialectic so unleashed that was 'the primary motor of human history'. The mental universe of Alexandre Kojève was a long way from that of the Daniel Lerners, Gabriel Almonds and their kind.

If this vision now appears to be something of an encumbrance for Fukuyama, perhaps that is because it was a theory of mortal conflict. Hegel and Kojève were each in their own time—Jena, Stalingrad—philosophers of war. Their legacy is too agonistic for the purposes of drawing a line between the newfound caution of the statecraft Fukuyama now recommends and the democratic hypomania of former friends at the *Standard*. The platitudes of modernization theory are safer. But there is a price to be paid for the drop in intellectual level to 'State-building 101'—the title, without excessive irony, of one of Fukuyama's recent essays. As a run-of-the-mill social scientist, he is never less than competent. There is even, in his criticism of free market recipes for development in poor countries, and call for strong public authorities, what could be read as a memory-trace of his Hegelian formation: the idea of the State as the carrier of rational freedom. But the miscellaneous proposals with which *America at the Crossroads* ends—greater reliance on soft power, more consultation with allies, respect for international institutions—are of a desolating predictability, the truisms of every *bien-pensant* editorial or periodical in the land. The most that can be said of them is that in offering a bipartisan prospectus for the foreign policy establishment, they seal a well-advertised vote for Kerry and understanding with Brzezinski, who co-edits *The American Interest* with Fukuyama. There is not the faintest suggestion in these pages of any basic change in the staggering accumulation of military bases round the world, or the grip of the US on the Middle East, let alone symbiosis with Israel. Everything that brought the country to 9/11 remains in place.

It is enough to look at the blistering essay by John Mearsheimer and Stephen Walt in the current *London Review of Books*—significantly, in no domestic publication—to see the enormous gulf between strategic muzak of this kind and genuinely critical reflection on American foreign policy, from thinkers who have earned the title realist. After starting his book under the aegis of Wilson, who brought the gospel of democracy to the peoples of the earth, Fukuyama ends it by enlisting Bismarck, who knew how to practise self-restraint in the hour of victory, as inspiration for his 'alternative way for the United States to relate to the rest of the world'.[8] What the Iron Chancellor, who had a grim sense of humour, would have made of his pairing with the Fourteen Points is not difficult to imagine. In such prescriptions, of Fukuyama and so many others today, America is not at any crossroads. It is just where it has always been, squaring the circle of philanthropy and empire to its own satisfaction.

April 2006

---

8   *America at the Crossroads*, p. xii.

POSTSCRIPT

Events since the composition of these essays have set off, as often since the seventies, another wave of laments in the Western media and American political class that US power is ebbing, amid criticisms of the Obama administration for irresolute handling of new threats to international security. The developments that have aroused the latest round of anxieties are too recent, most still lacking any clear-cut outcome, to permit more than brief comment. They divide into two main zones, the larger Middle East and Europe. What is to date the balance sheet in each?

At the centre of the Muslim world, the military overthrow of the elected government in Cairo, replacing unkempt rule by the Muslim Brotherhood with a return of the Mubarak regime under new management, has stabilized US positions in the country of greatest political importance to it, on which the tranquility of Israel as victor state depends. With the Sisi regime in place, closing tunnels to Egypt more completely than Mubarak did, Palestinian resistance in Gaza could once again be garotted, Israel launching a punitive invasion of the enclave, while American weapons and aid continue to flow to the signatories of Camp David. In Syria, on the other hand, US orchestration of the Gulf monarchies and Turkey for proxy warfare to dislodge Assad has so far proved less militarily effective than the Hezbollah fighters and Iranian supply-lines defending him along the critical axis from Damascus to Aleppo. With the rise of a radical Sunni insurgency in the vacuum to the east, extending into northern Iraq and seizing Mosul, the calculus in Washington has shifted—attention swivelling back to Baghdad. There adult supervision had proved too lax: the Maliki regime, flouting US counsels, now rested exclusively on a Shi'ite army and security system, both riddled with corruption. With jihadis installed in Fallujah and Ramadi, and threatening Erbil, the Obama administration wasted no time in removing Maliki for a more respectful instrument of American will and arming the new government with aerial attacks on ISIS positions. In Iraq, pacification of Sunni opinion, along the lines of the Bush administration's 'Anbar Awakening' of 2006–2007, is the next requirement. In Syria, much heavier bombing has been unleashed to halt the spread of ISIS control across the north of the country, in another advertisement of the president's indifference to domestic law.[1] Mustering its Arab clients into a coalition against jihadi forces fighting the regime in Damascus, while continuing to aim for the ouster of Assad himself, Washington has launched its fourth war of the century in the region.

Domestic fatigue precluding for the moment a return of ground troops to Iraq or the Levant, the lesson learnt in Washington is the mistake of letting them depart altogether,

---

1   For reflections from an impeccably mainstream jurist, see Bruce Ackerman, 'Obama's Betrayal of the Law', *New York Times*, 13–14 September 2014.

rather than leaving a residual force for emergencies behind. In Afghanistan, where Karzai showed no more eagerness than Maliki to accept such a fail-safe provision, Obama has made it clear the US is not to be trifled with. But securing a smooth passage to a more accommodating successor has not proved simple, with rival candidates mired in mutual electoral fraud—each professing the need for American troops to remain—needing to be spatchcocked together by US emissaries, and the Taliban undefeated. At the other end of the region, the dissolution of Libya, the showcase of humanitarian intervention by the West, into a maze of internecine feuds has underlined the difficulties of arm's length rather than direct control in revivalist and neo-tribal contexts. In these variegated theatres of conflict, American paramountcy has yet to find its equilibrium.

But on the strategically decisive front in the region, the Obama administration has reason for provisional satisfaction, as the current clerical government in Iran, buckling under the pressure of implacable sanctions and covert sabotage, signals increasing resignation to the American diktat that Israel must continue to enjoy a nuclear monopoly in the region, in exchange for a lifting of the blockade of the country. Common interests in shielding the recycled Shi'a government in Baghdad from ISIS hold out the prospect of wider cooperation, for which quiet Iranian help for the original American invasions of Afghanistan and Iraq offer a precedent—this time more openly and on a grander scale, with the aim of reconciling Teheran with Riyadh to make the Middle East safe for all its elites. Reintegration of Iran into the global economic order over which the United States presides would in all logic—policy-makers in Washington explain—spell a drawing down of Teheran's support for the regime in Damascus, and once ISIS is crushed, the decommissioning of Assad by another route. The Rouhani government, though plainly seeking an entente with the US, is not so immune to domestic criticism or the delphic directives of the supreme leader that any of this is a foregone conclusion. The dual objective of the talks in Geneva is not yet attained. But it has come closer.

In Europe the scene has been dominated by a political tug-of-war over Ukraine, where the weakness of a successor state, default product of the dissolution of the Soviet Union, has created a power vacuum of a classical kind—the West seeking to draw the country into a forecourt of the European Union, Russia seeking to check a further NATO expansion, encircling it from the South. In early 2014, the last-minute rejection by the corrupt Yanukovich regime, based in the eastern regions, of a trade pact with the EU, in favour of one with Russia, triggered its overthrow by a popular rising in the capital and the west of the country, followed by the rapid deployment of American diplomatic and security personnel to construct a reliable partner for Washington and Brussels in its place.[2] Riposting with the annexation of Crimea, regarded by virtually all Russians as attached to Ukraine only by recent accident, Putin has lifted his popularity at home. But by subtracting its population from the east of the country, he lowered Moscow's longer-term leverage in Ukraine itself, tempting him to cut his losses—any hope of regaining influence at the centre—by stirring Russian irredentism in the Donbass, attached to Ukraine some thirty years earlier. The result has been a rising against Kiev across much of

---

2   For documentation of this move, and analysis of the crisis in Ukraine, see Susan Watkins, 'Annexations', *New Left Review* 86, March–April 2014, pp. 5–13.

the east, part-spontaneous, part-instigated by Moscow, issuing into localized civil war in which rebel militias have been saved from defeat at the hands of the Ukrainian army, with unofficial assistance from American intelligence, by the arrival of unde-clared Russian troops and armour. As of the time of writing, in prospect is a military standoff, of relatively low intensity.

In the contest to gain the upper hand in Ukraine, the US and EU have the trump cards of pliable oligarchs, a favourable electorate, and *in extremis* a Western capacity for economic checkmate. For if Ukraine depends on Russia for its energy supplies, Russia depends for its capital investment and finan-cial stability on a global banking system controlled by America, interlocking vulnerabilities likely to exclude major escalation of hostilities by either side. These are not symmetrical. The ability of the US and EU to damage Russia exceeds the ability of Russia, short of an outright invasion, to damage Ukraine. Though Europe itself stands to suffer in some degree from the sanctions so far imposed on Russia, as the United States does not, American determination to punish Putin has once again shown how limited is the autonomy of any European capital when American primacy is on the line.

The crisis in Ukraine is a logical end product of the Clinton administration's decision to ignore the promises of its prede-cessor, and press NATO expansion to the East, against which many an unimpeachable veteran of the Cold War warned it. The prospect of a tacit Western protectorate in Kiev and the political model it would offer poses an unnerving threat to the Russian regime, as its reaction to the Orange Revolution had already made clear. Putin knows the cost of defying American will, and for over a decade bent to it. But after enduring one humiliation after another at the hands of a West ungrateful for Russian accommodations, it was always likely that in the end the worm would turn, and defensive reflexes acquire an aggressive edge. Classically, in such situations, rational calculation risks going by the board. But the demonstration effect of the sanctions against Iran stands as a warning to Moscow, a barrier against which it cannot afford to collide. In the great power conflict around the Black Sea, US protestations about Crimea, long a part of Russia, will pass. Ukraine remains the larger prize, even if it will be expensive to sustain, now within its grasp. A hegemon can sacrifice a pawn to gain a castle.

In the long run, more important for Washington than these skirmishes along the edge of the EU are two theatres of operation where deeper and more encompassing interests are at stake. The first is economic. For global capitalism as a whole, there is still no escape in sight from the logic of productive over-capacity relative to weak, debt-dependent demand. But within this system, the Treasury–Wall Street complex continues to control the diplomatic and monetary levers. To refloat the financial sector, Tokyo and Frankfurt are taking up the burden of quantitive easing, as the Federal Reserve moves towards its taper. But the structural priorities for the US are the free trade pacts it is pressing on the European Union at one end of the globe, and on Japan at the other end, to create a single commercial ecumene from the Atlantic to the Pacific, centred on North America. Neither is speeding to a conclusion, though if Obama does not shepherd them to the finish, they will remain on the agenda of the next administration. In the Far East, at least, where gains are potentially greatest for the US, the performance of the Abe government has been particularly encouraging: not only signalling readiness to dismantle Japan's traditional devices of economic protection, but to extend its diplomatic and investment reach from Southeast Asia to India, in a common wariness of China.

The second theatre is military. There, largely unnoticed, with a dramatic upgrading in the variety and accuracy of its nuclear armoury, the United States has regained something like the absolute strategic superiority in weapons of mass destruction it enjoyed for a time after the Second World War. In a further signature initiative, Obama has launched a 'nationwide wave of atomic revitalization that includes plans for a new generation of weapons carriers', which will cost up to a trillion dollars.[3] With the erosion of the Russian nuclear arsenal, and the much greater limitations of the Chinese, the US is not far from a first-strike capability that could in theory wipe out both without fear of retaliation.[4] If any such scenario remains beyond imagination, it continues to figure in the computations of what was once called deterrence. Such is the actual—technological—proliferation, of which the Non-Proliferation Treaty is a fig leaf.

20 November 2014

---

3   See William Broad and David Sanger, 'US Ramping Up Major Renewal of Nuclear Arms', *New York Times*, 21 September 2014, and the *NYT* editorial the next day, 'Backsliding on Nuclear Promises'.

4   See the successive studies of Kier Lieber and Daryl Press: 'The Rise of US Nuclear Primacy', *Foreign Affairs*, March–April 2006, pp. 42–54; 'The End of MAD? The Nuclear Dimension of US Primacy', *International Security*, Spring 2006, pp. 7–44; 'The Nukes We Need: Preserving the American Deterrent', *Foreign Affairs*, November–December 2009, pp. 39–51; 'Obama's Nuclear Upgrade: The Case for Modernizing America's Nukes', *Foreign Affairs*, July 2011 (postscript); 'The New Era of Nuclear Weapons, Deterrence and Conflict', *Strategic Studies Quarterly*, Spring 2013, pp. 3–14.

INDEX

Acheson, Dean G. 18n9, 37, 39–40, 57, 61n12, 79, 87n14
Act of Chapultepec (1945) 86
Adams, Brooks 7, 18n9
Adams, John 4
Adelman, Kenneth L. 110n13
Afghanistan
    future regime 256–7
    Operation Enduring Freedom 127, 133–4, 142–3, 222
    Saur Revolution 104–6
    US support for mujahedin 125–6, 197
    and the USSR 107, 113
Africa
    and the Cold War 69, 83n12, 98, 101
    colonialism 35, 70, 99–100
    US operations 223, 225–6
Al Qaeda 123, 126–7, 242, 246
Albright, Madeleine K. 179, 196n8, 201
Algeria 98
Allende, Salvador 94
Alsop, Joseph W. 36n11
America at the Crossroads (Fukuyama) 237–41, 243–5, 248, 250, 252–3

America in the World (ed. Hogan) 49n33
The American Interest (journal) 173, 249, 253
American-Russian Relations (Williams) 43–4
America's Economic Supremacy (Adams) 7, 18n9
America's Grand Strategy and World Politics (Art) 119n5, 209–17
America's Strategy in World Politics (Spykman) 13–16, 24, 52–3
Angola 100, 113
Arab Spring 141–2
Architects of Globalism (Hearden) 18n9
Argentina 87, 89
Aron, Raymond 207
Art, Robert J. 14n3, 119n5, 209–17, 225, 230–3
Asia
    and the Cold War 69–70, 74–80, 83n12, 93
    financial crisis 117
    US operations 16, 65, 127, 146–7, 182, 196, 206

see also China; Eurasia; Japan;
    Korea
Assad, Bashar al- 140–1, 144, 256,
    257
Atlantic Pact (1949) 58
Australia 77n5, 147, 196

Bacevich, Andrew J. 129n12, 235
Baghdad Pact 83–4
Bahrain 141
Balkans 202, 240
    see also Bosnia; Kosovo
Barnett, Thomas P. M. 219–26, 228,
    230–1, 232
Begin, Menachem W. 96
Beinart, Peter A. 164n8
Belgium 19, 99
Berger, Samuel R. 'Sandy' 121
Bin Laden, Osama 134
Bobbitt, Philip C. 165n8, 240
Bosnia 120, 176
Brazil 26n20, 88
Brenner, Robert P. 51, 108n11
Bretton Woods 25, 92, 152, 211
Brezhnev, Leonid I. 93, 107
Britain
    colonies 27, 70–1, 78, 80, 98–9
    economy 54, 57
    imperial preference 18, 19, 25
    and the Middle East 81n9, 82–3,
        84, 104, 144–5
    post–Second World War role 16,
        25–6, 62, 211
    during the Second World War
        17, 61
    and the US 170–2, 176, 195
Broad, William J. 261n3
Brzezinski, Zbigniew K.
    and Afghanistan 107
    and Clinton 116
    and Fukuyama 253
    and Ikenberry 179
    and the Ogaden Crisis 101

political strategy 197–209, 215,
    229, 230–1, 232–3
Bundy, McGeorge 88n16
Burma 76
Bush, George H. W. 111, 115, 116,
    204–5
Bush, George W.
    and Iran 222–3
    and Iraq 125, 169, 178, 240–1,
        244–5
    neo-conservatism 181, 183,
        205, 230
    and religion 41
    and Russia 131
    war on terror 46, 122, 127

Calleo, David P. 150n11, 235
Cambodia 97
Cambridge History of the Cold
    War (ed. Leffler and Westad)
    47, 48
Camp David Accords 96–7
Carter, James E. 'Jimmy' 95, 96, 97,
    102, 104n9, 198
The Case for Goliath
    (Mandelbaum) 174
Central America 6, 9, 86–7, 101–3,
    107
    see also Nicaragua; Panama
Cheney, Richard B. 'Dick' 230, 241
Chiang Kai-shek 25, 74
Chile 89, 94
China
    and Afghanistan 131
    alliance with 93–4, 96, 97, 182,
        221, 223
    civil war 74
    growing power 146–8, 152–3,
        164, 203, 212–13, 226–8
    Nuclear Non-Proliferation
        Treaty 115, 261
    post–Second World War role 16,
        25, 172

strategic encirclement 206–7,
   209
and Syria 140
trade with 18, 168
and the West 175, 184–5,
   193–4, 196, 232–3
The Choice (Brzezinski) 198, 202
Churchill, Winston S. 19, 21
CIA (Central Intelligence Agency)
and Africa 99, 100
creation and growth 37, 148
and Indonesia 79
and Latin America 87–8, 94n2,
   103n8, 114
and the Middle East 82, 84, 114
and money 73n2, 106, 125
and torture 78, 135n2
Civil War (American) 6, 193
Clark, Paul Coe 102n7
Clinton, William J. 'Bill' 116–22,
   163, 176, 177–8, 205, 259
Coatsworth, John H. 103n8
Cold War
in Africa 98–101
aftermath 113–14, 151–2,
   183–4, 191, 201, 238, 248
in Asia 60–1, 74–80, 91–2, 97
China and Russia 93–4
and colonialism 69–71, 123
covert operations 66–7, 71–3,
   82–3
economic order 51–6, 62,
   108–11, 116–17
historiography 43–50
ideology 31–6, 40–2, 95, 151,
   174–5
in Latin America 85–9, 94,
   101–3
in the Middle East 80–5, 94–5,
   96–7, 104–6, 125–6
military strength 63–6, 220
Soviet foreign policy 30–1,
   106–8

Truman Doctrine 29–30, 36–8,
   42–3, 53
a US project 58n10
and Western Europe 55–9,
   61–2, 91–2
Congo 99, 100, 101
*The Contours of American
   History* (Williams) 43–4
Cuba 9, 87–9, 100, 101, 102
Czechoslovakia 34, 67, 107, 110

Daalder, Ivo H. 195, 196n8
Dangerous Nation (Kagan) 192–3,
   195, 225
de Gaulle, Charles 21
Democracy's Good Name
   (Mandelbaum) 174, 178
Deng Xiaoping 97, 175
the Depression 11, 54
Diplomacy (Kissinger) 161, 162
Dismantling the Empire (Johnson)
   235
Doha Round 131, 145, 205
Dominican Republic 88
Dulles, Allen W. 66n19, 99n5
Dulles, John F. 33, 67
Dumbarton Oaks 25–6
Dutch East Indies 79

Eastern Europe
communism 20–1, 29–31
containment 35–6, 45
expansion of NATO 119–21,
   131, 176, 178, 201–2, 212
response to revolts 67, 107–8,
   110–11
see also Ukraine; USSR
Eden, R. Anthony 83
Egypt
and the Arab Spring 141
and Britain 80
current government 142,
   255

and Israel 84, 85, 94–5, 96–7, 124
Suez crisis 83
Eisenhower, Dwight D. 82–3, 99n5
El Salvador 102
The End of History and the Last Man (Fukuyama) 237, 246–7, 251–2
The End of the American Era (Kupchan) 184
Ethiopia 100–1, 113
Eurasia 59, 69, 72n1, 200–4, 206, 208–9, 216
Europe
    and the Cold War 46, 55–9, 61–2
    colonies 27, 69–73, 76–80, 98–100, 123
    economic alliance with US 145–6, 226–8
    expansion of NATO 111, 119–21, 131, 176, 178, 201–2, 211–12
    First World War 10–11
    and the Iraq War 244–6
    and the Middle East 136, 144–5
    post–Second World War economy 92–3
    power politics 190–1, 195–6
    resistance movements 19
    Second World War 16–20, 25–7
    see also Britain; Eastern Europe; France; Germany
European Union
    free trade pacts 226–7, 260
    and the Middle East 145
    and Turkey 131
    and Ukraine 258–60
    and US power 184, 186, 192, 202, 232
'The Exaggeration of American Vulnerability' (Thompson) 38n16

Financial Times (newspaper) 244
First World War 9–10, 227
Fisher, Louis 136n5
Foglesong, David S. 66n19
'Foreign Policy as Social Work' (Mandelbaum) 176
Forging a World of Liberty under Law (Ikenberry and Slaughter) 179–80
Forrestal, James V. 37n15, 56
France
    colonies 27, 35, 70–1, 76–8, 80–1, 98–9
    and the left 19, 29, 61–2
    and the Middle East 83, 84, 144–5, 245
    Nuclear Non-Proliferation Treaty 115
    post–Second World War economy 57–8, 92
    during the Second World War 20–1
Franco, Francisco 20–1
Friedman, Thomas L. 177
The Frugal Superpower (Mandelbaum) 177, 178
Fukuyama, Francis 173, 231, 237–53

Gaddis, John Lewis 38n17, 44–6, 52n2
Gardner, Lloyd C. 44, 52n2
GATT (General Agreement on Tariffs and Trade) 59, 116
Germany
    capture of Berlin 30n3
    East Germany 67, 107, 110–11
    and the Middle East 136, 145, 245
    post–Second World War economy 54, 58–9, 62, 91–2, 95–6, 152

and US hegemony 14–17, 21,
    29, 47, 202
Gleijeses, Piero 87n14
The Global Cold War (Westad) 47,
    49n33
God and Gold (Mead) 170–2, 224
Gorbachev, Mikhail S. 109–11,
    118, 175
Gordon, Lincoln 88n16
The Grand Chessboard
    (Brzezinski) 198, 200–4
A Grand Strategy for America
    (Art) 214n32, 216
Great Powers (Barnett) 219–26,
    228
Greece 19, 40n19, 42, 61
Guantánamo 135
Guatemala 87, 102
Gulf War 114–15, 121, 124, 128n12,
    139, 204–5

Haiti 9, 176, 245
Harding, Warren G. 11
Harper, John L. 22n13, 34n8, 47n30
Hearden, Patrick J. 44
Hegel, Georg W. F. 247, 252
Helms, Richard M. 87n14
Helsinki Accords 108
Hendrickson, David C. 128n12
Hiroshima 30, 32, 63
Hogan, Michael J. 37n15, 49n33
Hull, Cordell 11, 12, 26, 57, 81
Hungary 67, 107, 110–11

I
*The Ideas that Conquered the
    World* (Mandelbaum) 174, 178
Ikenberry, G. John 174, 179–83,
    193, 196, 230–2
India 80, 131–2, 147, 205, 207,
    223, 226
Indochina 76–8, 80
    see also Vietnam

Indonesia 79–80, 117, 213
*The Influence of Sea Power upon
    History* (Mahan) 7
Inter-American Treaty of Reciprocal
    Assistance (1947) 86
Iran
    and Europe 145, 245
    and Hezbollah 242
    Islamic Republic 104–5, 143,
        178, 257–8
    nuclear capability 137–8, 180,
        210, 222–3, 225, 231–2
    oil 82–3
    sanctions and cyber-war 138–9
    and Syria 141
Iraq
    Baath party 83–4, 139
    and Europe 81, 190, 244–5
    Gulf War 114–15, 121, 204–5
    insurgency 256, 246
    Iran–Iraq War 105
    Iraq Liberation Act (1998)
        121–2, 125
    Iraq War 127–32, 133–4,
        172, 196–7, 205, 214, 222,
        238–43
    regional power 142
    weapons of mass destruction
        169, 178
ISIS (Islamic State of Iraq and Syria)
    256, 257
Israel
    Camp David Accords 96–7
    and the Cold War 81, 94–5
    nuclear capability 115, 257
    and Palestine 142, 204–5, 212,
        255
    relationship with US 123–5,
        137–8, 178–9, 231–2, 243–4
    Six-Day War 84–5
    and Syria 139, 141
    Yom Kippur War 85
Italy 19, 29, 57–8, 61

Jackson–Vanik amendment 95
Japan
  and China 10, 16, 74–5, 207
  and the Cold War 35, 54–5, 57
  economic growth 76, 91–2,
    95–6, 152
  future role 184, 203, 212–13,
    260
  post-war reforms 60–1, 62
  Second World War deaths
    159n2
  and US power 14–15, 21, 146,
    147, 181, 211
  see also Hiroshima
Jefferson, Thomas 4
Johnson, Chalmers A. 128n12,
  147n9, 235
Johnson, Lyndon B. 40n19, 78
Jordan 85, 140

Kagan, Robert 4n3, 189–97, 225,
  229, 230–2, 238, 248
Karzai, Hamid 256–7
Kennan, George F.
  and China 74n3, 131n15
  and containment 33–6, 75n4,
    77, 79n7, 98n4
  and covert operations 67, 94n2
  and democracy 39, 60, 61n13,
    86
  and the Middle East 82n10,
    104n9
  and national security 37
  and religion 40–1
  on Roosevelt 21n12
Kennedy, John F. 33, 41, 77–8, 87–8
Kennedy, Robert F. 87n15
Keynes, John Maynard 26n19
Kiernan, Victor 6n7
Kimball, Warren F. 49n33
Kissinger, Henry A. 94n2, 107,
  161–2, 169n4, 179, 197–8
Kohl, Helmut 111

Kojève, Alexandre V. 247, 248–9,
  252
Kolko, Gabriel 21n12, 24, 44, 48,
  235
Korea 35, 75–6, 117, 160n2, 210,
  212–13
Kornbluh, Peter 94n2
Kosovo 120–1, 240
Krauthammer, Charles 244, 245–6,
  249
Kristol, William 238, 248, 249
Kupchan, Charles A. 183–8, 193n5,
  229, 230–1, 232
Kuwait 114

LaFeber, Walter 44, 86n13
Lake, Anthony 176
Latin America
  Cold War 85–9, 101–3
  resources 69
  US imperialism 14–15, 26, 35,
    65, 70–2
  see also Central America; South
    America
Layne, Christopher 129n12,
  206n19, 234, 235
League of Democracies 194, 195–6,
  231
Lebanon 80–1, 84, 124, 141, 245
Leffler, Melvyn P. 47–8, 53, 67n19,
  163
Legro, Jeffrey W. 163
Liberal Leviathan (Ikenberry)
  180–3
Libya 136–7, 140, 144, 145, 197,
  257
Lippmann, Walter 33, 72n1
The Logic of World Power
  (Schurmann) 23–5, 36n13
London Review of Books (journal)
  253
Lumumba, Patrice E. 99

Mahan, Alfred T. 7
Malaya 76
Maliki, Nouri al- 256
Mandelbaum, Michael 156n1, 174–9, 193, 229, 231, 232
Mann, James 136n5, 241
Manning, Chelsea E. 135–6
Mao Zedong 93, 97, 107
Marshall Plan 58, 79
Mayers, David A. 82n10
Mazzetti, Mark 135n2
McCormick, Thomas J. 42n23, 43n24, 44, 49n33, 58n9
Mead, Walter Russell 159–61, 167–73, 224, 229, 230–1
Mearsheimer, John J. 165n8, 253
Mexico 4–5, 9, 116, 117
Middle East
    Arab Spring 141–2
    and the Cold War 65, 70, 80–5, 94–5, 125–6
    disunity 142–3
    future policy 212, 231, 253
    Islamism 126–7, 164, 168, 172, 255–7, 246
    oil 42, 69, 216, 223
    war on terror 178, 191, 204, 242–3
    see also Afghanistan; Iran; Iraq; Israel; Saudi Arabia; Syria; Turkey; Yemen
Miscamble, Wilson D. 30n2, 60n11, 67n20, 79n7
Mobutu Sese Seko 99
Monroe doctrine 85
Mortal Splendor (Mead) 167
Mussolini, Benito 20–1

NAFTA (North American Free Trade Agreement) 116, 181–2
Nagasaki 30, 32, 40, 63
Nasser, Gamal Abdel 83, 84

The National Interest (journal) 173, 243
National Security Act (1947) 37
National Security Council (NSC) 37, 148
NATO
    and American hegemony 180–1, 210–11
    expansion to the east 111, 119–21, 131, 176, 178, 212, 259
    and Germany 59
    and the Middle East 136, 140
    and Russia 186, 201–2, 232, 258
Netherlands 78–9
New Deal 11, 22, 24
Nicaragua 9, 101–3, 113, 189, 250
Niebuhr, Reinhold 172, 173
9/11 46, 122–3, 127, 168, 175, 191, 204, 242
Nitze, Paul H. 33, 66, 95, 116, 119
Nixon, Richard M. 91–5, 107, 136, 162, 227
No One's World (Kupchan) 184–8
Noriega Morena, Manuel Antonio 114
Nuclear Non-Proliferation Treaty (1968) 115, 180, 261
Nye, Joseph S. 52n2, 165n8

Obama, Barack H. 41, 133–6, 138–9, 143–50, 196–7, 255–7, 261
Of Paradise and Power (Kagan) 189–92, 195
Offner, Arnold A. 29n1, 63n15
Ogaden crisis 101
Oil Crisis (1973) 95
Olney Corollary 85, 89
Open Door policy 5, 9, 10, 18–19, 44, 55, 216
Operation Desert Storm 114–15, 121, 124, 128n12, 139, 204–5

Operation Enduring Freedom 127, 133–4, 142–3, 222
    see also Afghanistan
Operation Odyssey Dawn 136–7, 140, 144, 145, 148, 197
Organization of American States (OAS) 86
Oslo Accords 141
O'Sullivan, John 4n4
Out of Control (Brzezinski) 198–200

Pahlavi, Mohammad Reza Shah 82, 104
Pakistan 80, 84, 106, 126, 134, 222
Palestine 81, 124, 126, 141–2, 204–5, 212, 231, 255
Panama 5, 103, 114, 115
Pearl Harbour 23, 191
Perry, Matthew C. 5
Pétain, Philippe 21
Philippines 76, 191, 213
Plaza Accord 1985 96
Poland 34, 108, 110
The Politics of War (Kolko) 19n10, 24, 44, 48, 63n15
Pollack, Kenneth 240
Popov, Vladimir 108n11
Portugal 100
Power, Terror, Peace and War (Mead) 168–9
Pravda, Alex 111n15
A Preponderance of Power (Leffler) 47, 53, 81n9
Princeton Project on National Security 179
Project for a New American Century 241–2
The Public Interest (journal) 238
Putin, Vladimir V. 131, 144, 221, 225, 258–9

Qatar 140, 142

The Radical Left and American Foreign Policy (Tucker) 53n4
Reagan, Ronald W. 102, 105, 109, 110n12, 208, 238
The Resurgence of the West (Rosecrance) 226–7
The Return of History and the End of Dreams (Kagan) 193–4, 196
Reverse Course 60
Reviewing the Cold War (ed. Westad) 49n33, 59n10
Rhodes, Benjamin J. 150
Rice, Condoleezza 241
Rio Treaty of Inter-American Defence (1947) 86
Roosevelt, Franklin D. 11–12, 20–7, 30, 38, 40, 81, 102n7
Roosevelt, Theodore 5, 161–2, 169, 173, 195, 224–5
Rosecrance, Richard N. 226–8, 232
Rumsfeld, Donald H. 241
Russia
    and Afghanistan 127, 131
    future role 184, 186, 196, 206
    and market economics 117–18, 145, 174–5, 221
    and the Middle East 115, 139–40, 141, 143–4
    NATO in Eastern Europe 118–21, 176, 201–2
    as threat to the US 193–4, 208–9, 232–3, 261
    and Ukraine 258–60
    see also USSR

Sadat, Anwar 85, 96
Saddam Hussein 105, 114, 121, 128, 131, 205, 241–2
SALT (Strategic Arms Limitation Talks) 93, 95
Sandars, Christopher T. 147n9
Sanger, David E. 261n3

Saudi Arabia 81, 109, 114, 125, 126, 140, 141
Savimbi, Jonas M. 100
Schroeder, Paul W. 128n12
Schurmann, Franz 23–5, 36n13
Second Chance (Brzezinski) 198, 204–6, 207
Second World War 15–20, 23, 54–5, 159n2, 191
Seward, William H. 5
The Shield of Achilles (Bobbitt) 240
Sisi, Abdel Fattah al- 141
Six-Day War 84
Slaughter, Anne-Marie 179–80, 196
Somoza García, Anastasio 87n14, 101–2
South Africa 98, 100
South America 69, 94, 101
see also Argentina; Brazil; Chile
space race 64
Spanish–American War 5
Special Providence (Mead) 159–61, 167–8
Spykman, Nicholas J. 13–16, 24, 52–3, 56
Stalin, Joseph 21, 30–1, 75
Steil, Benn 26n19, 57n8
Stephanson, Anders 6, 32, 33n8, 59n10, 164n8
Stimson, Henry L. 63n15
Strategic Defense Initiative 109–10
Strategic Vision (Brzezinski) 198, 206–7
Strauss, Leo 238, 247, 248–9
Stuxnet virus 139, 148
Suez Canal 83, 84
Syria
    Baath party 84, 139–41
    and Europe 145
    future government 142
    and Islamism 256, 242

    post-Second World War 80
    and Russia 85, 144

Taiwan 35, 93, 96, 97, 213
That Used to Be Us (Mandelbaum) 177
Third World
    and the Cold War 46–7, 70, 83, 98–101, 107, 113, 115
    debt 96
    and market economics 117
    see also Africa; Asia; Latin America; Middle East
Thompson, John A. 38n16, 49–50
Thompson, Nicholas 77n5, 87n14, 104n9
To Lead the World (ed. Leffler and Legro) 163
The Tragedy of American Diplomacy (Williams) 43–4
Trans-Atlantic Free Trade Agreement (TAFTA) 145–6, 228
Trans-Pacific Partnership 146
Treaty of Rome (1957) 59
Trotsky, Leon 108
Truman, Harry S.
    and Asia 74–6
    on the atomic bombs 40, 63
    and capital 54
    covert operations 87n14
    and Israel 81
    Truman Doctrine 29–30, 36–8, 42–3, 53
Tucker, Robert W. 49–50, 53, 128n12
Tunisia 141
Turkey 84, 131, 140–1, 206, 256
A Twilight Struggle (Kagan) 189
Twin Towers *see* 9/11

Ukraine 201, 258–60
United Nations

founding conference 26
and Russia 140, 144
Security Council 120, 121, 180
and US power 76, 81, 99, 101,
    115, 127, 239
Uruguay 89
USSR
and Africa 99–101
and China 93–4, 213
collapse 110–11, 113, 117–18,
    238, 248
economy 58, 108–10
Ermattungskrieg 32, 34–6,
    65–7, 110
foreign policy 30–1, 106–7
and Korea 75
and the Middle East 81, 82, 83,
    85, 104, 106
nuclear weapons 46, 63–4, 110
post–Second World War role
    16–17, 20, 25–7
repression 103n8
see also Cold War; Russia

Vietnam 44, 76–8, 92, 93–4, 97,
    160n2
Volcker, Paul A. 96

Wall Street Crash *see* the
    Depression
Walt, Stephen M. 253
Waltz, Kenneth N. 215

War on Terror 127–32, 133–6, 191,
    204, 242–3, 246
Washington Consensus 117
Watkins, Susan 115n2
We Now Know (Gaddis) 45–6
The Weekly Standard (journal)
    240, 252
Westad, Odd Arne 47–8, 49n33
White, Harry Dexter 25n19
Whitman, Walt 6
Williams, William Appleman 43–4,
    48n33
Wilson, Woodrow 8–9, 10, 20, 66,
    161–2, 169, 173
Wisconsin School 43–4, 48n33,
    49–50
Witte, Ludo De 99n5
Wolfowitz, Paul D. 241
Woodring, Harry H. 12
The World America Made
    (Kagan) 194–5, 196
World Trade Center *see* 9/11
Wright, C. Ben 35n10
WTO (World Trade Organization)
    116, 145, 182, 205

Yeltsin, Boris N. 118, 119, 120, 131
Yemen 84, 113, 141
Yugoslavia 19, 120–1, 144

Zakaria, Fareed R. 164n8, 205n19
Zubok, Vladislav 109n12